The Book
of
Granville

By the same authors

By Joseph E. Granville

A Schoolboy's Faith
Price Predictions (five editions)
Everybody's Guide to Stamp Investment
A Strategy of Daily Stock Market Timing for
     Maximum Profit
Granville's New Key to Stock Market Profits
Granville's New Strategy of Daily Stock Market
     Timing for Maximum Profit
How to Win at Bingo

By William Hoffer

Caught in the Act (with William W. Pearce)
Midnight Express (with Billy Hayes)
Saved! The Story of the Andrea Doria
Volcano: The Search for Vesuvius

The Book
of
Granville

Joseph E. Granville
with William Hoffer

St. Martin's Press / New York

Design by Barbara Richer

Library of Congress Cataloging in Publication Data

Granville, Joseph E. (Joseph Ensign), 1923–
   The book of Granville.
   1. Granville, Joseph E. (Joseph Ensign),
1923–   . 2. Investment advisers—United States—
Biography. 3. Stock-exchange. I. Hoffer, William.
II. Title.
HG4621.G73   1985   332.6′2 [B]   84–18275
ISBN 0–312–08902–3

First Edition
10 9 8 7 6 5 4 3 2 1

For Karen.
There are no accidents.

Winners and losers, gamblers and boozers,
If they zig every time they should zag,
If they follow the news or the obvious views,
They're caught, baby, holding the bag.

—"Bagholder Blues"

CONTENTS

PROLOGUE

Richard Fant was a graduate of the Harvard School of Business, where he was elected to membership in Phi Beta Kappa. He was a conscientious, dutiful worker who, by his mid-fifties, had labored his way up the traditional pathway of success to become director of the research department of the prestigious Wall Street brokerage firm of E.F. Hutton & Company.

An impeccable dresser, Fant complemented his conservative suits with an ever-present slide rule that he used to calculate the potential profits of various large corporations. It was his job accurately to forecast those profits, in the belief that a company's future earnings would alter, for better or worse, the price of its common stock. Based on the work of Fant's department, Hutton's stockbrokers all over the world urged their clients to purchase certain stocks. Fant's words influenced billions of dollars of investment capital, and he felt deeply the pressure of the responsibility.

His day's work started with a departmental meeting. As he pointedly toyed with his Phi Beta Kappa key he listened to his staff members express their opinions about various companies. Occasionally he took up his slide rule to make a quick calculation.

Fant was a stock market fundamentalist, a true believer in guiding his clients toward investment success. He was bullish on America. He earned money the old-fashioned way. When Fant spoke, he wanted his clients to listen.

For a period of six months in 1959, Fant supervised a team of analysts involved in a study of Ryder Systems, the truck rental firm. An army of researchers went out on ambitious field trips to interview key corporate officers and to study the company's facilities. As is the normal outcome of such exercises, they returned with a favorable attitude, glowing about the positives, glossing over the negatives.

The result of this half year of labor was a manuscript numbering more than fifty pages that was to be printed and circulated to Hutton's top institutional accounts to persuade them to invest heavily in the stock of Ryder Systems. It was by far the most ambitious undertaking of Fant's promising career.

As he crossed through the research department on his way to deliver the manuscript to the printer, Fant happened to stumble against my desk. Though I was assigned to the department, I was not really considered a part of the team. My job was not to delve into the inner workings of corporations. That was the realm of Fant's respected fundamental analysts. I was what is known as a technical analyst; my job was simply to study the statistical data that emanated directly from the stock market.

In a brokerage firm, the technical analyst is akin to a tea-leaf reader. In some circles, we are known as "elves"—little men who compute the daily results of stock trading and are supposed to remain relatively unobtrusive.

But when Fant bumped his knee on my desk it reminded him of my existence. He remembered that I was a necessary nuisance because, to his chagrin, there are a few investors who actually heed the words of technical analysts. He realized that a favorable technical opinion on Ryder Systems, though unnecessary, would buttress the report's optimistic outlook even further.

"Joe," he said, "would you write up a brief technical opinion on Ryder Systems? I need it right away because I have to get this report to the printer within the hour."

"Yes, Mr. Fant," I replied, grabbing my copy of *Horsey's Stock Charts.* This is merely a compilation of graphs depicting the short- and long-term price fluctuations of the most popular common stocks.

As Fant went back to his office I began what I called a "three-minute exercise," a simple study of the price patterns of a given stock. I believe that such patterns reveal the mix of investor optimism and pessimism concerning the stock, and are therefore far more valuable in predicting future prices than are the giant research reports of the fundamental analysts.

On that day, in January of 1960, Ryder Systems' common stock was selling for $32 per share, down a couple of points from its recent high of 34. One look at the chart sent the word *Sell!* screaming through my head. The chart revealed what I called a parabolic rise —when the price at the 32–34 area fell, it indicated that there was too much investor confidence in the stock. It had nowhere to go but down, like a waterfall, for there was no evidence of further price support above $14 per share.

I quickly typed a paragraph detailing my opinion that Ryder Systems would drop from 32 to 14.

"Here you are, Mr. Fant," I said, dropping the page onto his desk.

He scanned the paragraph quickly, his eyebrows registering his disbelief at my impertinence. He dismissed me with a curt thank you, and hurried off to the printer.

The Ryder report came out three days later beautifully bound in simulated leather and stamped in gold with the name of each of Hutton's top institutional investors. It concluded with the official opinion of Fant's research department that it was an excellent time to purchase the stock of a company with such fine growth potential.

The report conspicuously lacked my technical opinion.

Richard Fant was a sincere person, but he was sincerely wrong. A week later, the stock began to drop in price—not much at first, but the slide gradually gained momentum.

Richard Fant was also a worrier. He actually thought that worry could raise the price of a stock. As the stock of Ryder Systems began to drop, he worried and worried and worried. But the stock did not know that, and it kept going down.

As the stock headed toward $25 per share, Fant began to absent himself from the office. He phoned his departmental instructions in to Bob Stovall, a liquor analyst who sat at the desk behind me.

"Where's Mr. Fant?" I asked Bob one day.

"He's not feeling well," Bob admitted. "As a matter of fact, he may have a stomach ulcer."

The stock didn't know about Fant's intestinal problems and it continued to go down. And the more it went down the more he worried.

By the time the stock got down to $20 a share Bob told me that Fant's condition had been diagnosed as stomach cancer. But the stock did not know that. It continued to plunge, and so did Fant's health.

The day the stock dropped to under $20 per share, Bob and I took off from work to attend Fant's funeral. I marveled that a man could worry himself to death by placing his trust in a philosophy that was so patently false.

Thirty days after the funeral Ryder Systems hit $14.50 per share. Fant's six months of work was fatally wrong; my three-minute exercise was absolutely correct. Two years later it had sunk to $8 a share, 75 percent under Fant's recommended buy price.

I have never seen a more graphic illustration of my contention that the stock market and Wall Street are antithetical entities. The stock market is life; Wall Street is death.

Destiny, I have always believed, is the natural unfolding of harmonic chords that fulfills the symphonic pattern of the Supreme Composer. From the day I went to work for E.F. Hutton & Company on October 4, 1957, I knew, in broad outline, the melodic score that Destiny had written for my life.

Success in the market is predicated upon the ability to predict the future course of stock prices, and that means predicting the future mood of people—the people who buy and sell stocks. From my earliest moments my mother had encouraged me in the spectacular enterprise of predicting the future. It was her fervent desire to know the future that led her down countless bypaths of life and exposed me to the strange strategies of the occult. Although I would use reason rather than mysticism to predict the course of the stock market, I would remain enchanted with the accuracy of various unconventional forecasting mechanisms.

There was, as well, a more traditional basis for my fascination. The market was a game played out in numbers. Games were my father's lifelong passion, and he nurtured the same love in me. Forecasting the stock market is serious business, but it is also an encompassing, enjoyable pastime that has never lost its sportsmanlike aura for me.

The market is a high-stakes poker game like none other in the world. What more enjoyable occupation could I envision?

Not being a mystic, how could I foretell the extent of the notoriety that would result from my love affair with the stock market? Even to those of us who make a career out of predicting the future, Destiny does not reveal her entire plan at one time.

Who could foresee that my eyes would view the market from an entirely different perspective than those of my associates; that this unique vision would enable me to apply simple mathematics to predict accurately the major moves in stock prices; that I would forever alter the fortunes of tens of thousands of investors; that I would become a media star; that my work would detonate mighty explosions in the world financial community; that my affair with the market would tear apart my family; that nearly three decades of studying the market would bring me equal doses of pain and euphoria?

I could know none of that when I went to work on Wall Street after failing a broker's aptitude test.

I knew only that every event in my thirty-three years theretofore was a prelude to this life-and-death encounter.

There are no accidents.

The Book
of
Granville

1.
GENESIS

Dorothy Dartmouth Crehore was born on May 17, 1895, on the campus of the famous university in Hanover, New Hampshire, that inspired her middle name. Her mother, Sara Buck Crehore, was the adopted daughter of an heiress of the Toy Bickford Company, a munitions firm. Dorothy's father, Dr. Albert Cushing Crehore, was an inventor and a distinguished professor of atomic physics whose quest in life was to win the Nobel Prize.

When Dr. Crehore left Dartmouth for a teaching post at Columbia University, he moved his family into the home of his mother-in-law, Julia Toy Buck. The house in Yonkers, New York, was jammed with artifacts from Mrs. Buck's world travels. To escape the clutter, Dr. Crehore built a laboratory and observatory on the downslope of the backyard. From then on he spent far more time in his laboratory than in his home. To his wife and most of his children he sometimes seemed almost a stranger, but to his eldest daughter, Dorothy, he was an adventurer.

Dorothy spent long hours in the laboratory with her father as he exposed her kindred, inquiring mind to a wondrous universe. They studied the minute world of microscopic organisms, where life was carried on as tenaciously as in the human sphere. They studied the moon, the planets, Halley's comet, and the mysteries beyond the solar system, all of which seemed to diminish the significance of human pursuits. Father and daughter asked of one another, but never answered, the questions of existence: What? How? And most of all, why?

Dr. Crehore was lonely when Dorothy went away to finishing school but he took solace in his laboratory work—until the day he mixed the wrong batch of chemicals and blew out one side of the building. He was unhurt, but he never bothered to repair the lab. Perhaps he already knew that he would be moving away soon.

Dorothy, meanwhile, attended the Baldwin School in Bryn Mawr, Pennsylvania, where she was a classmate and friend of Cornelia Otis Skinner, who would later become a noted writer and humorist. At Baldwin, Dorothy adopted the classic pursuits of a lady of gentility. She studied voice, developing into a polished lyric soprano. She also took up painting and poetic composition. In short, she cultivated all the arts, bringing to their study the same questions her father asked in atomic physics. Dorothy pondered the past, but even more she wondered about the future.

As she studied beauty, Dorothy became one herself. She had the high cheekbones of a model, dark, expressive eyes, and a smile that combined social grace with just the right hint of the coquette. She was unfashionably slim, however, suffering from a form of anemia that sometimes kept her bedridden for days. She had to take a liquid dose of hydrochloric acid with all her meals.

She was twenty when her parents divorced. Dr. Crehore, thereafter wedded only to his work, took a professorship in Cleveland and left his family behind. His ex-wife ordered the remains of his laboratory torn down, leaving only a concrete slab that soon became overgrown with weeds.

Though decades would pass before she was reunited with her father, Dorothy always remembered the wonders that she had seen in his laboratory. She knew that life held exciting mysteries, and she meant to study them. Though many of her less attractive friends had already married, Dorothy was content to wait for the right suitor and concentrate on her own interests.

When you are endowed with a historic name you cannot easily escape the notion that destiny has called you out for greatness. George Washington Granville dreamed such visions but never had the chance to act them out. He spent most of his working life running a grocery store.

As did his own father, however, George Washington Granville intended to bestow upon his firstborn son a name that would set him apart from the masses and spur him to great achievement. He was thwarted when his first two children turned out to be Blanche and Ethel. Following those disappointments, he sought a change of venue, moving his family from Norfolk, Virginia, to Mount Kisco, New York. It was there, on November 4, 1892, that his son finally entered the world, four days before a presidential election.

An unbending Republican, he settled upon the name of Benjamin Harrison Granville. When Harrison lost the election to Grover Cleveland, however, a quick alteration seemed in order. Inspiration struck as the family drove its carriage near Sleepy Hollow in Tarrytown, New York, and the son was renamed Washington Irving Granville. The baby came to be called Irving, or Irv.

It was his mother's wish that he become a minister, but Irving was naturally drawn to the world of finance. At the age of seventeen he dropped out of Mount Kisco High School to take a job as a messenger boy for the New York Produce Exchange in Manhattan, gradually working his way up to the position of teller. He was naturally gregarious and endowed with an amazing supply of energy. It was obvious to all of his associates that he would ascend to a position of great responsibility. Such an understanding was much to Irving's liking. It had always been his goal to become prosperous and famous.

For a time the Great War interrupted his plans. He served as a signalman on the cruiser U.S.S. *Seattle,* then returned home in 1919 nattily attired as one of America's conquering heroes.

In the weeks and months following the war it was fashionable to hold receptions in honor of returning servicemen. Thus it was that Irving and his younger brother, Hutton, received notice that "Mrs. Charles Henry Buck, Mrs. Albert Cushing Crehore, and Miss Dorothy Dartmouth Crehore will be at home on Saturday, the second of December, from four until seven o'clock at Four Hundred and Nine North Broadway, Yonkers, New York."

Irving, handsome in his Navy uniform, charming the drawing room with easy repartee, could not keep his eyes off the dark-haired beauty who returned his gaze with a strange look of presentiment. Six months of picnics, dances, and church socials followed.

On June 19, 1920, Dorothy walked solemnly down the second floor stairway of her home in Yonkers, through an aisle of ribbon and roses, past a string trio, to the library. She wore her mother's wedding gown of ivory satin and antique lace.

The couple honeymooned in upstate New York, and the birth of their firstborn son, William Osler Granville, less than seven months later, was the type of quiet scandal upon which Dorothy seemed to thrive. Two years later, I arrived on the scene.

Diligence and dedication soon brought my father to the position of cashier at the Liberty National Bank and Trust Company. In those days banks printed their own money, and dad was duly proud of the oversized bills resplendent with fancy scrollwork, signed at the bottom with the distinctive, ornate script of "W. Irving Granville."

In 1927 he was named a vice-president of the bank. These were highly successful years for him. Beyond his salary he was privy to the inner thoughts of the financial community and he began to speculate successfully in the stock market. Brokers were allowed to lend their customers as much as 90 percent of their investment; thus, for a $1,000 investment almost anyone could purchase $10,000 worth of stock and parlay it into a modest fortune, assuming, of course, that the prices of his stocks continued to rise.

Years of prosperity seemed to stretch ahead. Dad was only one of the many investors whose confidence drove the Dow Jones Industrial Average from 155 to 386 between 1927 and 1929. Throughout his life he was enchanted with all sorts of games. He thrived on competition, whether in golf, bowling, cards, croquet, Ping-Pong or checkers. Nor was he averse to placing a wager upon the outcome. The stock market seemed like an ideal game to him, where the potential profits were limitless.

Dad was so clever with his stock portfolio that he began to invest money for his mother-in-law as well as for his elder sister Blanche, who was national sales manager for the Spencer Corset Company. Earning more than $100,000 a year, Auntie Blanche was hailed as the highest-paid businesswoman in the country.

This was somewhat disconcerting to dad, who had always intended to be the star of the family. He loved Auntie Blanche and never begrudged her success. Nevertheless, he took particular pride in his ability to handle a considerable portion of her personal finances. Auntie Blanche depended upon her younger brother for his astute investment advice. Subsequent events were thus as great an emotional blow to dad as they were a financial setback.

When he returned home from his office one Monday evening in 1929, dad was uncharacteristically glum. It was apparent even to me, at the age of five. He customarily held court at the dinner table, entertaining the rest of us with stories and quips, but this night he only stared vacantly into his soup bowl, speaking to no one during the entire meal. Then he returned to his study where he placed a call to Auntie Blanche and spoke to her for hours in a hushed tone.

The following day he was even more distraught. There was a palpable tension between him and mother. Once again he spent the evening talking with Auntie Blanche.

Only later, of course, did I come to appreciate the reasons for my father's sudden change in personality. The stock market topped out on September 3, 1929, reaching a high point of 386 in the Dow Jones Industrial Average, the loftiest peak it had ever ascended. But mountains are surrounded by valleys. The very height of the rally set the market up for a steep plunge.

The great bear market began gradually, stocks drifting lower until the Dow settled at the 300 level. Then, on October 28, 1929, the average dropped 38 points from 298 to 260. The following day, Black Tuesday, it plunged another 30 points to 230. By November 13 it had dropped to 198. Insofar as the average represented all common stocks, the market had lost 50 percent of its value in the span of two months.

Dad was caught in a typical squeeze. When the value of his stocks dropped, his broker had no alternative but to issue a margin call, requiring him either to put up more cash or sell some of his holdings to repay the debt. Since dad's situation was identical to that of most speculators, this sudden surge of margin calls resulted in a tumultuous selling spree that only drove the market down at a more accelerated pace. There was a "sucker rally" late in the year that set investors up for further losses when the second cycle of the crash came. By December 1930 the Dow-Jones Industrial Average had plummeted to 169.

Dad lost $30,000 of his own money and at least twice as much more that he borrowed from Grandma Buck and Auntie Blanche. The family survived only because our relatives were comfortable enough to write off their losses and aid us in recovering. Dad was grateful for the assistance, but it cut deeply into his manhood. At one point in 1930 he was ready to take a gun to his head, but mother talked him out of it.

It was years before he fully recovered from the shock.

2.
FIRST CHRONICLES

I rested quietly in the blue armchair, just as I had been directed to do. The silent upright Victrola caught my attention, setting off in my imagination the glorious harmonies of Tchaikovsky's Fourth Symphony. I let the music flow inside of me, background for my task. I was to remain stationary for the full hour from 11:00 A.M. until noon on this particular day, February 8, 1939. As a fifteen-year-old boy it would have been impossible for me to sit still that long had I not shared my mother's interest in the experiment.

Though we were members of the First Methodist Church of Yonkers, mother did not confine her spiritual pursuits to mainline respectability. On Sunday mornings while dad played golf, mother was likely to be found at any one of a number of local churches, from Catholic to Presbyterian to Baptist to Christian Science. She had no intention of joining any of these churches, but she was determined to become aware of their philosophies. She was particularly impressed with the writings of Mary Baker Eddy, the founder of Christian Science. What intrigued her was that the prophetess seemed to have an ability to predict the future. If there was one thing mother wanted to know, it was the future.

To this end she began to pursue an ancient philosophy that would bewitch her for the rest of her life: astrology. In the cycles of the planets mother could discern recurring patterns, and she realized that the study of patterns was the key to predicting the future. With precise mathematics one could, for example, calculate exactly when the sun would rise the next morning, when the moon would be full, or when Saturn would eclipse a star. But mother, of course, took the process much further. She believed that the cycles of the planets influenced the daily lives of human beings on the small speck of the universe that they inhabit.

From astrology she moved on to the study of Tarot cards, palm reading, and numerology. She attended the lectures of Manley Hall, the famous theosophist. She participated in seances. She became conversant on such esoteric topics as the lost continent of Atlantis, reincarnation, the *Bhagavad Gita*, Rosicrucian philosophy, the secrets of the pyramids, and Platonic thought.

Somewhere amid her quest for mystic knowledge mother learned of a fascinating man who lived in Virginia Beach, Virginia. Edgar Cayce, while still only an unsophisticated farm boy, had recognized in himself an unusual ability to predict the future. At first he had no plans to capitalize upon this special talent, but his fame spread to the point where he was forced to adopt the practice as a full-time job. Every day he reclined upon his sofa in Virginia, entered a self-induced trance, and dictated to a secretary the impressions sent to him from what he called the "universal consciousness." He gave medical readings for ten dollars; for twenty-five dollars you could purchase a life reading.

Mother sent him forty-five dollars, requesting medical readings for herself and my brother Bill and a life reading for me.

All that Cayce knew about me was my name and my date and place of birth. Mother told me to try to keep my mind free of confusing thoughts during the entire hour. I was to concentrate quietly on who I was and what I wanted to do with my life. That was easy, because I was a precocious child and in a general way I had always known my grand goal. It was very similar to the dreams of my maternal grandfather and of my own dad.

And so, as Tchaikovsky's Fourth Symphony built to a crescendo in my mind, I silently repeated my own special litany for the full hour: "I am Joseph Granville. Someday I'm going to be famous."

Two weeks later the readings came in the mail. Cayce proclaimed my personal motto to be *Deus et Fidelis*, "God and Fidelity." According to the universal consciousness, I had lived at least four previous lives under that banner.

In ancient Egypt I "directed the song, the dance in the temple of Sacrifice, as well as in the Preparations of music for the Temple Beautiful."

As Abner, I was "among those who were close to the king who was proclaimed after Saul—or a friend of, a companion of David; and raised to one in power—yet the experience became both an advancement as well as a retardant.

"For the entity allowed self, and the power of self, to become as the greater influence."

The third incarnation, as reported by Cayce, was overpowering to my fifteen-year-old intellect. My name had been Eucuo. " . . . The entity," Cayce reported with reverence, "was in the land during those periods of hardship, during the activities in what is now called the period when the Master walked on the earth.

"There we find the entity was among the shepherds who heard the cry of 'Glory to God in the Highest—Peace on earth and good will to men.'

" . . . Hence he beheld Him as a Babe!"

In my most recent life I was Cormant Bruce the Swift, leading English crusaders in song as we fought to liberate the Holy City.

All of these previous lives had prepared me for the present existence. " . . . The entity," dictated Cayce, "is endowed innately with a many-sided disposition; being highly sensitive, and inclined to be dramatic—though very much in the position where, in whatever endeavor the entity undertakes, he will not be in the background but toward the front."

The conclusion of the reading took my breath away. The universal consciousness urged me to hold to my motto, "God and Fidelity."

"Hence hold to that as indicated in the seal, that must be the motto; as to realizing, becoming aware and giving expression of same in music of what that vision meant which the entity did experience. Again set that to music, and thy praise, thy glory, thy activity will be such that HE will never again be forgotten!

"We are through with this Reading."

To any fifteen-year-old boy this would be an overwhelming prophecy; to me, especially, it undermined what little humility I possessed. One of my most difficult problems in communicating my message to others is that I have an aggressive speaking style—a touch of the demagogue. Later years would teach me that the message is far more important than the man, but in childhood I did not understand that important truth.

My quest for notoriety was, I think, already underway when I was born on August 20, 1923. My father was tremendously successful in those years. When I was still a toddler he moved us into a magnificent home on Lincoln Terrace in Yonkers, the last house at the end of a cul-de-sac.

Dad was justifiably proud of the house, for it reflected his propserity. Mother loved it because its backyard rose to adjoin the property of my grandmother's house. Midway up the hill was the ruined foundation of my grandfather's laboratory, which brought my mother warm memories.

My older brother Bill and I liked the house because it offered limitless areas for exploration and adventure. Bill appropriated much of the basement for his own workshop. He would spend hours there tinkering with his bicycle or with an old radio. The upper areas were my domain, in particular the third floor, where I had a bedroom all to myself. I felt as though I had my own little castle at the top of the world.

On Bill's ninth birthday someone gave him a small volume entitled *Minute Biographies*. I was only seven, but mother had taught me to read several years earlier, and the brief accounts of the lives of famous people were written simply enough for me to understand. I took the book for my own, studying it repeatedly, underlining passages that potentially applied to me.

Here were vignettes of many American presidents and other world political leaders. Here were brief descriptions of authors and composers who achieved that magical goal of fame at an early age. One of my particular favorites was Edgar Allan Poe, and I often urged my mother to read to me from his works; my favorite Poe story was "The Gold Bug," a nickname that would later be applied to me by various Wall Street reporters.

The composers fascinated me the most, because my early life was devoted to music. My own path to fame appeared to lie somewhere in this field, either as performer or composer, and I coveted the early notice achieved by Bach, Handel, Chopin, and Mozart. Beethoven's incredible triumph over adversity was inspiring.

I was a child who frequently found himself in trouble. At the age of three I set the house afire by throwing matches into the woodpile under the front porch. I proudly announced to my second-grade class that I had been born in Jerusalem. When I was a bit older I purposely spooked the milkman's horse so that it overturned the wagon and spilled hundreds of bottles into the gutter. On another occasion I ordered my Great Dane to attack a neighbor man whom I disliked. One of my accomplishments was to run naked through the hallway just as our minister came to visit. I was a happy child and my parents loved me, but I could not avoid the impulse to create troublesome, attention-getting situations. I had a natural abhorrence of the word *average.*

All children vie for attention, but there was a special compulsion within me to make the world take note of Joe Granville. I did not care whether the reaction was favorable or unfavorable, only that it be loud. My childhood days were never happier than when Bill and I drove through Yonkers in a fancy cart pulled by Heliotrope, a Shetland pony shipped over to us from England by our accomplished Auntie Blanche, or when I starred as Mozart in a third-grade play, resplendent in a velvet suit made by my mother.

One of my mother's astrologically inclined friends once asked me, "If you had to choose one of the following—money, fame, or happiness—which would it be?"

"Fame," I replied quickly.

The woman stared deep into my eyes, her pupils glazing over in prophetic ecstasy. "Your wish will be fulfilled," she announced. "But you will pay a high price for fame."

Yonkers is built upon a hill above the Hudson River. As I grew older it was a simple matter to climb out the window of my room onto the roof and gaze at the island of Manhattan sixteen miles to the south. I often sat there with Bill, smoking Kools stolen from my mother's purse, dreaming of the day when I would conquer the great city that stretched out in the distance.

This quest for achievement was nurtured by my parents, who tried to steer my attention-getting behavior into nondestructive forms. My father's wish was clear. He envisioned me as a financial magnate, perhaps following his lead in banking. He encouraged me to study his library of financial volumes, and my curiosity led me through his entire collection of the *Alexander Hamilton Business Course*, comprising more than a score of leather-bound volumes on everything from accounting to speculating in the stock market.

My father saw so much of himself in me that my pranks did not surprise him; he himself had always counted on being rich and famous. Though the stock market crash of 1929 interrupted his dream, he still took delight in associating himself with historic events and famous people, as though notoriety were infectious. As often as he could he included me in his escapades, such as the night—in fact it was New Year's Day—in 1932 when he woke me in the wee hours and bundled me into the car. We drove to the Hudson River and parked at the end of a new highway. By dawn we were the vanguard of a long line of waiting automobiles. Dad grinned with pride when officials cut the red ribbon and he pulled the car forward, the first person to drive across the George Washington Bridge.

I never saw my father more starstruck than the Sunday morning in June of 1936 when he called home and asked mother to rush me over to the Siwanoy Golf and Country Club in Bronxville. It seemed that the great Babe Ruth, now a retired legend, had shown up that morning ready to play golf. The club arranged a foursome for him and dad had made certain that he was one of the members chosen.

I caught up with them on the third hole and spent the rest of the day caddying for my father and studying the great home-run hitter. The Babe embodied all my dreams of glory and riches.

As a golfer, however, Babe Ruth was a failure. Whenever he hit one of his frequent poor shots, he let out a stream of curses. After he exhausted the standard four-letter epithets he used some highly creative phrases that were new to my ear at the age of thirteen. Then and there I adopted the same technique whenever I played golf. A foul mouth did not improve my game, but it made me feel as grown-up and colorful as the great Babe Ruth.

I thought about the incident often. It occurred to me that someone famous did not need to conform to society's norms of decorum. Perhaps, in fact, the nonconformity came first and was one of the precursors of fame.

Mother also groomed me for the limelight, but in a gentler manner. She was my first piano teacher, drilling me in the mechanics of the keyboard on our Mason-Hamlin piano in the music room at the front of the house. From the first she encouraged me to reach out to the world of fantasy, to be less than content playing the music of the great masters. I was always happiest when I improvised; often I would sit on the roof and compose original pieces.

All through these years, mother held season tickets to the White Plains County Center and took me to see and hear reigning artists —Rachmaninoff, Hofmann, Kreisler, Heifetz—even Nelson Eddy. One evening we sat in the front row awaiting the appearance of Ignace Paderewski. After a long delay his doctor came onstage and announced that the virtuoso had suffered a stroke. He died a few days later.

Frequently mother would invite well-known artists to our home. One of them was Lewis Lane, director of musical research for NBC. During a bout with the chicken pox in 1938, I completed a forty-eight-page violin sonata, which I sent on to Lane for his comments. I received a four-page letter in return that crushed me with its opening line: "First of all, your sonata is *too long.*" I have always tended to confuse quantity with quality.

I was a good keyboard improviser, but sight reading came with difficulty. This was my first indication that perhaps music was not my intended career.

Mother and I loved to read together about the lives of the composers. Though my earliest dreams were to join their company, I was bothered by the recurring theme of personal despair in their lives. So many of them died young and penniless. Schubert once sold a composition for a meal. Mozart was buried in a pauper's grave.

By the time I was fifteen my musical interests had shifted from classical to jazz. Ditties like "Lazybones," "Ida," "Margie," and "Ain't She Sweet" seemed to have more commercial potential than piano sonatas, and by that age I was growing more aware that sooner or later I would have to earn a living.

Perhaps it was my father's devastating experience with the stock market that made me so sensitive to the economic realities that lay behind every human pursuit. The effects of the 1929 crash were felt for a decade. Everyone had a newfound respect for money. It was difficult to get. A poignant example of the psychology of the times occurred in 1938 when Lowell Eisenhower, a blood relative of the future U.S. president, was our houseguest for a week. He was a dashing figure, in the mold of Errol Flynn. He earned a superior income working for Wilding Pictures, yet he took a day off to go to New York City to beat up a man who owed him four dollars.

After suffering his bitter losses in the great crash, dad suppressed his fantasies of getting rich through speculation and returned to the more plodding regimen of hard work. He took a job with the Fidelity Investment Association, which marketed secure savings plans to investors. He proved to be a superstar as a salesman because he believed in thrift, now more than ever. He refined the art of imperceptibly nodding his head as he spoke to his prospect. Invariably, the customer was soon nodding his own head in approval of the wisdom of the plan. The house overflowed with sales trophies. During the height of the Depression he won a trip to the 1933 Chicago World's Fair for mother and himself, journeying there on a company airplane. He was named manager of Fidelity's New York office.

But as mother already knew and dad was learning, life moves in inexorable cycles. No upswing lasts forever. The Treasury Department looked askance upon Fidelity because its savings plan was in direct competition with the sale of government bonds. At the height of its success, Fidelity was forced out of business by the Securities and Exchange Commission. The president of the company committed suicide.

Once again dad had to turn to Auntie Blanche for help. She appointed him as manager of the New York office of the Spencer Corset Company. He joked that he took the job to "support" his family, but his bitter irony was obvious.

My increasing awareness of the necessity of earning a living helped my father's practicality win out over mother's emphasis on the arts. Music, I decided, must remain an avocation. I realized that I would have to find some other path to fame.

I often envied Bill, who seemed to have found his niche early in life. He was the mechanic of the family. He acquired an old 1931 Henderson motorcycle, on which he spent hours tinkering. I loved to ride with him, partly for the feel of the cold air blowing into my face, partly for the attention-getting racket that we created. But I was clumsy with a wrench or screwdriver, and how much fame could a mechanic hope for?

I became an incessant reader, searching books for clues to my future. I studied my mother's vast collection of mystic writings. On those frequent days when she was ailing we sat together on her bed, poring over astrology magazines, the writings of Mary Baker Eddy, or the *Bhaghavad Gita.*

In all of my mother's books there was a common message: Human life is generally lived on one particular plane of awareness. But normal consciousness is not necessarily the only sphere of existence. Some humans are capable of tapping into sources of information that are unknown to most others. Mother's books argued that there were unique, often ignored dimensions of existence to be explored.

On days when mother felt well enough she set up her easel outdoors and I often sat by her side and read. Our discussions frequently turned toward the occult. One day we found ourselves on the hill behind our house, so engrossed in our activities that evening overtook us. As mother hurried to finish before the sunlight faded completely, I lay on my back and gazed at the emerging wonders in the sky. A pale yellow moon rose above the horizon.

"Mother," I asked, "are there people on the moon?"

"There could be," she said.

"If there are, can they see us?"

"Perhaps."

A faint star caught my attention. I knew that stars were far more distant than the moon. I knew that the light from the nearest star took four years to reach us.

"Mother, if there are people on a planet that's four light years away from us, and if they have a big enough telescope, and if they are watching us, would they be seeing things that happened here four years ago?"

"I suppose so."

I pondered that for a moment before I asked, "Well, if there are places in the universe where you can see the past, where do you go to see the future?"

Mother put down her paint brush and gazed at me. "I don't know," she said. "Maybe that's why you're here. Maybe it's your job to find out."

Our maid was a stout Scot named Grace Bennett. She worked from 6:00 A.M. to 10:00 P.M. six days a week caring for the house and the family and still found time to be my closest friend. We went shopping together and often indulged in our shared passion for the movies. At home we played cards or tinkered with my chemistry set. Ironically it was Grace—not my father or mother—who introduced me to my first promising career. When I was six she took a summer vacation back home to Scotland. Upon her return she presented me with a simple little red stamp album and a large packet of assorted stamps. I set to work immediately gluing stamps into their proper places, not realizing that I was destroying their value by failing to use peelable hinges.

Here was a world of color and excitement! I was fascinated by the large denominations of some of the stamps, particularly the inflation-plagued Deutschmarks. I could picture myself in a king's treasury, counting out overwhelming sums of pounds, marks, francs, and rubles.

I had to have more stamps. For weeks my mother knew where to find me on a rainy day. I would be in granny's attic searching for old letters, tearing off the stamps and soaking them in water to remove bits of envelope from their backing. The hunt was successful beyond my dreams; I found some stamps that predated the Civil War.

Hearing of this, my great-grandmother raided her own attic and presented me with a carton of stamps she had accumulated during her three trips around the world. The greatest prize was a beautiful set of British Colonials of all colors and styles. Again, I promply pasted them into my album, destroying what value they had.

A few years later I was in Getty Square in Yonkers, where, in a second floor cubicle, I found the Collectors Stamp and Coin Shop, owned by a certain Dr. Neuburg, a Jewish refugee from Hitler's Germany. Noting my interest, the old man invited me to inspect his private collection of several thick albums gloriously stocked with stamps from all over the world. His was no haphazard collection. He had stamps in blocks of four, whole sheets, and complete unused sets of stamps, all neatly mounted in symmetrical rows.

The next day I brought my own collection to show to him. He frowned at the condition of my album and taught me how to mount a stamp with a gummed hinge in order to preserve its value. He was impressed by the devotion I showed to the hobby. He pointed out several of my stamps that would be worth two or three dollars apiece if I had not glued them onto the page.

Dr. Neuburg introduced me to *Scott's Standard Postage Stamp Catalogue,* which was revised annually to identify the current market value of thousands of stamps. Looking through back issues I soon realized that the prices of most stamps rose invariably from one year to the next.

My knowledge of the hobby grew so fast that at the age of fifteen I published a small article in *Stamps* magazine about the Edward Pound, a relatively rare British issue I had found in a Yonkers shop.

At school, the classroom bored me; I was far happier with extracurricular activities. Sometimes I entertained for assemblies, performing my own compositions on the piano. I always auditioned for the plays, once landing the lead role of Prince Charming in *The Nutcracker Suite.* I promptly fell in love with my co-star, Ruth Knight. My fondest memories of school are the kissing-scene rehearsals.

The presence of girls was the highlight of school for me, but there were few other compensations. Events came to a crisis in 1939 when I was a sophomore at Gorton High School.

Regardless of the distractions of my surroundings, I have always been able to lock myself into my own world when I found reality boring. I had perfected the technique of outwitting long-winded preachers by following the notes in the hymnal up and down with my eyes, searching for patterns. Now I applied the same technique in the classroom. My geometry teacher frequently found me in the back of the room playing rock, paper, scissors with a fellow sufferer or reading the *Phantom Detective Magazine.* Geometry was a subject that should have fascinated me, for I had a great appreciation for all of nature's patterns. But this teacher presented geometry by rote. I did not want to be told to memorize a rigid set of rules. I wanted to experiment, to test the rules before I blindly accepted them.

I flunked geometry, therefore.

My parents were always mildly upset with my occasional Cs or a rare D. But failing a subject was out of the question if I was ever to be accepted by a first-rate university. Mother and dad realized that they had to find a school that would challenge me.

Nor was I their only concern right then. This was the very time when the Fidelity Investment Association was under investigation by the Securities and Exchange Commission. Dad was worried about losing his job.

Mother suffered one of her periodic physical setbacks and was bedridden for some time.

Bill became disoriented. He seemed unable to remember the simplest matters. He experienced bouts of insomnia and irrational anger. Doctors diagnosed dementia praecox, the juvenile form of a degenerative disease often caused by vascular problems in the brain. There was hope for a full recovery, but for a time, at least, Bill had to be hospitalized. My parents reluctantly placed him at the West-port Sanitarium in Connecticut. We visited him occasionally and often talked with him by phone, but it was difficult for all of us to live without him.

Europe was moving toward an encompassing war. Mother pre-dicted that the United States would be drawn into the conflict just at the time when her sons were of prime draft age. There was constant discussion of death and destruction.

Sometimes in the evenings Grace told us frightful stories of World War I. As a young girl in Edinburgh she experienced terrible nights of horror when German dirigibles bombed the city. After listening to Grace recount her stories I would go to bed and shiver whenever an airplane flew overhead. I would squirm in bed for hours, trying to get comfortable.

Suddenly, somehow, I would be standing outside in the yard, gazing up at my mother and Bill, who had managed to climb onto the roof. They sat at the apex, chatting and smoking cigarettes. Then mother would begin to slide down the steep slope, unable to control herself. Bill always reached out to help her and then he also lost control. As the two of them tumbled toward the edge of the roof I screamed. I could only attempt to catch one of them. Whom should I save? My mother? Or my brother?

Before they hit the ground I would always wake to cold, damp-ened bedsheets.

New York Central's *Pacemaker* cleared the network of tracks beneath Manhattan, sped along the banks of the Hudson River, and emerged into the upstate countryside, carrying me off to a new life. With a copy of *Esquire* under my arm I made my way to the smoking car, feeling more mature than my sixteen years. Throughout this long September day in 1939, I kept my eyes at the window, enjoying the new sights. There was so much of the world to see, so much of God's creation to enjoy, so many interesting people to meet. I vowed that I would experience it all.

As Albany gave way to Schenectady and Syracuse I grew sleepy and philosophical. I wondered what awaited me in Woodstock, Illinois, where my parents had enrolled me in the Todd School for Boys, whose most illustrious alumnus was Orson Welles. The previous year, Welles had achieved notoriety—and panicked a good part of the populace—with his Halloween radio production of H. G. Wells's *War of the Worlds,* and I fantasized the great actor returning to his alma mater and directing me in a play. I prayed that Todd would not be merely a more exclusive copycat of the unimaginative public school system. I wanted to learn, but I was impatient. Through my voluminous reading I had already taught myself most everything that was considered fundamental. I wanted to move into unexplored spheres.

After spending a night in Chicago I arrived in Woodstock the next morning. The school bus picked me up at the station and drove me to the campus. I was introduced to headmaster Roger Hill, who had been like a father to Orson Welles. Then a designated student took me on a tour of the several buildings that would constitute my home for the next two years.

I felt comfortable immediately. The repressive "babysitting" atmosphere of Gorton High did not exist here. Todd adjusted its programs to the interests of individual students. The print shop captivated me. I learned to operate the linotype machine, and the occasional burns from spurting hot lead did not deter me. As I worked I could fantasize my own name spelled out in the byline of a work of poetry or prose, or perhaps a prize-winning scientific thesis.

By now I had learned to live with what I had come to see as a unique trait of those in my family. I was not a one-issue person. The world was chock full of interesting pursuits and it seemed impossible for me to concentrate on any one field for long. I was fascinated by chemistry, but the harmonies of atomic theory carried my interests back to music. Thoughts of a musical career were always dashed by my concern about money.

I would then shift into my economic frame of mind, wondering whether I could learn to forecast the machinations of the financial world with greater precision than my father had managed. Money, to me, was synonymous with fame. Thoughts of fame would push me onto the stage in one of Todd's many theatrical productions, or set me to work at the typewriter composing a poem or working on an article for the school paper. Sometimes I was so confused about my future that I entertained thoughts of being a generalist, of *specializing* in *everything*. But that was a paradox, and only set my mind spinning once more to the infinite variety of potential human pursuits.

I could only hope that as time passed I would learn to concentrate my efforts, and as my first year at Todd took form, I was able to center my attention more and more upon chemistry. This was due in part to my discovery of the explosive properties of sodium.

One of my favorite applications of this knowledge was to drop a speck of sodium into a bottle half-filled with water, slam on the cork and thrust the bomb under someone's chair. The reaction was simple. The liquid changed from water to sodium hydroxide. In the process it liberated hydrogen into the plugged-up atmosphere of the bottle. The resultant explosion was a thing of joy and beauty, and a wonderful attention-getter.

Such exploits were not condoned by the administration at Todd, but my chemistry teacher, Mr. Marsh, was a hellion himself who once sprayed the campus with shrapnel when he placed black powder in the carburetor of a derelict Ford truck. This was the kind of teacher I could relate to, and his own spirit of adventure encouraged him to give me a free hand.

He also gave me a key to the chemistry lab.

Only a handful of the approximately 100 students smoked, but the school was liberal enough to set aside an area for habitués on the road behind my dormitory. Before long I was the acknowledged leader of the "Tobacco Road Gang."

My hydrogen bombs were the subject of discussion one evening as I sat idly in the smoking area with my pals Jim Thurston and Richard Ruxton.

"What would happen if you took a larger piece of sodium and flushed it into the toilet?" one of them asked.

"I don't know," I replied. "A bigger explosion, I guess."

This was an irresistible challenge. Temporarily assuming the identity of my hero, Humphrey Bogart, I formulated a plan. Under cover of darkness we made our way to the second floor chemistry lab and selected a lump of sodium as large as a golf ball. Suppressing our giggles, we climbed a staircase to the top floor, flushed the sodium down the toilet, and ran.

Fortunately for us, the reaction occurred a half second before the French teacher entered the ladies' room one floor below. The deafening blast blew the seat clear off the toilet. Bits of masonry pelted the room. The pipes ruptured, sending water cascading through the hall and down the stairways.

Since Mr. Marsh knew that I possessed a key to the chemistry lab, he could have quickly identified the ringleader of this plot. But if he had any suspicions, he kept his counsel. Perhaps he realized that creative teaching necessitated experimentation.

Organic chemistry interested me the most, for it is the stuff of which life is made, and Mr. Marsh fostered the development of my own hypothesis, which I called the CHO theory. I believed that any carbon-hydrogen-oxygen compound could be synthesized by the process of polymerization, rearranging the molecular structure by placing it under severe pressure.

The CHO theory took further shape during Christmas vacation when my parents sent me for a short visit with a very special man, my grandfather, Dr. Albert Cushing Crehore. He lived in a small house on Euclid Avenue in Cleveland, where he spent most of his time refining his atomic theories. Semiretired at seventy-one, the kind, portly gentleman still lectured frequently at the Case Institute of Applied Sciences.

In the space of a week grandpa did his best to indoctrinate me into his pet hypothesis. He could never bring himself to believe the prevailing theory that electrons were in constant orbit around an atomic nucleus. "Niels Bohr is wrong!" he ranted. Grandpa believed that electrons were a static part of the nucleus until excited by an outside stimulus. He wrote several treatises on the subject and attracted a few converts, but was generally considered to be eccentric in his views.

What particularly impressed me about the old gentleman was his undiminished drive for international recognition. He made no secret of his goal—the Nobel Prize in physics. He felt that he had worked hard for it and that it was rightfully his.

True to family tradition, he encouraged me to follow my own inclinations in whatever field I eventually decided to pursue. He was pleased with my current interest in chemistry and chuckled with a faraway look in his eye when I told him about blowing up the toilet.

He gave me a list of all the carbon-hydrogen-oxygen compounds and advised me to explore the potential uses of my CHO theory. As I studied, I devised a clear and practical goal. I wanted to synthesize vitamin A, become rich, and win the Nobel Prize in chemistry. In my mind it was now a contest to see who would win the Nobel first, grandpa or me.

As I did with everything, I looked at the project on an economic level. The Eastman Kodak catalog of rare organic compounds listed the current price of vitamin A as $10 for one-tenth of a gram. At that rate a pound would sell for $45,600. My plan was to synthesize a few pounds of vitamin A and retire.

My parents had moved to Westport, Connecticut, to be closer to Bill. They purchased a country home on Green's Farm Road, which mother immediately named Dream Acres. It was smaller than the Yonkers house, but comfortable and idyllic. It was heavily wooded on one side; the other faced onto a great, open field. Dad was quick to erect a flagpole in front and almost as quick to set up croquet wickets in the backyard near an old red barn.

When I arrived in Westport for summer vacation my parents were lovingly proud of a volume of poetry I had composed over the course of the year. Dad contracted with the Fleming H. Revell Company to publish my collection of verse under the title *A Schoolboy's Faith*, in which I placed a special dedication to Bill. The contract called for a printing of 1,000 copies to sell at one dollar a piece, but dad planned to purchase them all at the author's 40-percent discount and place them in local bookstores.

It was a thrill like no other, in the spring of 1941, to see my byline on *A Schoolboy's Faith*, the handsome dust cover exhibiting both my portrait and signature.

One of the first notices appeared in a Cincinnati newspaper, and the reviewer was impressed with the insights of a young author. Back home, the *Westporter* called me Westport's challenge to Orson Welles. Dad saw to it that local bookstores were well supplied, and the limited edition soon sold out.

It felt to me as though Edgar Cayce's prediction was close to fulfillment.

War had not yet come to the United States in the spring of 1941 when I graduated from Todd, but the draft was a reality that could not be avoided by any healthy young man. Bill had recovered so completely from his difficulties that he was accepted by the Marines.

Still undecided over the plethora of careers available to me, I took a year off from school. For a few weeks, as Westport's budding author, I was feted at cocktail parties. I always requested a Manhattan at these events, because I did not know the name of any other cocktail.

I joined a theater troupe in New York known as the Valdes Players and toured small cities playing Ibsen, Noël Coward, and other standard authors. I wrote a three-act comedy entitled *Hot Tropics*, but it remained unpublished.

Meanwhile, the draft came ever closer to me. I was ready to serve my country, but not anxious to accelerate the process. As a delaying tactic I signed up for the Navy's V-1 program, which allowed me to attend college for at least a year prior to active duty.

My choice of schools was made simple by the fact that Bill's girl friend, Shirley Wilcox, had enrolled at Duke University in Durham, North Carolina. Unbeknownst to anyone, I was passionately in love with Shirley, so I, too, enrolled at Duke.

As I waited for the college year to begin, the idyllic country environment set my mind to scheming. The previous year the post office had issued seven unique sets of commemorative stamps honoring the nation's heroes. To me this Famous Americans collection was like a new volume of *Minute Biographies* with glue on the back. I pictured my face on them.

More so, I pictured money in the family purse. The Famous Americans sold for their face value of ten cents apiece at the post office. I knew that relatively few of them had been printed. There were 70 stamps on each sheet. I calculated what might happen if we bought 110 sheets of each of the 35 stamps, took care to preserve them, and held them for investment. This plan would require an outlay of $5,390—money that was dear to my parents but nonetheless available from mother's inheritance. Extrapolating a one-cent-per-year rise in value for each stamp, I predicted a 10 percent annual return in an era when banks were paying 2 percent on savings accounts.

Dad was pleased with the industry I exhibited in filling sheets of papers with columns of numbers, but he was not disposed to take investment advice from his eighteen-year-old son. He vetoed the plan.

Only six years later the stamps had a market value of $45,908. I had underestimated their rapid rise. We could have realized a profit of more than 850 percent in six years, but it was not to be.

My romance with Shirley Wilcox met the same fate. Days before I was to leave for Duke she changed her plans. But I was already committed, so I journeyed to Durham alone in September 1942 and entered the university as a chemistry major.

Still enthralled with my CHO theory, I neglected any facet of study that was irrelevant. I failed algebra because I sat in the back of the room working out organic transformations. My French grades were dismal. This did not concern me, for I placed a far higher value on one spectacular achievement than on the generalized accomplishment of earning a diploma. That first semester I hoisted many a beer mug to the future success of my CHO theory.

But I began to experience more and more problems with its practical application. I probably still hold the record for glass breakage in the Duke chemistry lab. In one semester the chemistry department added $450 to my school bill to cover their losses. One day it all came to a head. There I was—all set up for an ambitious experiment, beakers and bottles and test tubes arrayed on the workbench in every direction—when a co-ed came up to ask what time I would pick her up for the Saturday night dance. As I whirled around, my elbow caught the entire edifice and down it went—$90 lying in brittle bits on the lab floor.

As the school year drew to a close I decided to drop my chemistry major and, with it, the pursuit of my elusive CHO theory.

Late in the semester I chanced upon a copy of *Looking Backward*, by J. E. Handshaw, which described his life as a stamp collector. In one chapter he recounted how he had purchased a bulk supply of half a million U.S. stamps, sorted them, and sold them for a handsome profit.

I had $200 in my bank account and subscriptions to several stamp collectors' magazines. In these I found many classified ads offering stamps for sale by the pound. One ad, for example, offered a mixture of 28 pounds of U.S. stamps for $10. Once more my fantasies took hold of me. At 4,500 stamps to the pound, I set a goal of amassing 223 pounds, or 1 million stamps. If each stamp increased in value by a penny a year, I would have an annual income of $10,000.

Mother never forgot that summer. Almost every day huge mailbags full of stamps arrived at Dream Acres. I sat in the middle of my room, tearing into each new treasure sack, tossing stamps into paper bags carefully labeled for identification. There were paper bags blanketing the floor, all over and under my bed, on every bookshelf, in the closet, and spilling out into the hallway. I had stamps in my pockets, in my socks, in my hair. The hub of all this was a mountain of unsorted stamps rising ever higher in the center of the room.

Before long I had accumulated 250,000 stamps, one-fourth of my goal.

I took to hanging around the post office on State Street to see what new stamps were being issued. Inevitably the postmaster learned of my interest and one day invited me to his office and exhibited the contents of his big, black safe. Tucked away inside were sheets of the old 1922 regular issues in their original, mint condition. They had been out of circulation for more than a decade and their value had grown exponentially. Many varieties of the 1940 Famous Americans series were also here in their pristine state. They were all still available at their original price.

Most of my cash was tied up in a quarter million assorted stamps, but this was too good a chance even for dad to ignore. The next morning I raced to the post office with our combined cash resources in hand and bought every obsolete stamp I could find.

We held the collection for many years before finally selling out for a substantial profit.

All of this activity took place during the month of June. I had to report back to Duke on July 1 for indoctrination into the V-1 program.

3.

SECOND CHRONICLES

Five-thirty in the morning, every morning, found me in my naval fatigues staring in stuporous disbelief at the captain who insisted on this primitive ritual of roll call. Adding injury to insult, he then took us on a forced run before breakfast. The only compensation I could see was that the girls were very impressed with the dress whites I had to wear to class.

I was a premed major now, foundering in a sea of physics, trigonometry, and anatomy. At lunch I might attempt to lift a forkful of dripping Salisbury steak to my mouth, but the stench of formaldehyde on my hands would transform the hamburger into the cat I had just dissected.

I knew that I would never become a doctor, but I did not know what other course of study to pursue. Like so many of my peers I simply marked time until my Uncle Sam decided what to do with me.

Young American men, my brother included, risked their lives all over the world even as I cursed the predawn mornings in Durham. Bill, a radio technician in the Marines, proudly wore battle ribbons from New Caledonia, New Hebrides, and the Marianas, and boasted a set of corporal's stripes. But the Navy held me in reserve, presumably for the ultimate assault of the war. Not until the spring of 1944 was I ordered to boot camp in Plattsburgh, New York.

The Plattsburg stay was mercifully short. For some reason hidden deep within the naval bureaucracy I was ordered to finish boot camp in Asbury Park, New Jersey. En route, I enjoyed a few days' liberty at home in Westport.

The uncertainty of what awaited me weighed on my heart. I would surely be sent to the Pacific; the war against Germany was on the wane. The Japanese, though beaten, were committed to suicidal defense, relinquishing one small island at a time at an increasingly severe cost in young lives from both sides. Ahead of us all lay the prospect of the invasion of Japan itself, which would surely be the bloodiest battle in all history. In preparation for this inevitable holocaust, the services were conscripting every available man.

I had always been a fatalist. If the time of my death was approaching, so be it, the reasonable part of me said. Death was nothing to fear. Like my mother, I believed that death was merely a doorway to another plane of existence.

Yet the emotional part of me cried out to live, to experience all the wonders that the future held—if there was a future.

I was in this confusing, depressed state of mind when my parents brought the Reverend Ernest A. Reese and his two daughters home for Sunday dinner. My first glimpse of the elder girl, Kitty, was unforgettable. She lay in the hammock stretched between two of our pine trees and stared at me with undisguised passion.

Kitty and I took in a William Bendix movie that night and fell in love immediately. We wrote to one another as I finished boot camp, and we enjoyed a reunion in Westport before I was sent off to midshipman school at Northwestern University.

With the war staring me in the face I took my naval studies seriously, particularly enjoying courses in gunnery and communications. Most of all I lived for the arrival of Kitty's letters from Smith College.

In January 1945 I returned from Chicago proudly wearing the sparkling insignia of an ensign. Kitty was home on vacation and dad brought her to the train station, where she ducked under a restraining rope to rush onto the platform and greet me with a meaningful kiss.

We were ecstatic when orders arrived assigning me to a four-month communications course at Harvard, not far from Smith College and Kitty. We never missed a weekend together. After class on

Friday I caught a train to Northampton, dropped my suitcase at a small boarding house, and rushed over to Tenney House, where I entertained on the sitting-room piano until Kitty came downstairs. One special weekend I surprised her with an engagement ring, purchased with money borrowed from dad.

During my stay at Harvard I rekindled another love. I happened to pick up a copy of the 1945 edition of *Scott's Standard Postage Stamp Catalogue* and noted how greatly stamp prices had increased in only three years.

Suddenly I had the idea for my second book! The economics of stamp collecting were rather simple. I believed that I could accurately predict the prices of certain postage stamps five years in advance, and, if I could, the service would be a boon to the growing number of investors.

The key was to concentrate on stamps that were in limited supply. Each year the U.S. government designs and prints a number of stamps to commemorate historic events or to honor memorable people or organizations. These are stamps keyed to a particular date, such as an anniversary, and for this reason commemoratives are almost never reissued.

Therefore, from the very moment that a commemorative is placed on sale in the nation's post offices, it begins to diminish in supply. Eighty-five percent of all commemoratives are used for postage, canceled, and can never again regain their mint, or unused, condition. The remaining 15 percent of the issue is purchased by collectors, but this supply shrinks through age, wear, theft, and disposal. After a few years only a small number of top quality mint stamps remain in the hands of collectors and dealers.

Clearly, there is a diminishing supply of U.S. commemorative stamps held in mint condition.

But look at the other side of the equation. There are millions of stamp collectors throughout the world. The hobby is so fascinating that it easily creates lifelong devotees. It teaches them about world governments, currencies, and languages. It embodies the disciplines of history, geography, and biography. It fosters an appreciation of art. Nearly one out of every ten Americans has a stamp collection of some kind. Even my commander-in-chief, President Franklin D. Roosevelt, was an avid collector.

There is thus a constantly *decreasing* supply of U.S. commemorative stamps that are demanded by *increasing* numbers of collectors. The law of supply and demand decrees that, over a period of time, the value of these stamps must certainly rise.

Stories of the wisdom of investing in stamps are legion. One of my favorites is the tale of financier Arthur Hind. In 1929 Hind boasted holdings of $19 million that he had invested in blue chip stocks, government bonds, and real estate. Another $1 million—5 percent of his fortune—was invested in his stamp collection. He died during the height of the Depression, after the value of his holdings had severely eroded. When his assets were liquidated in a series of notorious auctions, all of his stocks, bonds, and real estate holdings brought in $3 million, having lost nearly 85 percent of their value. But his stamp collection sold for more than $1 million, now representing 25 percent of his estate. His stamps retained all of their value amid the worst economic conditions the country had ever known.

And when general economic conditions are good the increase in stamp values can rival the wildest fluctuations in the stock market. For example, if my father, instead of speculating in the stock market, had purchased 2,000 copies of each U.S. commemorative stamp issued between 1912 and 1929, he would have invested a mere $2,380 in seventeen years. He would have been 100 percent certain that he bought those stamps at the bottom of the market, for he would have obtained them at the post office for face value. They could never shrink below that value because they would always be usable for postage, if nothing else.

Dad's modest investment would have weathered the crash of 1929, because stamp collecting is an inexpensive diversion that gains in popularity whenever people have less money to spend on more lavish forms of entertainment. By 1940, according to *Scott's*, his initial investment of $2,380 would have skyrocketed to $108,013, an increase of 4,500 percent in less than 30 years.

I could not escape the conclusion that investing in U.S. commemorative stamps was far safer and potentially more lucrative than buying gold, silver, diamonds, furs, or stocks and bonds. Stamps were a sure thing!

The investor, however, must look upon stamps as a long-term

commitment. The sensible course of action is to buy systematically, take care to preserve the stamps in proper condition, and sell each issue between ten and fifteen years after purchase.

The stamp market, like all markets, fluctuates in a cyclical manner. When it comes time to sell his stamps the investor needs to look for an approaching bull market top if he is to benefit from the best price. No one had ever attempted to predict such price peaks. The stamp business had no way of measuring the general ups and downs of its market.

Wall Street had, over the years, solved this problem by devising a number of indices to signal trends in the stock market, the most famous being the Dow Jones Industrial Average. I realized that Nassau Street, the area of Manhattan where the most influential stamp dealers were centered, needed the same sort of indicators.

So, to mimic the Dow Jones Average of thirty industrial stocks, I created what I called the 20-Blue Chip Index, which I envisioned as a barometer of the entire stamp market. For the list I chose what I considered to be the twenty U.S. commemoratives that seemed best to reflect the trend of stamp prices as a whole.

I added together the 1941 prices for these twenty stamps, as listed in *Scott's,* then calculated the necessary divisor that would establish the 1941 value of my 20-Blue Chip Index at 100.00. Each year, by totaling the current value of all twenty stamps and dividing by the same divisor, I could calculate the rise and fall of the market.

Dow Jones did not rely upon a single average, so neither would Joe Granville. My second indicator calculated the value of full sheets of stamps (usually 100 to a sheet). This 20-Recent Sheet Index concentrated on the more valuable new commemoratives, representing the most volatile portion of the stamp market.

I began to codify my theories into a thick manuscript that I entitled *Price Predictions.* I hoped that I could finish it before I shipped out to the Pacific.

Kitty and I were married on May 5, 1945, at the First Congregational Church in Greenwich, Connecticut. Bill, home from the Pacific and resplendent in his Marine uniform, was my best man. He also lent me his Mercury convertible for the honeymoon.

My bride and I left in a rainstorm for a rented cottage at Candlewood Lake, near Danbury. The spring air was cold and damp, the storm worsening, when we arrived. We turned on a small gas heater in the cabin, put Chopin on the phonograph, and snuggled together under the covers. Finally sated, we fell asleep in one another's arms.

My eyes blinked open with alarm the next morning. The cozy surroundings of the cabin were replaced by the antiseptic white of a hospital room. Our gas heater had flamed out during the night, nearly suffocating us. We were discovered, lying naked on the floor of our cabin, just in time. I was angry at this stupid interruption of our honeymoon and snapped at the nurse for forbidding me to smoke.

Time accelerated in the next few weeks. Each day I reported to the Port Director of New York for duty, returning in the evening to our small rented room on Eighty-third Street in Manhattan. I always managed a few hours work on the manuscript of *Price Predictions* before making love to Kitty.

I finished the book before I received orders to ship out for Pearl Harbor via San Francisco. I gave the manuscript to my mother with orders to have it printed at the Hour Press in Norwalk, Connecticut. Kitty, crying hysterically, put me on the train to San Francisco and returned to her parents' home for the balance of the summer.

The misfortune of the Japanese was my own salvation. President Truman's agonizing decision to unleash the atomic bomb on Hiroshima and Nagasaki brought the war to a precipitous end. More than 100,000 people were killed in the two cities, but the awesome use of power made the invasion of Japan unnecessary and saved maybe a million other lives. *C'est la guerre.*

Since I was one of the last men sent to the Pacific, I would be one of the last to leave. My job would be to help clean up the aftermath of war and allow the fighting men to return as soon as possible. I was assigned as a communications officer on Roi Namur, a small island in the Marshall archipelago about sixty miles north of Kwajalein.

We called it the Battle of Boredom.

Mail call was the highlight of the day. I looked forward to the frequent letters from Kitty, who had returned to her studies at Smith College. Mother sent me a very special present—a copy of *Price*

Predictions, which she had copyrighted on my twenty-second birthday. It was selling very well in the New York bookstores, particularly around Nassau Street.

There was little to do on Roi Namur except work, sleep, drink, and gamble. During my brief stay at Pearl Harbor I had the thrill of playing cards with Commander Oswald Jacoby, an expert at both bridge and poker. I obtained a copy of his classic book on poker and applied its principles successfully for the duration of my service. I had my entire paycheck sent to Kitty, supporting myself on my poker winnings.

Since I was a published author myself, I was assigned the job of hopping around to the nearby islands to write human interest stories for stateside consumption and, in the process, to augment the liquor supply of our Officer's Club. On one of these trips I witnessed a memorable drama that would later figure in one of the greatest mistakes of my life.

Every island had a grass shack devoted to a twenty-four-hour poker game. I invariably found the action and sat in whenever I could. One night I had to wait for an empty seat and used the time to study the habits of the opposition. One of the players was a captain whom I noted for his conservative betting pattern. During the hour that I waited for a seat the captain never bet more than twenty dollars, and he always dropped out immediately whenever he had a weak hand.

Finally a seat became available to the left of a young, unsmiling lieutenant commander with a dark five o'clock shadow on his face. I placed my bankroll of $800 onto the table, threw in my $10 ante, and prepared myself for action.

It was the captain's deal and he called five-card stud. He dealt everyone one card face down and one card face up. His own king was the highest card showing and he promptly bet $100. Based on his conservative pattern of betting, I had to assume that he had another king face down. Three of the other seven players called his bet, including the lieutenant commander to my right, who had a queen showing. Since the bet represented one-eighth of my capital, and since I had a weak hand, I folded.

The captain dealt the remaining players their third card, face up. No one caught a pair, so his king was still high. He bet another $100.

Everyone folded except the lieutenant commander, who called the $100 with an inscrutable expression fixed upon his face.

Two more cards spun out from the deck. Neither player paired up. Again the captain bet $100 and again the lieutenant commander called the bet. To everyone at the table it seemed obvious that the younger officer had a second queen in the hole, since he continued to match the captain's heavy bets. There was now $880 in the pot.

The captain dealt the final card face up. The lieutenant commander now had a pair of deuces showing, presumably to go with his pair of queens. The captain had no pair showing.

The lieutenant commander bet $100. The captain, sensing a bluff, matched the $100 and raised the pot another $100. With no hesitation the lieutenant commander saw the $100 raise, counted out the remaining $500 in front of him, and tossed it all into the pot. There was now $1,780 in the middle of the table.

Moments passed in silence. It would cost the captain another $500 to see the lieutenant commander's hole card. Finally the captain dropped his shoulders in resignation and folded his hand.

As he reached across the table to rake in his huge pot, the lieutenant commander accidentally nudged his hole card off the table. It fell to the floor near my feet, face up. Naturally I glanced at it. It was not a queen after all, but the ten of hearts. The lieutenant commander had pulled off a superb bluff, beating the captain's apparent pair of kings with a mere pair of deuces and the guts to push hundreds of dollars into the pot.

The memory of that bluff would come back to me years later as I attempted to assess the nerve of that same lieutenant commander after he had worked his way up to become president of the United States.

"My health is at a very low ebb now and it will take lots of good food to put me back on my feet," I wrote to my parents on October 13, 1945. "I haven't had a glass of milk since I left the States, nor a piece of lettuce. Recently (two days ago) an insufficient supply of chlorine was discovered and a medical analysis of the drinking water has revealed a large quantity of polio germs. Two other men came down with fever yesterday, but I know my illness is not from this source, and is, I hope, merely in line with the terrifically hot weather we have been having and the run of bad food that has been ours for the last few days.

"How much longer this staying here is going to last no one knows.

I just came back from Tarawa ten days ago and I caught some kind of fever down there. Nevertheless I have to stand my watches and tonight I have the midnight watch and am very weary. I do so want to go home."

I collapsed on duty that night, doubling over from severe abdominal pain. Doctors diagnosed malaria.

I did not reveal to my parents the worst part of my malady. It was increasingly painful to sit down because of a burning sensation in my right testicle. Over a period of days it began to swell. By the time I reported to sick bay it was the size of a golf ball. For days I lay naked in a hospital bed, unable to stand even the slight pressure of clothing on my expanding testicle. Whiling away the time by perusing medical books, I found one that pictured an African native so deformed by elephantiasis that he had to push a wheelbarrow around to support his giant testicle.

My condition quickly became the major topic of discussion on the island. Everyone was taking bets on how large Granville's testicle would grow. By the time it reached the size of a grapefruit I was near hysteria, visualizing myself going through life with a wheelbarrow.

The ailment was probably a complication of malaria, but the Navy doctors never could reach a clear diagnosis. I did not care what it was, only that the condition be arrested. Finally, when they made a pincushion of my behind, shooting me up with 100,000 units of penicillin a day, the testicle begin to shrink back to normal size. The doctors told me that I would be sterile.

For a time the deadening routine of Roi Namur was a threat to my emotional health also. I found myself slipping into a functional coma. I stood my watches. I gambled and drank. I ate and slept. I did absolutely nothing that was productive.

It finally occurred to me that each passing day was a twenty-four-hour portion of my life. Why should I waste it? Was there something I could do with my free time that would begin to build a career for me back home?

When dad sent the welcome word that *Price Predictions* had completely sold out, I decided to set to work on a second edition. My first predictions were 85 percent accurate. I had correctly predicted the beginning of a new bull market in stamps. As I sought to extend the basic concepts of *Price Predictions*, I developed a theory that was to become central to all of my future work.

Analysis of any market is a difficult task. Price fluctuations are merely the reflections of the emotional reactions of human beings —the buyers and sellers who create the market. Anyone can trace the ebb and flow of emotions in the past performance of a market, but predicting them ahead of time is far more difficult. Human emotions are complex. To predict a market, therefore, one must develop as intricate a system of indicators as possible. There is strength and safety in numbers.

The two indicators I had already developed were good, but more would be better. For my third indicator, then, I created the Used Index, because mint condition stamps represent only a portion of the market. I carefully chose representative stamps of the past fifty years that had demonstrated an ability to hold their value even when in used condition.

Then I plunged into the job of creating the most comprehensive list of all, the Master Sheet Index, which included all 10 of the Army-Navy stamps issued in 1936–37, all 35 of the Famous Americans series, all 13 of the Flag series of 1943–44, and many others. In all, 145 varieties made up the Master Sheet Index.

Now I had four major indicators of stamp market activity, but I was still not finished. Following the lead of Dow Jones, which combines the values of its Industrial, Transportation, and Utilities averages to create its list of sixty-five stocks, I combined my indicators to form the 4-Index total, which finally gave the stamp world a complete barometer of price activity.

I was so engrossed in this work that I could think of nothing else. When I finally returned in March of 1946 Kitty and I immediately embarked upon a second honeymoon. We holed up in a motel room in Culpeper, Virginia. We were surrounded by the glories of nature. Beneath our feet were wondrous natural caverns; stretching above us the Blue Ridge Mountains offered spectacular vistas of springtime in the Shenandoah Valley. We could hike, canoe, golf, or laze in the warm sun. But we were strangers to one another. The wartime tingle was gone. We both knew it immediately, but tried to ignore the death of love.

Oblivious to the beautiful countryside around me, I worked ten hours a day to refine my manuscript, which ran three times longer than the first edition.

After the short, disappointing vacation Kitty returned to her studies at Smith. I went home to Westport and delivered my manuscript to the publishing company. I remodeled the barn at Dream Acres into a small studio apartment, but this activity proved futile. Kitty moved in for a short time that summer; however, she continually found excuses for visiting her mother. For her part, Kitty's mother increasingly pressed me with questions about my future. She reminded me constantly that I had no money.

Kitty and I soon parted by mutual agreement. Like so many of our generation, the marriage was a hysterical reaction to war. When the war ended, so did the emotional tie.

I found myself more disturbed by this failure than I would have thought. *Price Predictions* was a great success, selling out more quickly the second time. Harry L. Lindquist, the publisher of *Stamps* magazine, asked me to write a series of articles for him. At the age of twenty-three I was a recognized authority in the field of stamp investment, but I was unsettled.

My life was hollow.

4.
NUMBERS

One sunny morning Oddlot the caveman chanced upon a lump of stone that reflected the daylight with a pleasing yellowish sparkle. Humming a primitive ditty, he set to work assembling a collection of the bizarre rocks, which he cached safely away at home.

Being a bachelor, Oddlot had to leave his cave unguarded for long hours each day as he hunted for a tasty pterodactyl. He worried that his unscrupulous neighbor Nasdaq might discover his hiding place. How could he be sure his treasure was not tampered with?

Somewhere in the recesses of his prehistoric brain Oddlot conjured a method of monitoring his collection. He pulled a stone from his pile, placed it to one side, and scratched a mark onto the wall of his cave.

He had invented counting.

Soon his wall was covered with marks, each representing a golden rock on a one-for-one basis. Every night when he returned home he counted his stones, making sure that he still had one for each mark on the wall. After a time he came to realize that there was a rhythm in his head as he counted. The second stone seemed to be different from the first—and of course it was. The first was number one; the second was number two.

He had invented numbers.

Oddlot was pleased with his accomplishment and lay down to sleep, realizing once again that he was *so* lonely.

Nasdaq was poor in worldly goods, but he did possess three wives, five daughters, and more sons than Oddlot could count. The daughters particularly interested Oddlot, and one day he approached Nasdaq with a proposition. He would give Nasdaq one of his prized lumps of rock in exchange for a daughter.

"Fair enough," Nasdaq grunted, proud of his business acumen. They had invented the market.

Weeks passed. Enamored with the delights of marriage and of counting, Oddlot reasoned that if one wife was good, two would be twice as good. Toting another lump of gold over to his neighbor, he proposed a second deal, equal to the first.

"Not so fast!" Nasdaq growled. He had noticed that the glint in his neighbor's eye outshone the precious stone. "If you want one more daughter, you must give me two stones."

Nasdaq had invented inflation.

Oddlot stifled an impulse to crush Nasdaq's skull with the stone, seeing himself outnumbered by the uncountable sons. "I'll think about it," he said, stalking off.

"One daughter, two stones," Nasdaq called after him. "Or I'll sell you my oldest wife for one stone."

We can never know what Oddlot decided, for the historical record ends here. But the story illustrates a concept often overlooked by those who do not have a mathematical bent. To many, numbers are dull, dry, meaningless abstractions. But to Oddlot and Nasdaq numbers represented basic human realities. Numbers offered a means of quantifying the swings in their behavioral patterns. The emotions of love, lust, greed, and jealousy were intertwined with their argument over a number.

Without the realization of what they represent, the study of numbers is meaningless; with it, the study is all-encompassing. It was to this study that I found myself inexorably drawn as I searched for my own lump of gold. I became engrossed in statistical studies because I was increasingly aware of the ability of numbers to signal human behavior *in advance.*

With only loose plans for the future, I applied for readmission to Duke. Due to the postwar glut of students I had to wait a year to return to the scholastic life, so I took a small apartment in New York and hunted for a job.

Harry Lindquist of *Stamps* magazine was sufficiently impressed with my investment philosophies to make me his protégé. Harry was president of the New York Athletic Club, where he often took me to poker games with such notables as actors Brian Donlevy and Alan Ladd, and Theodore Steinway, the piano magnate. A great sportsman, Harry took me to Madison Square Garden for the famed Milrose Games. At a special dinner commemorating the centennial of the first U.S. postage stamp, Harry had me seated at the head table with Steinway and Cardinal Spellman. He even arranged private luncheons for me with ex-King Farouk of Egypt and Alexander Kerensky, the exiled Russian who headed the provisional government during the time between the overthrow of the czar and the victory of Lenin's Communist forces. Both of these fallen leaders were avid stamp collectors.

Wherever we went Harry introduced me as the first man to put philately on an investment basis. He knew that I had helped my readers earn money and he wanted me to do the same. I had paid the printing bills myself for my two editions of *Price Predictions,* and Harry wanted me to write on a more professional basis. He worked out a contract for a third edition to be published under Harry's own imprint and he gave me a cash advance against royalties.

In the meantime I found a sixty-dollar-a-week job with a Manhattan consulting firm that specialized in hospital fund-raising. My job was to estimate the cost of each room in a proposed new hospital building and then help write the brochure that would form the basis of the campaign.

Regardless of the reality of the situation, my task was to "prove" statistically that the hospital was desperate for money. For example, the firm was hired to raise $1 million for an addition to a hospital in Staunton, Virginia. When I studied its balance sheet, however, I discovered the hospital was operating at a healthy profit. How could we raise $1 million when the hospital did not need it?

The answer was creative numerology. The bulk of the income came from endowments and other gifts while the operating revenues, like those of any hospital, were far lower than expenses. So we simply ignored the outside income and proved that the hospital's operating revenues were insufficient to fund the building project. Our brochure made a strong case for charitable need, and the $1 million fund-raising campaign was successful.

I was a willing participant in this legal scam, but it taught me a lesson. It is risky to trust the financial figures of any organization. The larger the company, the greater the risk, for there is more leeway.

It is not that all accountants and executive officers set out to lie deliberately (though some certainly do). They merely search for the most attractive means of reporting corporate finances. Given any accounting choice, they will always opt for the one that appears the most favorable. The better the company looks on paper, the more secure are the jobs in the executive suites. Thus the numbers in a corporate report tend to reflect the very human emotions of greed and lust for power. Even before I realized that there were *other* reasons to ignore corporate reports, I came to distrust them on this basis.

To read the truth in numbers, one must search for pure, honest data.

I was in hot pursuit of such data every evening as I labored over the hefty manuscript for the third edition of *Price Predictions*. Harry added an interesting challenge to this project, asking me to see if I could correlate the fluctuations of the stamp market with those of the stock market. Edward Dewey had just published his book *Cycles*, a comprehensive description of the patterns of oscillation exhibited in nature, politics, the arts, and all phases of economics. Following its publication, Dewey established the Foundation for the Study of Cycles to carry on the work he had so ably begun. Dewey lived in nearby Greenwich and was gracious enough to meet me to discuss our mutual theories.

The stock market seemed to move in a rough four-year cycle. A rising bull market typically lasted about two and a half years, followed by a falling bear market of somewhat shorter duration. The stamp market, on the other hand, seemed keyed to an average cycle of nine years. The first phase was a four- or five-year bull market of sharply rising prices. Then came a four- or five-year bear market of modestly falling prices. Though momentum shifts sometimes coincided with major changes in stock market trends, I could not draw a clear correlation between the two.

What I could state with conviction, however, was that the stamp market appeared to be a much better investment vehicle. Stock prices, as measured by the Dow Jones Industrial Average, showed little or no long-term growth. Each bull market cycle merely brought the Dow back to, or only slightly above, its previous peak. But stamp market highs trended considerably above their previous highs.

This was easy to understand. The stock market is continually infiltrated by new supply. Major corporations print billions of new shares of common stock each year, watering down the market, whereas a commemorative stamp, once issued, can never increase in supply.

I detailed these theories in a series of articles for *Stamps* magazine entitled "Financial Cycles—How They Affect Philately and the World." The third edition of *Price Predictions* included this material as well as my first stock market prediction. Based upon cyclical theories, I forecast a bear market in stocks that would bottom out in 1949. The prediction proved to be beautifully correct.

I returned to Duke University in September 1947, this time to major in a field in which I knew I could excel—economics. I poured myself into my studies, enjoying them immensely in spite of the fact that I found myself questioning most of the classic theories.

The world, economically speaking, is a great bazaar. Ever since man first pounded a stone into a special shape and called it "money," financial life has revolved upon one simple principle—the principle at work in the bazaar. Theoretical economists are fond of spinning out a variety of truth-clouding terms such as *prime rate, M-1, M-2, supply-side,* and many others that all amount to so much flotsam. They claim that all of these factors are necessary to understand the happenings within the financial community.

But the more I waded through the theories of Adam Smith, Ricardo, Malthus, and Marshall, the more I understood why economics is nicknamed "the dismal science." The conclusion was inescapable: Economists, in general, do not know what they are talking about.

In the first place, 90 percent of their studies deal with the past. History is important, but only when applied to the present. Economics seems to fail at this task, because when a theory meshes perfectly with a past economic era it rarely applies to the present or the future.

Second, the diversity of economic theory creates total confusion in the practical, political world. At any given time one can quote diametrically opposing viewpoints from dozens of highly respected economists. What good is that?

The third, most telling shortcoming of economics is its obvious, dismal failure to change things for the better. One of my most ambitious projects at Duke was the production of an eighty-page study detailing the problems of what I called the A and B countries —the haves and the have-nots. I was disturbed by the realization that there is more than enough food in the world to feed everyone —yet every night *most* of the global population goes to sleep hungry. Millions of human beings starve to death every year in the B countries, while millions of tons of food in the A countries rot on the garbage heap. Something has to be terribly wrong with a system of thought that cannot solve this dilemma.

As so often happens when a basically good concept is thrown into the scholarly arena, economists over the centuries have so managed to cloud the simple truth of their discipline with refinements, appendages, augmentations, and postscripts that they forget the original premise.

As I sat at my desk drinking a beer and smoking a cigarette, attempting to cut through all these distortions, I formulated my first rule of economic study: Keep it simple.

Boiled down, economics still rests—and always will—upon a simple fundamental tenet. In the economic world the law of supply and demand is enforced with a vigor and equality unmatched in any courtroom. In the bazaar of life, potential buyers and sellers constantly haggle over price. Whether the commodity is Persian rugs, apples, soybeans, Saudi Arabian crude, alligators, toothbrushes, radial tires, sauerkraut, video games, stamps, or common stocks, the price will rise if there are more buyers than sellers; the price will fall if there are more sellers than buyers. The study of economics is the study of the law of supply and demand. Period.

I always came back to the law of supply and demand whenever I mused upon the stock market. The majority of people who follow its ups and downs are hooked by the first half of its name. They follow *stocks*. They study corporate earnings reports, dividends, and price-earnings ratios. They watch the international business climate. They buy or sell on the basis of today's financial news—fluctuations in interest rates, the government's economic indicators, and the

Gross National Product. They even concern themselves with the effects of elections and revolutions. All of these factors are then congealed into theories as to how they will affect the earnings of a given corporation and, by extension, the price of its stock.

To me, it all seemed like hogwash. The key word in the term stock market is *market*. It matters not what commodity is being sold. As it happens, that commodity is common stock. But a market is an auction between a potential buyer and a potential seller. The only thing that matters is whether the buyer wants to buy more than the seller wants to sell, or vice versa.

When an order comes into a brokerage house the broker sends that order to the floor of the New York Stock Exchange for execution by a stock specialist. For example, if the specialist has an order to buy 100 shares of AT&T at $60 per share and he also has an order to sell 100 shares of AT&T at $60, the transaction is an easy one.

But suppose he cannot match the order so easily. Perhaps the potential buyer is so anxious to obtain the 100 shares of AT&T that he tells his broker to make the purchase at the market price. The broker discovers that the specialist does not have any sell orders at $60 per share, but does have 100 shares that the owner is willing to sell at 60⅛. The transaction is completed and the price of AT&T has risen 12.5 cents per share because the buyer was more anxious to buy than the seller was to sell.

On the other hand, suppose the owner of the 100 shares needed money to pay his taxes and did not want to quibble about price. And suppose that the potential buyer is not willing to pay $60 per share, but will buy at 59⅞. The transaction is completed and the price of AT&T falls 12.5 cents per share because the seller was more anxious to sell than the buyer to buy.

There is no more beautiful demonstration of the law of supply and demand than the stock market.

From the moment I began my serious study of economics, my attention centered upon the great crash of 1929, which had so affected my father. I was determined to understand the reasons for the event, and I read everything I could find about this tumultuous era.

What drove the market to an all-time high on September 3, 1929?

There could only be one answer. There were more buyers than
sellers, creating a condition of excessive demand. In Frederick Lewis
Allen's classic history of the 1920s, *Only Yesterday,* I found a profile
of my father and millions of other speculators who had created the
conditions of excessive demand:

> The American could spin wonderful dreams—of a romantic
> day when he would sell his Westinghouse common at a fabu-
> lous price and live in a great house and have a fleet of shining
> cars and loll at ease on the sands of Palm Beach. And when he
> looked toward the future of his country, he could envision an
> America . . . set free from poverty and toil. He saw a magical
> order built on the new science and the new prosperity: roads
> swarming with millions upon millions of automobiles, airplanes
> darkening the skies, lines of high-tension wire carrying from
> hilltop to hilltop the power to give life to a thousand labor-
> saving machines, skyscrapers thrusting above one-time villages,
> vast cities rising in great geometrical masses of stone and con-
> crete and roaring with perfectly mechanized traffic—and
> smartly dressed men and women spending, spending, spending
> with the money they had won by being far-sighted enough to
> foresee, way back in 1929, what was going to happen.

With this obvious rush of optimism behind it, how could the
market have turned around so swiftly? Again, there could be only
one answer. There were suddenly more sellers than buyers, and a
condition of excessive supply was created. In the latter months of
1929 that supply increased exponentially as brokers issued margin
calls, forcing speculators to sell more and more stocks to cover their
losses. When the slightest bit of detrimental news caused a mild
sell-off, the speculators just had to be squeezed. What goes up must
come down.

This seemed like a simple truth in retrospect. Why had no one
foreseen it?

I found little evidence of economic wisdom in the pronounce-
ments of those who were supposed to understand the meanderings
of the market. In the seven weeks between September 3 and October 24, 1929, after the market had peaked and was wavering prior

to the plunge, one economist after another forecast a great new upward swing.

"Some pretty intelligent people are now buying stocks," said R. W. McNeel, director of McNeel's Financial Service. "Unless we are to have a panic—which no one seriously believes—stocks have hit bottom."

Charles E. Mitchell, chairman of National City Bank of New York, proclaimed, "The industrial situation of the United States is absolutely sound and our credit situation is in no way critical. . . . The market values have a sound basis in the general prosperity of the country."

Even the great John D. Rockefeller was caught holding the bag. The day after Black Tuesday, Rockefeller said, "Believing that fundamental conditions of the country are sound and that there is nothing in the business situation to warrant the destruction of values that has taken place on the exchanges during the past week, my son and I have for some days been purchasing sound common stocks."

Early in 1930, the first full year of the Great Depression, President Herbert Hoover's Treasury Secretary, Andrew Mellon, predicted "a revival of activity in the spring."

Commerce Secretary Thomas Lamont declared, "There are grounds for assuming that this is about a normal year."

In March Hoover himself predicted that *unemployment would be ended in sixty days.*

How could so many people have been so completely, disastrously wrong?

And then, as I studied further, I came across a startling, intriguing fact. There had, indeed, been a handful of perceptive investors who *had* foreseen the crash. Joseph Kennedy left the market in 1928, recognizing the blue chip bubble for what it was—an inflated bag of gas that had to burst.

Bernard Baruch was the most astute, selling out in July 1929 and sitting out a straight-up market for the next six weeks. When stock prices crashed in October, Baruch was grouse-hunting in England with $9 million in his pocket—and out of the market.

Had these men merely been lucky or had they predicted the future course of the stock market? Did they know something that few others knew?

Gradually I came to realize that the single most sure characteristic of the stock market was its rhythmic pulsations, which seemed to follow the laws of physics, harmony, and nature. The market does not rise forever in an unbroken line. It breathes. From day to day, week to week, month to month, year to year, and even over decades the market ebbs and flows. The classic statement came from J. P. Morgan when he was asked what he expected the market to do in the future. He replied: "I expect it to fluctuate." The crash of 1929 was merely a severe example of a regularly recurring cycle.

Each day in the market presents a furious battle between the bulls —those who foresee prices rising—and the bears—those who foresee prices falling. During any given day, week, month, or year either the bulls or bears will predominate and the market will rise or fall accordingly.

Stocks are not bought or sold in a vacuum. Each transaction requires a buyer and a seller, one of whom has correctly guessed the wisdom of the deal and one of whom has erred. The investor who guesses right will make a profit; he is automatically a part of the smart money crowd. The investor who guessed wrong will be caught holding the bag. In 1929 Bernard Baruch was the epitome of the smart money and my father was a typical bagholder. The mix of smart money and bagholders is constantly changing. Nevertheless certain investors tend to remain in one group or another. Why are some so astute and others so chronically wrong?

In any market the obvious winning strategy is to buy at a low price and sell at a high price. Winners buy stocks from losers when the price is low and sell them back when the price is high. This is an easily understood basic concept. Yet in practice it is extremely difficult to implement.

It is a simple matter to buy low-priced stocks. They are low-priced because there is an excessive supply. People want to sell them. It is just as simple to sell high-priced stocks. They are high-priced because there is an excessive demand. People want to buy them.

To do so, however, smart money has to force itself to go against the majority viewpoint. Low stock prices reflect a general opinion of poor business conditions, and vice versa. To win at the stock market game, then, one must have the emotional fortitude to act in opposition to the crowd. Theorizing is easy; putting up your money is difficult.

During the course of a bull market, 80 percent of all stocks rise in price. During a bear market, 90 percent of all stocks fall in price. But such major fluctuations in market psychology are extremely difficult to predict. *If* one could learn to correctly label the current thrust of the market, he could say good-bye forever to the bagholders and join the smart money crowd.

That is a very big *If*.

Nikolai D. Kondratieff was Deputy Minister of Food in the provisional government of Alexander F. Kerensky, who ruled Russia after the fall of the czar. Because of his concern for feeding the Russian people in an era of postwar revolutionary chaos, Kondratieff became a student of economic cycles. After Lenin came to power, Kondratieff founded the Moscow Business Institute, which he directed from 1920 to 1928. Here he carried on his studies of the fluctuations of commodity prices in France, Germany, and the United States.

In 1926 Kondratieff authored a monograph entitled "The Long Waves in Economic Life," which was translated into English in 1935. The Russian's work fascinated me because his theories seemed to mesh with my mother's studies of numerology and my own interest in market cycles. At Duke I began to do independent study of Kondratieff and his long waves.

In this monograph he identified a long-range cycle of commodity price patterns that lasted anywhere from fifty to fifty-six years. He noted that commodity prices had peaked in 1814, 1864, and 1920. Students of Kondratieff came to realize that the beginning of a crash in commodity prices correlated with a stock market crash from five to nine years later. The commodity peak of 1814 was followed in 1819 by the most severe depression in U.S. history up until that time. Nine years after the 1864 commodities peak the Panic of 1873 forced the stock market to close for a full week. What had happened nine years after the 1920 commodities peak was fresh in my mind.

The crash of 1929 was as disastrous to Kondratieff as it was to anyone. Lenin's successor, Stalin, was quick to proclaim the stock market debacle a sign of the demise of capitalism and the rise of a new world reign of communism. Yet there in his backyard was a Russian economist who proclaimed that capitalism was subjected to such cyclical lows every fifty years or so and always rebounded from them. Stalin could not tolerate the notion that capitalism would recover and thrive for another fifty years. Kondratieff was arrested and either executed quickly or shipped to Siberia.

But he left behind a remarkable legacy. The key point to remember is that Kondratieff published his paper in 1926. Based on the long-wave cycles of commodity prices, Kondratieff's work *predicted the stock market crash of 1929.* That made me speculate whether Joe Kennedy and Bernard Baruch were fluent in Russian.

This was a great revelation to a twenty-three-year-old scholar and I filed it away in my mind. It was heartening to note that the fifty- to fifty-six-year cycle was long enough to predict relative prosperity for decades to come. If Kondratieff was correct in his thesis, the next peak in commodity prices would not occur until the mid-1970s. If Kondratieff's students were right, the stock market would not experience a major crash until the 1980s. That seemed remote enough to cause me no anxiety.

I graduated from Duke in July 1948 and returned home to Westport to find my parents out back in the studio apartment of the barn playing bridge with a houseguest, an attractive young woman named Paulina Delp. Polly was the daughter of a banker in Palmerton, Pennsylvania. My parents met her while on a trip to Atlanta, where Polly was performing on tour for the Three Arts Club in New York. When mother learned that she was living at the Three Arts Club while studying piano at the Juilliard School of Music, and learned of her other wide artistic interests, she invited the girl to come to Westport to paint with her.

Mother may have had an ulterior motive, for shortly after I arrived, she and dad excused themselves for the night. Polly and I lay on the carpet before the embers of a dying fire and talked about our dreams. I read several selections to her from *A Schoolboy's Faith.* Before long we were kissing furiously.

Polly never opened her paintbox during the brief visit. We spent the few days together walking, talking, and necking. When I kissed her good-bye at the train station she extracted a promise that I would visit her the next week at her parents' home in Pennsylvania.

I walked up the steps of her home listening to Polly playing Rachmaninoff brilliantly. During dinner her father interrogated me about my economic theories. His conservative banker's mind was unimpressed with my brash dismissal of the main body of economic thought. I knew that I had made a poor impression.

After dinner Polly and I walked in the park. Despite her father's antagonism I was smitten. Here was a woman who shared my interests in the piano and in all forms of art. She had a natural appreciation of symmetry and beauty—and she was a beauty herself. I proposed to her that night, but she deferred her response.

As soon as I returned to Westport I applied for admission to Columbia University as a graduate student in economics, so as to be in proximity to the Juilliard School of Music. Weeks passed before I heard from Polly. Finally she sent a curt letter saying that she felt it wise that we never see each other again.

I could neither understand nor accept this rejection. As the school year neared, I took a dismal room in a dilapidated hotel simply because it was near the Three Arts Club. Half-heartedly I reentered the scholastic routine, but much of my study time was eroded as I hung out around Juilliard or the Three Arts Club, hoping for a glimpse of my beloved.

Another big distraction was my growing reputation in the world of stamps. The two-volume third edition of *Price Predictions* was published in August to the delight of my limited but loyal readers. Harry Lindquist arranged an autograph party at Brentano's on Fifth Avenue, with huge signs in the window announcing the event. I continued to churn out articles for Harry's *Stamps* magazine and enjoyed my modest celebrity status. I was a featured speaker at a forum on stamp collecting conducted by the *New York Sun* and also appeared frequently at smaller gatherings of stamp devotees.

My studies at Columbia fell to the side. I did not wish to teach and could see little practical use for the mishmash of economic theory presented to me. I gave up my room and, with it, my hopes of changing Polly's mind. Dad kept an apartment at 140 East Fortieth Street for those nights when his workload kept him in the city late, and I moved in there to try my hand as a free-lance writer, specializing in stamp investment.

I had carved a big niche for myself in a little field. As the reigning expert on stamp investment I came to the attention of *Collier's* magazine, which featured me and my theories in a five-page spread published in April 1949. It noted my accurate track record with stamp prices, and also pointed out that I had correctly predicted the 1949 bear market on Wall Street.

Shortly after the feature appeared I received a call from a man named John, the son of a vice-president of New York Central Railroad. The *Collier's* article had impressed him and he had a proposition for merchandising my unique abilities.

We met at my apartment. John was fifteen years my elder, so it was extremely flattering when he proposed the formation of the Granville Stamp Corporation, with me as president. Among his ideas was the manufacturing and selling of a metal box, for the proper preservation of investment stamps.

He told me about an adventurer named Mush Moore who had announced plans to drive a dogsled from Fairbanks, Alaska, to Portland, Maine. John's idea was to contract with Mush Moore to stop off at every city along the way to mail letters with a special Granville cachet, which we would then sell to collectors to commemorate the odyssey. He had persuaded a friend to produce an animated television series called "The Adventures of Mush Moore" that would add to the lore of the trip. The TV series would be created under the aegis of Granville Productions, a subsidiary of Granville Stamp Corporation.

To a twenty-five-year-old already touched by a ray of limelight and hankering for more, this was irresistible. I agreed immediately.

The first task, my new partner explained, was to sell stock in the corporation to members of my family. I did so, managing to raise $20,000 from my parents and Auntie Blanche. With the money we opened an office on East Fortieth Street. John and I both drew generous salaries. We hired one of my Duke fraternity brothers to research the TV script. Other funds went for a secretary's salary, a retainer to Mush Moore, production costs for the TV series, and magazine ads for the Granville cachet.

The world, of course, proved to be little interested in Mush Moore and even less so in Granville cachets. Before long most of the money was gone, and nothing was coming in.

Just about the time our bank balance hit zero, John ended up in the Charles B. Towne Center for the Cure of Alcoholism and I was

$20,000 in debt to my family. Mush Moore eventually completed his journey, but by then the Granville Stamp Corporation had been canceled.

In March 1950, when everything else seemed so dismal, Polly suddenly called and said she would like to see me again. I was astounded. More than a year and a half had passed since her "Dear John" letter, but I was still in love with her and we made a date immediately.

Over dinner Polly told me that her father was very impressed with the *Collier's* article and never stopped talking about me. I decided that maybe he was not a bagholder after all.

It was as though the long separation had never happened. The same magic was at work for both of us. We saw each other nearly every day until she graduated from Juilliard in June and left for a camp counselor's job in New Hampshire.

She was gone only a short time when war broke out in Korea. Once again fearful of the future, I called her immediately and said I was coming up to New Hampshire to marry her. This time she said yes. Despite a ticket for speeding through a twenty-five-miles-per-hour zone at eighty-five, I arrived the next morning. Within a few days mother joined us to play the organ and witness the wedding. We were married on July 11, 1950.

Faster than a speeding bullet I proved the Navy doctors wrong by impregnating Polly. Now I became serious about increasing my income. In November I published the first issue of the *Philatelic Investment Letter*, a sort of monthly version of *Price Predictions*. I advertised in Harry's magazine. Each subscription brought me five dollars a year. I could never get the circulation above 500, but that provided a base income supplemented by magazine articles.

Both the *Letter* and my editions of *Price Predictions* were so esoteric that they were of interest only to the professional. I had nothing to sell to the general public, so I was intrigued when a literary agent contacted me and suggested that I expand my market by writing a popular book that would persuade millions of Americans to become stamp investors. She obtained a contract for me from Hermitage House and my time in 1951 was divided between my monthly *Letter* and the new book. *Everybody's Guide to Stamp*

Investment, I was convinced, would bring me to the forefront of the economic world.

Our daughter, Leslie, was born only three days before our first anniversary and our eldest son, Blanchard, followed the next year. We named him after my Auntie Blanche, in part because we needed a loan from her to help us move from Manhattan to a more suitable child-rearing environment.

Everybody's Guide to Stamp Investment was published in October 1952 and condensed in *Omnibook* magazine. Though it was named one of the outstanding "how-to" books of 1952, it earned only modest royalties. It suffered from a growing criticism of my work by the purists of the hobby who did not appreciate my investment angle. Consequently it received horrible reviews in the stamp columns of both the *Times* and the *Herald Tribune*—the kiss of death to any philatelic book.

Nevertheless, with Auntie Blanche's help, we bought a three-bedroom tract house in Ramsey, New Jersey, for $13,900. I converted one of the bedrooms into an office that housed my stamp safe and the Vari-Typer I used for my *Letter.*

As Polly entered her third pregnancy in four years, I scraped for an existence. My latest venture, the Granville Stamp Features Syndicate, proved to be another disappointment. Few newspapers wanted to publish stories about postage stamps.

I took a part-time job with the *Ridgewood News,* covering local events. That at least kept us supplied with milk for the babies.

In the midst of all this activity I managed a small profit by purchasing investment stamps for a number of clients, including the literary agent who had sold *Everybody's Guide* for me. I regularly made the rounds of the Nassau Street dealers searching for stamps that I believed would most benefit from the current bull market. I purchased them in wholesale lots and retailed them to my clients, pocketing the difference. Because I was almost 100-percent correct in my predictions, all my clients made respectable profits.

I, on the other hand, was still working for nickels and dimes.

Nothing could shake my belief that stamps were a tremendous investment. But in the world of investments, they were small time. I had given the stamp world its first supply of comprehensive investment advice, but the low level of demand for the advice ensured that I would always be underpaid.

Yet my demand for income was increasing exponentially, in direct proportion to the size of my family. Leslie and Blanchard were great consumers of groceries, and the arrival of Leona in 1954 and Sara in 1956 gave me two more mouths to feed. Once I tried my luck at bingo at the local Catholic church and won enough money to buy milk for a week.

Out of desperation I took a job with the printer in Ridgewood, New Jersey, who produced my monthly *Letter.* But I never saw myself as a career printer, though I enjoyed the work. My goal was to find a larger field where my abilities to quantify behavioral patterns and analyze the resulting numbers would be more appreciated. So I began to reconsider the stock market. If it held certain inherent disadvantages, perhaps those were outweighed by its popularity. Millions of investors rode its ups and downs and always came back for more. If I could apply my talents successfully to the stock market, the potential for notoriety was limitless.

I was intrigued, therefore, when I read in the newspaper that the world's largest stock brokerage house, Merrill Lynch, Pierce, Fenner & Smith, was offering an aptitude test for aspiring employees.

At the appointed time I arrived at the Pine Street office for the examination. I did my best to provide the proper classical answers to questions about interest rates, dividends, yields, bonds, and a host of other subjects that seemed to me to have nothing to do with the stock market.

A tingle coursed through my body a week later when I came home from work to find a brown envelope with the Merrill Lynch logo in the upper left-hand corner. I wanted to savor the moment, so I grabbed a cold beer and retreated to the backyard to escape the clamor of the kids. Here was the letter that would launch me on my Wall Street career, the natural culmination of my heritage and experience.

I took a long swig of beer and tore open the envelope to read that I had failed the test miserably. It was the considered opinion of Merrill Lynch that I had no future working on Wall Street.

Years after my tears dried I would come to appreciate how correct that assessment was. I did not belong on Wall Street because I was a winner. Wall Street, I would learn, is structured to make you a loser. But more than a year would pass before I began to learn that truth.

And so I landed a job at Avon Products in Suffern, New York, just across the state line. I earned ninety dollars a week running a printing press and supplemented that by shuttling some of my fellow employees to and from work in my Volkswagen microbus.

Avon was generous enough to allow me to use the press on weekends for my own work. I was able to cut my overhead on the *Philatelic Investment Letter* and even printed and bound the fourth edition of *Price Predictions* myself. Polly took a job as an organist for our church, St. John's Episcopal, and also acquired a few private students.

Life settled into a grind. I put in long days at Avon and somehow found the time for my monthly *Letter*. I also set to work on the massive manuscript of the fifth edition of *Price Predictions*. It ran nearly 2,000 pages long and weighed fourteen and one-half pounds.

Money was such an overriding consideration that fantasy took hold of me. My favorite television show was "The $64,000 Question," where ordinary people could get rich instantly by answering a series of difficult questions on a given, exotic topic. I wrote to the producers applying as a contestant in the category of stamps.

I received a "maybe" answer in the mail and that was enough to get me going. Each day I took my copy of *Scott's Standard Postage Stamp Catalogue* to work and studied it at every opportunity. Before long I knew *everything* about stamps! I could discourse on the engraving process, the proper selection of inks, the relative merits of flat-bed versus rotary printing, and counterfeiting. I knew the history of every U.S. postage stamp ever printed. But I was never summoned to appear on the show.

The toll of all this effort was exacting. One night in the summer of 1957, as I was watching television with the family, I suddenly tumbled to the floor, doubled over with excruciating pain in my chest and stomach. I could barely breathe. Perspiration flowed onto the carpet. Polly screamed and called an ambulance.

As I lay in bed recovering from a relapse of malaria, I had plenty of time to ponder the future. I came to a critical decision. I *had* to find a better job, and the only way I could do so was to quit Avon so that I could devote full time to the search. It was a gamble, but I knew I had more to offer the world than was as yet evident. My future lay somewhere in that great land of Manhattan that I had dreamed of conquering as a boy.

My feet ached from pounding the city pavement in search of an employer hungry for an economist who understood the machinations of the postage stamp market, could run a printing press, and play the piano at the Christmas party. I had been on this discouraging quest for weeks, dropping off my résumé at innumerable personnel offices and employment agencies without success.

Finally one agency set up an appointment for me with the McGraw-Hill Publishing Company, which needed a statistical analyst who could study the metals industry and write a periodic newsletter. It was obvious to them that I could do for metals what I had done for postage stamps, and they offered me the job at $9,000 a year.

This was nearly double what I had been making at Avon. The temptation was acute, but a warning note sounded in my brain. Where was the future in the job? I could not envision any more fame and fortune in this field than I had achieved in postage stamp investment. I asked for one night to think it over.

Polly was aghast that I had not accepted the job immediately. How could I return home to my wife and four children penniless and jobless, and *think about* an offer of $9,000 a year?

We were arguing the issue when the phone rang. It was a man from another employment agency, informing me that he had an appointment for me the following day with a brokerage house.

"What kind of brokerage house?" I asked.

"A stock brokerage house. It's E.F. Hutton & Company."

I was such a Wall Street neophyte that I had never heard of the firm. "What does the job entail?" I asked.

"They need someone to write a daily market letter."

I fairly shouted into the phone. "You tell them I'll be there!"

The following morning I was ready early, carefully dressed. On an impulse I grabbed the 2,000-page manuscript of *Price Predictions* just before I left the house. On the train to New York I buried my nose in the *Times*, trying to memorize the current price quotations for the leading stocks. I rode the subway to 61 Broadway, took the elevator to the eleventh floor, and announced to the receptionist that I had an appointment with Mr. Sylvan Coleman.

She led me down a hallway, her heels clicking off the faded brown linoleum, to the glass-enclosed cubicle where the senior vice-president of Hutton's Wall Street headquarters held court. I knocked on the door, introduced myself, and shook hands with a tall, half-balding man with a hawkish nose and extremely sharp, humorless eyes.

Coleman asked all the standard questions about my education and job experience, which suddenly seemed rather drab to me.

"Do you know anything about Wall Street?" he queried.

Sensing a chance to lighten the atmosphere, I chuckled and replied, "Well, sir, I think so. But last year I flunked Merrill Lynch's aptitude test."

Coleman did not seem to see humor in the announcement. He scowled.

"What's the yield on General Motors today?" he suddenly barked.

"Roughly five percent, sir," I answered, blessing the *Times*.

"What does that mean? How do you compute that?"

"You divide the price into the dividend, sir. That tells you what percentage you are making on your investment, like the interest rate in a bank account."

Despite my correct answers to a series of basic questions, Coleman seemed dubious that a thirty-three-year-old printer could write a market letter for E.F. Hutton. He explained the duties of the job. Hutton was one of the largest "wire houses" in the country, meaning that every day it teletyped a constant stream of data to its branch offices and clients nationwide. The teletype came alive each morning at 8:00 A.M. with Hutton's morning wire, a statistical summary of how the stock market had performed the previous day. Coleman needed someone to prepare that morning wire.

"Do you think you can handle a job like that?" he asked.

"Well, Mr. Coleman," I replied, "here's a statistical job I've just finished." I dropped the manuscript of *Price Predictions* on his desk. The thud echoed dully off the frosted glass walls that separated his office from the general din of the research department.

He thumbed through a few pages and noted the myriad of statistical tables I had devised to monitor the stamp market. For a moment he was lost in thought.

"Well, son," he said finally, "if you are ambitious enough to inflict this much punishment upon yourself, I guess we can teach you about the stock market."

He would hire me, he said, on four week's probation. For a month I would practice writing the morning wire, but my efforts would not go out over the teletype. After a month, if I proved my ability, I would begin to write the actual wire. Starting salary was $150 per week.

I accepted on the spot.

Polly was incensed that I had spurned the McGraw-Hill offer, which paid $1,500 a year more. But there was never a doubt in my mind. Here was an opportunity to display my analytical and writing abilities from the inside of the biggest financial game in the world.

From now on I would devote myself tirelessly to the study of numbers that reflected the minute-by-minute shifts in the emotions of millions of investors throughout the world. I knew not where the study would lead, but I could sense that I, like Oddlot the caveman, had stumbled upon something of very special value.

5.
ECCLESIASTES

On October 4, 1957, the day the Russians shocked America by beating us into orbit with Sputnik, I started work on Wall Street. I had to be at my desk by 7:10 A.M., and on that first morning I realized that the early schedule was a blessing. The trains were nearly deserted at that hour, allowing me a quiet interlude with the *Wall Street Journal* and my new copy of Gerald Loeb's *The Battle for Investment Survival*. Loeb was a senior partner at Hutton and would now be one of my co-workers. As I read the book I fantasized that someday my own byline would appear on a stock market book.

I was determined to inundate myself with all available stock market information, to bring with me as few preconceptions as possible, and to learn by observation. Each morning the early train gave me time to collect my thoughts, to filter out the static of misinformation that is so rampant on Wall Street, and to study the clear harmonies of the market.

Though the market does not open until 10:00 A.M., Hutton's office was buzzing by seven. Brokers plan their strategies, study yesterday's New York quotations and overnight action in world markets, and most of all make lists of clients who might be persuaded to pour additional funds into the market this day. This is lesson number one: The name of the game in any brokerage house is commissions.

At 7:00 A.M. I reported to Carl Hess, a young oil analyst who had risen quickly to the position of director of the research department.

"Your first task," Hess said, "is to watch the market today and then write a closing wire." The closing wire is a bare statistical summary of the day's trading, similar to the round-up story that runs daily in the business section of a newspaper.

Hess assigned me a small desk in the middle of the research department. All around me other researchers were sipping coffee and setting about their tasks. The research department is a critical adjunct to any reputable brokerage firm. The firm justifies its relatively inflated commission rates by providing the investor with a fleet of analysts who study every nook and cranny of the business world and guide the client toward investments that seem to have profit potential.

Their days are spent digging into company reports and financial statements, searching for clues to predict the probable future performance of individual firms. This is generally boiled down to a key statistic known as the price-to-earnings ratio. It is computed by dividing the company's current earnings per share into the current price of the share.

The assumption is that stock prices move in concert with company earnings. For example, if a company's stock currently sells at $20 per share and that company's current earnings are $2 per share, the p/e ratio is ten. If the company then doubles its earnings to $4 per share, the fundamental conclusion is that the p/e ratio, which has suddenly dropped to five, will seek to regain its previous level of ten and, in the process, the price of the stock will double to $40 per share. Thus, by forecasting the future earnings of any given company, the brokerage house analyst believes that he can make accurate predictions of the future value of that company's stock.

At Hutton, as at almost all brokerage houses, the p/e ratio reigns as the supreme deity of stock analysis. It is the *raison d'être* of the research department.

Such analysis was not to be part of my job. I was to concentrate only on the facts and figures of daily market action, reporting statistics on the fluctuations of what are known as stock market indicators. The most widely followed of these indicators is the Dow Jones Industrial Average, which is a weighted average of the stock prices of thirty of the nation's most respected corporations. There was little for me to do until the exchange opened, so I left the analysts to their esoteric work and toured the suite of offices.

Soon I discovered the boardroom, which, from the moment the exchange opened until it closed precisely at 3:00 P.M., would be a hub of activity. The focus of attention here was the mechanical display that covered one full wall. On the board were listed, in alphabetical order, 100 of the most prominent stocks. Next to each stock was a place for the opening, high, low, and closing prices of the day.

Facing the board was a row of chairs for those investors so caught up in the game that they had to follow changes in the price quotations from minute to minute. Behind these seats was a roomful of desks for the brokers. Off to one side was the ticker tape that would record every transaction of the day. Anyone interested in a stock not popular enough to be listed on the board would have to check the ticker tape for the details of the latest transaction in that issue.

Returning to my desk, I lit a Marlboro, sipped at a cup of coffee, and perused a variety of financial publications, attempting to orient myself to this new world.

There was a tangible sensation of pessimism in the room, reflected in the financial stories that I studied. Prices of common stocks had been dropping for months, as indicated by the Dow Jones Industrial Average, which slipped from a high of 520 in June to 419 in early October. And there seemed to be no end in sight to the market's slide. A few months earlier Secretary of the Treasury George Humphrey had predicted that the nation was entering a depression that would "curl your hair."

Brokerage firms detest bear markets. The more the market slides, the more difficult it is to draw fresh investment money into the game. The average broker's commissions fall off in direct proportion to the Dow Jones Industrial Average.

On that very first morning, however, I found it difficult to share the prevailing pessimism. What goes down must come back up again, I reasoned, rewriting Newton. This bear market had continued for many months and must certainly run its course soon. I was not audacious enough to voice this opinion that day, but I looked forward to studying the events of the next few months to see if I could detect signs of a turnaround.

Shortly before 10:00 A.M. I returned to the boardroom to view the onset of the day's trading. Investors jammed the available seats. Behind them the brokers sat ready at their desks. Some were on the phone; others in conference with clients. But there was a common denominator. As the clock hand pointed toward 10:00 A.M., everyone in the room had at least one eye fixed upon the board.

This sophisticated gambling den had a palpable, electrified atmosphere. The latest prices of various stocks rolled into position with a metallic clang, like the changing data on the departure board at Grand Central. Each change brought a mixture of grins and worried expressions from the assemblage of winners and losers.

"Hey, Randy! What's the latest on American Motors?"

The question came from a red-faced, plump gentleman in a slate gray, tailored suit. It was directed toward a stockbroker who stood off to one side of the room, hovering over the ticker tape. Randy slid a portion of the tape through his fingers, searching for information concerning the most recent transaction in American Motors. Suddenly he stopped, studied the tape, turned, and yelled out, "Eight and five-eighths!"

"My God!" stammered the questioner. "Sell. Sell!"

Randy scurried back to his desk to execute the order.

I leaned against a wall, lit a Marlboro, and tried to comprehend the intensity of it all. The market pulsated with life. Prices on various stocks would rise steadily for a short time, then suddenly turn and plunge. I realized that all over the country tens of thousands of investors and brokers, at this very moment, were studying these changes and acting upon them immediately. Millions of dollars were being won and lost as I stood gaping at the board.

I had always known that the market was susceptible to long-term fluctuations in one direction or the other, but I was amazed to feel the mood swings that altered the course of market action almost minute by minute.

The numbers that flashed upon the board were not meaningless abstractions to Randy and his client, nor to the dozens of others in the boardroom that morning. Rather, they were the quantifications of human emotion. Prices did not rise or fall on their own initiative. They could only be affected by changes in the collective mood of the nation's investors. These numbers were alive.

By 10:05 that morning I knew that I had discovered my lump of gold.

The bulk of Hutton's clientele consisted of long-term investors but, being a wire house, Hutton also attracted droves of traders who followed the market with daily fervor. The most intense of these were the day traders who, if they felt that a particular stock was going to rise on a given day, bought in the morning and sold in the afternoon, pocketing their profit (if they were correct) or accepting their loss (if they were wrong) in a matter of hours. Instinctively I gravitated toward these short-term traders. They were where the action was.

These were archaic days in the stock market, compared to present times. There was no up-to-the-moment computerized information available at the touch of a finger. The investor had to rely upon the slow, ponderous input of data from the big board and the stock ticker. The most widely followed barometer of stock market action, the Dow Jones Industrial Average, was computed and posted only once every hour. To a day trader, an hour's lag in vital information could mean thousands of dollars in profit or loss.

One of my first services to the boardroom habitués was to compute the Dow average every half hour. This was a simple task, yet it gave me a great understanding of the internal workings of the market. To compute the average I would gather the latest prices on each of the thirty stocks included in the industrials. Checking their prices against yesterday's close, I would compute how many net points had been gained or lost in the thirty stocks.

The final step was to employ the current divisor in use by Dow Jones. When I first joined Hutton the divisor was 4.56. In other words, it took more than a 4½ point swing in any Dow Jones stock to move the industrial average a single point.

In order to keep the average relative, Dow Jones is forced to alter the divisor whenever there is a significant change in one of the thirty stocks. For example, when the Manville Corporation filed for bankruptcy in 1982, it was removed from the list of thirty Industrials and replaced by American Express. Because American Express was selling at a higher price than Manville, the divisor had to be adjusted upward in order to avoid an immediate false jump in the average.

Similarly, when a company splits its stock or declares a stock dividend, the per share price of that stock is lowered due to the additional number of shares in circulation. The Dow divisor must thus be lowered.

Over the years the cumulative effect has been to lower the divisor dramatically. Today it takes a move of about 1⅜ of a point in any Dow stock to move the average 1 point. Few people realize it, but the average is three times more volatile than it was twenty-five years ago. This is why we observe so many double-digit swings in the average today.

Back in 1957 a 5-point swing was a big move. My services in computing these moves were greatly appreciated in the boardroom and made me a particular favorite with the day traders.

Meanwhile, I practiced writing the morning wire and, unbeknownst to me, Mr. Coleman sent my work out to selected brokers around the country for their private opinions. Those reports were highly favorable, and beginning with the first week of November 1957, the official E.F. Hutton morning wire was signed "Joseph E. Granville."

Amid the din of the research department, where the analysts studied their corporate data, I soon came to realize that I was a second-class citizen. The primary theme of the department, as it is up and down Wall Street, is fundamental research. This is the traditional study of corporate information in order to predict future profits and relate them to the almighty p/e ratio of a given stock. Fundamental analysts often spend months researching a single corporation.

At my small bare desk in the midst of these scholarly, respected pursuits, I held forth as Hutton's one and only technical analyst. Often I was not even accorded the courtesy of the appendage "analyst," and was sneeringly referred to as "the technician." Even worse was the nickname "elf," implying an insignificant little tyke who practiced the art of sorcery.

The technician was regarded then in most brokerage houses as a barely necessary evil. My job was to study the market statistics and quantify them into an overview of current performance. The fundamentalists sometimes conceded that technical analysis could be useful for short-term forecasting, but they were adamant in their belief that it had little to offer in the field of long-range market forecasting.

I quickly came to believe that there was something radically wrong with this concept. Fundamental analysts follow companies, believing that there is an inexorable link between the performance of the company and the performance of its stock. Perhaps there is, to a small degree, but by studying companies the fundamentalists seem far removed from the nub of the problem. I already distrusted the statistics available from corporate documents, and I came to believe in their complete futility in market analysis.

A company issues stock in order to obtain capital for its operating expenses. Once the stock is issued it takes its place on the open market and has little, if anything, to do with the company. To be sure, the company often pays a quarterly dividend to its stockholders, but that dividend is generally far less than the interest anyone can obtain at the corner bank. A few people purchase stock in anticipation of the dividend, but most people do not. The majority buy stock in anticipation of an increased price, so it can then be sold for a profit. Many people will sell even if it is the day before they would qualify for a dividend check.

The New York Stock Exchange is a market, in many ways no different than a Turkish bazaar. It is a grand auction point where otherwise meaningless pieces of paper are exchanged by buyers and sellers. There are only two things that can influence the price of any commodity in any market. The first is supply; the second is demand. There is no third thing.

Therefore, the performance of any individual company, or of the business community in general, has little or no effect upon stock prices. A stock can only rise in price when a preponderance of investors wish to accumulate it. Likewise, it can only fall in price when a preponderance of investors wish to distribute it. The reasons behind the accumulation or distribution are totally irrelevant. If an investor can correctly identify the current level of supply and demand, he can earn handsome profits in the stock market without knowing a thing about companies.

I discovered an immediate, effective method to monitor current trends in supply and demand—a method pioneered by earlier technicians that proved far superior to the laborious studies of my co-workers in the research department. Mr. Coleman wanted me to make occasional stock recommendations in my morning wire and, though he was a fundamentalist, he knew that morning wire readers —the short-term traders—were looking for technical opinions. One of the accepted methods of technical forecasting was the study of price charts, and it was to this study that I turned.

My bible was *Horsey's Stock Charts,* a monthly periodical that charted the past performances of the prices of 1,500 individual stocks. I took the book home with me and studied it late into the night after Polly and the kids had gone to bed. The excitement built within me, for I could see in these charts the graphic display of human emotions. Here was supply and demand in a pictorial representation *that could predict the future!*

For example, let's assume that the price of a share of Coca-Cola has been oscillating between $10 and $20 over an extended period of time. There are very human reasons for this.

Whenever the price falls to 10 it attracts a significant number of investors who have seen it as high as 20 and reason that they can double their money on the next rise. Those who had bought at 20 are locked in, human psychology dictating that very few of them will sell at a 50-percent loss. Thus at 10 there are more buyers than sellers. This is a point of support. This is the level where demand takes over from supply.

But what happens when the price rises to 20? Those who bought at 10 are tempted to take their profit. Those who bought at 20 and held on all the way down to 10 are now ready to breathe a sigh of relief and dump their stock before it plunges once more. If the stock chart shows that 20 is the point where price tends to stabilize on the upside, then 20 is the point where more people want to sell than buy. This is a price ceiling. This is the level where supply takes over from demand.

A price chart is not a meaningless graph; it is a pictorial display of human emotion as it searches for a balance between optimism and pessimism.

The most significant development to look for on a chart is a *breakout.* Any alteration in the pattern is a clear signal that investor confidence has changed in one direction or the other. If Coca-Cola breaks out to a high of 22, drops off to 15, and then turns upward again, it is a good buy because the chart indicates that the levels of supply and demand have been altered to the upside. But if it crashes through to 8 and only rises back to 15, sell it, for it is likely to drop back to or below 8 on its next downswing.

Chart reading is considered by fundamentalists to be one step removed from Tarot card reading. To me, however, it seemed a clear display of how real people regard a stock. Moreover, I came to realize that the value of chart reading went well beyond individual stock performance. A chart of the Dow Jones Industrial Average or of the broader Standard & Poor's Composite Index of 500 stocks could signal the performance of the entire market.

As I studied *Horsey's Stock Charts* I identified several formations that always seemed to signal major changes.

The first is the *breakout series.* When a stock moves above previous price ceilings it is likely to move up further. The longer the series of breakouts, the more bullish is the pattern. If, in its daily, weekly, monthly, and even longer cycles of fluctuation, Coca-Cola broke through to a price ceiling of 22, dropped to 15, rose to 25, dropped to 18, and rose to 30, its chart would reveal a series of upside price breakouts that clearly signaled an increase in investor confidence.

The *flatbase breakout* occurs when a stock suddenly jumps to a new high after an extended period in the doldrums. The longer the base period of little or no change, the greater the potential for rapid growth once the breakout has occurred. I found a classic example of this in the chart of Shahmoon Industries, Inc., a manufacturer of cast-iron pipe and fittings. From 1946 through 1954 the price of Shahmoon remained in an extremely narrow range, from 4 to 10. Then in the first quarter of 1955, after an eight-year flatbase period, it rose above $15 per share. For the next six months it fluctuated between 12 and 13, never dropping back below the $10 *ceiling* it had maintained for nearly a decade. This was the time to buy, the $15 breakout being a clear signal of change. In the final two months of the year it began the rise that had been signaled in the spring, closing out 1955 at about $25 a share. By April 1956, Shahmoon stock was worth $50 a share. A smart investor could have quadrupled his investment in six months by spotting the flatbase breakout; he did not need to know a thing about the company.

Just as charts reveal the beginnings of major price trends, they also graphically forecast the endings. Two patterns are particularly important. The *head and shoulders* formation is simply a combination of three intermediate peaks wherein the second peak is higher than the first and the third is lower than the second. The second peak forms the head, while the first and third form the shoulders. In terms of market psychology, the third, lower peak reveals a lesser degree of investor confidence and forecasts a sharp drop in price.

The pattern with the most potential for profit and loss is the *parabolic curve.* It begins with a modest upsurge in price that grows in momentum until it can be seen shooting almost straight upward on the chart. Such a curve was traced out by Shahmoon Industries in its phenomenal rise in 1955 and 1956, when it climbed from $12 to $50 a share after its flatbase breakout. A chartbook illustrates that stock prices follow the laws of physics. What goes up must come down. Furthermore, the faster it goes up the faster it will come down. After peaking at $50 a share Shahmoon dropped to 32, then rose back to 43, forming a lower right shoulder that clearly signaled the demise of the parabolic curve. The stock collapsed back down to $10 a share late in 1957.

It was just as difficult for the fundamental analysts to accept the value of chart reading as it was for me to ignore it. As a result, I found myself on a course far divergent from my co-workers, and during my first few months at Hutton it would have appeared to the casual observer that I was a badly misguided minority of one.

By early 1958 all the fundamental analysts were in a sour mood. The nation was in the depths of a recession. It was easy to be bearish, as most people always are at the very bottom of the market cycle. Listening to all the gloomy talk that permeated the research department and the boardroom, I realized that this was how it had to be. For a bear market to reach bottom, the vast majority of investors must be pessimistic or they will not sell. And if they do not sell, the market cannot reach bottom. Conversely, for a bull market to reach the top, the vast majority of investors must be optimistic. It is a paradox that can mean glorious profits for anyone with the fortitude to swim against the tide.

In February 1958, when everyone else at Hutton was full of foreboding and ill will, my charts suddenly showed reason for optimism. The fundamental analysts could not see beyond the gloomy predictions coming from all segments of the business sector and from the most respected economists in and out of government. But my charts belied them all. They showed signs of bottoming formations, reverse head and shoulder patterns, higher ceilings and higher bases. In other words, they revealed that people had begun to accumulate stocks. The Dow itself had risen 35 points above its bear market low of 419.

By now I realized that in the stock market timing is everything. Perhaps the best advice an investor could ever read was the classic third chapter of Ecclesiastes. Verses one and six are especially pertinent:

> *To every thing there is a season, and a time to every purpose under the heaven . . .*
>
> *A time to get, and a time to lose; a time to keep, and a time to cast away . . .*

This was clearly a time to get. In my morning wire I strongly recommended the purchase of several depressed stocks whose chart formations showed signs of upside activity.

When he read my wire, Mr. Coleman called me into his office. "Joe," he said, "I don't get the feeling that you're watching everything. Don't you see the worsening statistics on factory output, unemployment, and housing starts? I want you to pay more attention to the list of major economic indicators. Can't you see that the tide is going out?"

Prepared for the criticism, I was armed with *Horsey's Stock Charts.* I thumped its cover and replied, "Well, Mr. Coleman, according to these charts the tide is coming in."

Mr. Coleman gazed at the chart book with a grimace on his face. "Joe, I think you're getting off on a track here that is difficult to explain to people."

He assigned me the task of keeping him abreast of current economic news, thereby forcing me to study it. Dutifully I reported to him all the monthly fluctuations of the government's list of ten leading economic indicators.

My morning wire, however, continued to ignore the increasingly bearish tenor of those misleading indices. Bolstered by the support of Gerald Loeb, the senior partner who had extra clout because of his popular stock market book, I made additonal buy recommendations based on my charts. Some were blue chip stocks, but most were lesser-known corporations that, on paper, were in obvious financial trouble.

"You can't recommend a stock like that!" one of the fundamentalists chided me about American Motors. "The company is losing money."

"They're always losing money at the bottom," I pointed out.

For several months the gloomy economic conditions persisted, the market continued to remain in the doldrums, and I looked like a fool. Gerald Loeb encouraged me to keep faith in my predictions. We frequently had lunch together to escape the pessimistic aura that permeated the office.

This was my first encounter with an investment psychology whose proponents have hounded me ever since. Despite their emphasis on long-term forecasts, fundamental analysts exhibit extreme nearsightedness in their examination of the market. They never seem to see the big picture. It has often taken months—even a year—for my market predictions to prove themselves correct. The market is such a devious mistress that she has countless ways to mask her real intentions. During this inevitable waiting period I am often subjected to furious criticisms and periodic news stories that proclaim my "death" as a market analyst. Yet once the market confirms my predictions these same critics fall strangely silent.

This recurring scenario gave rise to one of my major axioms: Losers have short memories; winners have long memories.

Edward F. Hutton sat in the front row next to his daughter, actress Dina Merrill. He was in his seventies by then, but he made a point of attending the meeting that day at the uptown office at 650 Madison Avenue. It was May 14, 1958. After months of apparently uncertain action the market was clearly beginning an upswing and I basked in the glory of having been the first to predict it. Accordingly, I had been invited this day to address the senior officials of the firm on the subject, "1958 Stock Market Projections."

I reiterated my forecast of a 1958–59 bull market to a room full of fundamentalists. They listened politely. But when I turned to a particular group of stocks to recommend, their expressions became openly skeptical. I had been pondering an increasingly severe problem facing the United States government. Because of our nation's insistence upon keeping the price of gold fixed at $35 an ounce, we were losing increasing amounts of the precious metal to overseas markets. Demand was fast outstripping supply and the inevitable result was rising price. It was an elementary deduction that the U.S. government was going to have to lift its freeze and allow the price of gold to rise to its natural level. The price, after being held down at an artificial flatbase for so long, would skyrocket in a powerful parabolic curve.

With such pent-up demand unleashed, the logical next step would be to tap new sources of supply. Therefore, stocks of gold mining companies would become the new darlings of investors.

I displayed a series of charts to the audience of brokers and analysts. The South Africa gold mining stocks were so obscure they were not even contained in *Horsey's Stock Charts,* but I had obtained some crude charts from White, Weld & Company. The charts proved to me that a few smart investors had reached the same conclusion as I had. All the gold mining stocks had achieved modest upside breakouts after years of flatbase performance.

"The conclusion is obvious," I declared. "Thar's gold in them thar stocks."

Mr. Hutton shook my hand afterward and mumbled something about a "brilliant presentation." A few days later when I handed Mr. Coleman a paper entitled "The Gold Dilemma" he vetoed its publication.

Over the next two decades the price of gold would rocket from $35 to $875 an ounce. Shares of Dome Mines increased in value from $7 to $100. American South African shares multiplied their value by 4,500 percent. But Hutton failed to predict the coming bull market in gold and thereby cost its clients millions of dollars in potential profits.

As the year progressed the emerging bull market gained momentum. Without exception, the stocks that I had recommended moved upward. The star performer was American Motors, which shot from 10 to 96⅞, but the complete list was nearly as impressive. Adjusting for the effects of stock splits, page 71 shows the results of stocks that I recommended in my morning wire of April 22, 1958.

Hutton's other analysts jumped onto the bandwagon late in the year when the bull market was already aging and I was beginning to grow wary. Only those clients who had followed the guidance of my morning wire were able to achieve maximum profits.

STOCK	BUYING PRICE	SELLING PRICE	PERCENT PROFIT
Alco Products	16	22¾	42.2
American Motors	10	96⅞	868.8
Baldwin Lima	11	18⅝	69.4
Bigelow Sanford	9	21⅝	139.8
Bohn Aluminum	16	35	118.8
Bond Stores	16	24⅝	53.9
Braniff Airways	9	17⅝	95.9
J.I. Case	17	26⅝	56.6
Celanese	16	41⅛	157.1
Commercial Solvents	11	19½	77.3
Congoleum	10	14¾	47.5
Continental Motors	8	13¾	71.9
Crown Cork	19	41	115.7
Cudahy	10	17¼	72.5
Dome Mines	16	22	37.5
Electric Auto Lite	28	55½	98.2
Great Western Sugar	24	32⅞	37.0
H. L. Green	25	47½	90.0
Holland Furnace	11	15¼	38.6
Kresge	28	35	25.0
Northwest Airlines	14	46⅛	229.5
Schenley	22	45½	106.8
Singer Mfg.	39	66⅜	70.2

(Continued)

STOCK	BUYING PRICE	SELLING PRICE	PERCENT PROFIT
J.P. Stevens	21	43⅞	109.0
Stokely-Van Camp	17	22	29.4
Trans World Air	13	24⅝	89.5
Underwood	17	40	135.3
Walgreen	33	55½	68.2

Exuberant over my success, Polly and I contracted to have a large home built for us in Country Club Estates, the prestige address in Ramsey. We had a fifth baby on the way and could use the extra room.

The years prior to my job at Hutton had been lean. Polly and I had built up a number of debts and for a time the bulk of my paycheck was allocated toward paying those off, as well as financing our new home. Paul joined our family in August, our fifth child and second son. I was particularly warmed when Mr. Coleman, despite our ideological differences, sent Polly a beautiful bouquet.

As I gained confidence in my ability to forecast stock trends, and as our financial reserve increased, the temptation to dabble in a few personal investments became overwhelming.

I believed that the market was in the beginnings of a major bull era and set out to find a vehicle for turning a small amount of cash into a large hoard. If the general level of demand was increasing, I reasoned, a stock that was in limited supply would benefit most from buying pressure. So I searched for a stock with low capitalization— that is, a company that only issued a small number of shares.

"Extraordinary!" I exclaimed to myself as I ran my finger down the capitalization column in *Standard & Poor's Stock Guide.* Here was a firm called American Beverage Company, listed on the American Stock Exchange, which had a capitalization of only 150,000 shares—a ridiculously small number. Even the tiniest public firms often have millions of shares in circulation.

With such a flimsy capitalization I figured that each share must be priced rather high. I walked over to the Amex ticker and searched for a price on American Beverage. It was such an inactive issue that I could find no transaction on the tape.

In the back of the boardroom I finally found a broker who could give me a quotation. American Beverage was selling for only $1 a share.

As I walked back to my desk the realization suddenly hit me that for $75,001 anyone could buy a controlling interest in American Beverage that very afternoon.

I mentioned the stock to a few friends in the boardroom and, just for the fun of it, three of us decided to pool our money and buy 1,000 shares. Within fifteen minutes this unprecedented demand drove the price of American Beverage to 1½, increasing the value of the company by 50 percent.

For a time very little happened to the stock. It pulled back to 1⅜, then jumped to 1¾. I bought additional shares periodically, eventually holding 600 shares at an average price of about $2 per share.

My friend Dick Calvert, who was in the liquor business, came in on the game, buying 1,000 shares at 2½.

This sudden interest in American Beverage seemed to create a momentum all of its own. After a few months the stock was quoted at 4½.

In those days I suffered from a touch of acquired fundamentalism. Despite the success of my technical studies of the market I had not been able to escape completely the influence of Mr. Coleman and the plethora of fundamental analysts who surrounded me. With the stock at 4½ I pondered whether I should sell out for a nice profit or gamble on a further rise. I decided to find out a little bit about American Beverage.

It was a snowy day in February 1959, the kind of day when little happens on Wall Street and I could get away for a two-hour lunch. "Dick," I said to Dick Calvert, "why don't we go over to Brooklyn and take a look at American Beverage?" Since he was facing the same decision I was, he agreed to come along.

We emerged from the subway into a Brooklyn blizzard, searching for the address that was listed as the corporate headquarters of American Beverage Company. After several wrong turns we finally located a battered old building, the second floor of which housed the entire facilities of the firm.

When I introduced myself as an analyst from E.F. Hutton &

Company the manager welcomed me cordially. He took the two of us on a tour of the assembly line, where a few tired-looking women in white smocks bottled and packed the one and only product of the company. It was called Celray and the manager described it as a sort of celery-flavored beer.

"Want to try it?" he asked enthusiastically. He pulled two bottles from a refrigerator and gave them to us. I took note of the fact that he did not grab a bottle for himself.

Taste is certainly a matter of opinion. No doubt Celray had a following, but Dick and I couldn't bring ourselves to compliment the manager on his concoction. But he didn't seem to notice, and talked on about American Beverage's plans for expansion. The firm was going to purchase a bottling company in Texas and introduce Celray to the Southwest.

We retreated as fast as possible. Back at Hutton, Dick and I sold out immediately for 4½ per share. The next week the stock skyrocketed to 9¾.

I kicked myself for bowing to the tenets of fundamental analysis. If I had not gone to Brooklyn I would probably have held my stock until its chart showed the end of the rally. I had paid attention to the company, rather than the stock, and my temporary amnesia to the basic assumptions of technical analysis cost me about $3,000.

From this time forward I resolved to pay no attention whatsoever to companies. I would concentrate solely on stocks. I would ignore all the traditional Wall Street numbers—corporate earnings, dividends, and p/e ratios. I would study no quarterly reports. I would screen out all the general business and political news. I would care not whither the prime rate fluctuated, or where the wholesale price index lodged for the month. I would filter out the static of all this irrelevant information and listen only to the internal music of the market itself. I would be a pure technician.

When the market spoke I would get down on my knees and say, "Yes, Master."

The continual study of the ups and downs of price movements was reminiscent of my childhood game of following the pattern of notes in the church hymnal to distract myself from the pain of a boring sermon. Thus I was led to the intriguing correlation that existed between the market and the world of music. My study of these relationships was the subject of a lecture I presented in December 1961 at the New School for Social Research in New York.

"There is a predictable order in the universe," I declared. "All motion is governed by physical laws. There are no accidents. Stock price movements exhibit a mathematical rhythm that is strikingly similar to that found in the greatest music. Johann Sebastian Bach could have been a great technical analyst if he lived in today's world."

To illustrate, I produced a chart of the first seven bars of Bach's "Jesu, Joy of Man's Desiring." I assigned the number one to the lowest note in the theme and charted the progression of the melody, humming it to my audience. When diagrammed in this manner, Bach's harmonious composition exhibited all the expected movements seen in a stock price chart:

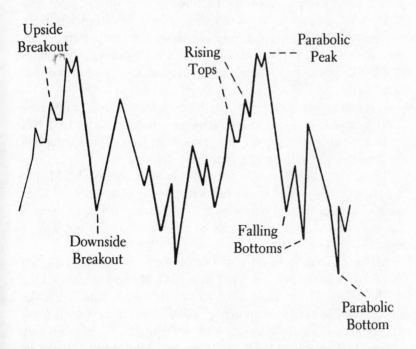

Assigning numbers to each note, the melody of the first seven bars is graphed on the following points: 4,5,6,8,7,7,9,8,8,11,10,11,8,6,-4,5,6,7,8,9,8,7,6,5,6,4,3,4,5,1,3,5,7,6,5,6,4,5,6,8,7,7,9,8,8,11,10,11,8,6,4,5,6,2,8,7,6,5,4,1,4,3,4.

Here were upside breakouts, rising bottoms, downside breakouts, and declining tops. "If Bach showed a trained stock chart technician portions of his composition the technician could predict the next patterns of the melody with a high degree of accuracy," I said. "This is because music and the stock market both follow the laws of physics."

Here are some of those basic physical laws and how they apply to the stock market:

1) A body at rest tends to remain at rest. A stock that sits on a flatbase is likely to remain there until some important change takes place, altering the pattern of accumulation and distribution.

2) A body in motion tends to remain in motion. This is called price momentum. If a stock has been going nowhere for an extended period of time and suddenly scores an upside breakout—suddenly moves—it is likely to continue to move.

3) What goes up must come down. When a stock rises in price over a period of time that very rise will alter the pattern of accumulation and distribution. Buyers at a low price become sellers at a higher price. That change in orientation is signaled by a downside breakout.

4) It takes more energy to go up than to come down. It might take a stock more than a year to double in price, but it can give back half of that advance in a period of weeks—even days. This is why bull markets are generally longer than bear markets.

There was a logical reason for each new note that Bach added to his composition—the human ear demanded it in order to fulfill its innate sense of natural harmony. There is an equally logical reason for each new change in the price of a stock—it fulfills the laws of natural harmony.

My speech was received with a combination of reactions ranging from skepticism to awe, but there were few lukewarm observers. One of the believers was Abe Cohen from Larchmont, New York, the publisher of an independent market newsletter called *Investors Intelligence.* His is a unique service among the myriad of such advisory letters. Abe does not advise his readers about the market; rather, he tells them what all the other advisers are saying. Abe and I became friends that day. Our paths would cross again.

* * *

"Joe, could I join you for a cup of coffee?"

The question came from Sam, a polite but humorless man in his late sixties who ran the elevator.

"Sure, Sam," I answered. "I was just on my way down to the coffee shop for a break."

We rode down together, got our coffee, and found a small table. Sam clearly had something on his mind, but he had difficulty launching his topic. He stared at his coffee cup for a few minutes before he spoke.

"Look at me," he said. "I'm sixty-nine years old and I'm making seventy-five dollars a week." A quivering note came into his voice. "You would never believe that at one time in my life I was worth $875,000 on paper."

"When was that?"

"In 1929. Just before the crash."

My mind flashed back to my father, and I asked the question of Sam that I had often posed to dad. "Sam, why didn't you sell?"

"I've regretted that all my life and I've asked myself that same question many times. I didn't sell because I only had $875,000. I always wanted to be a millionaire." Sam sipped his coffee and sighed. "I came so close," he whispered.

There are millions of Sams in the stock market. Most investors seem to have a problem selling, partly because Wall Street constantly urges them to buy, and partly because it is human nature to cling to things. They fail to realize that a paper profit is no profit at all until the stock is sold. Instead, they retain the stock out of greed, hoping it will go higher. Too often they wait so long that their paper profits dwindle to zero.

I was determined that followers of my Hutton wire would not experience that pain. Whenever I recommended a stock to buy, I followed it carefully thereafter until the time was right for a sell signal.

The very word *sell* made me a maverick at Hutton. It is alien to the conventional broker's vocabulary. The furthest a fundamental analyst was likely to go was to indicate that a company was in a "period of difficulty" or that it was "not a recommended buy," and even these mild euphemisms were rarely employed.

Most of my sell utterances went completely against popular belief.

They were so out of line with what the rest of the research department was saying that my desk became a little island surrounded by ideological hostility.

This, of course, failed to silence me. Early in 1958 I had issued a buy recommendation on American Motors, which, in the course of the next eighteen months, rose from 10 to more than 90. I watched it carefully, noting an apparent peak of the parabolic curve at 96. When the stock next reached a lower peak, at 85, my morning wire advised the reader to sell American Motors.

That very afternoon an elderly gentleman, one of our customers, sought me out at my desk. He was very disturbed. "Don't you realize that I can't sell my American Motors right now?" he said.

"Why not?" I asked.

"I have had such a gain in the stock that if I sold now I would have a tremendous tax problem."

I showed him the evidence on the stock chart and warned him that a stock coming off such a tremendous parabolic curve is likely to drop with incredible speed. But he would not listen and stormed off.

In a matter of days American Motors jumped back up to 96, and I could feel the other researchers pulling for a greater rise in order to see me proven wrong. After all, under the leadership of George Romney, American Motors was posting record profits and had resumed paying a dividend.

Four months later, after American Motors had dropped from 96 to 35 on its way back down to 15, the same elderly gentleman returned to my desk.

"Mr. Granville," he said, "I have a confession to make."

"What's that?"

"I no longer have a tax problem. My profits have been wiped out."

There is another tactic, shunned by fundamentalists, that I increasingly urged my followers to apply: the technique known as selling short. Most people think they can make money only when they buy a stock and it rises in price. But since the market falls as often as it rises, this gives the average investor only half a game to play. Short-selling enables the investor to profit from a falling market. Yet this technique is little understood, and is discouraged by most brokers.

Suppose that you have inside knowledge that the price of cows is going to collapse from its current level of $1,000 a head all the way down to $200 a head. You would like to translate your knowledge into cash, but how do you do this?

You do just the opposite of what you do in a rising market. In a rising market you buy first and sell later. This is the procedure most people understand, and it is the way most people play any market. They buy and then at some later time they sell.

But you are smart, and you want to sell a cow for $1,000 before the market collapses. The only problem is, you don't happen to own a cow. What can you do?

You can borrow a cow. Go to your next-door neighbor who has a herd of them and offer him a small stipend for the loan of Bessie. He's not averse to a second income, so he says, "Fine, she's in the third stall on the left."

You go down to the third stall, take the cow by the neck and lead it to the local cow market. And you sell it. How much do you get for Bessie? One thousand dollars. And you put the money into your pocket.

At this point in the equation you owe your neighbor one cow and, of course, he wants her back.

Let us suppose that your knowledge turns out to be correct. The cow market collapses and the going price is down to $200. Beautiful. You've got $1,000 in your pocket, so you go back to the cow market and buy one cow. How much does that cow cost you now? Two hundred dollars.

Now you have a cow to return to your neighbor, and you are left with $800 in your pocket. You go back and knock on your neighbor's door and say, "I'm here to return your cow."

Actually, he does not get Bessie back, he gets Elsie instead. But a cow is a cow is a cow. Your neighbor says, "Third stall on the left."

You put Elsie back into Bessie's old stall. Now you are even with your neighbor. You are even with the cow market. You have $800 in your pocket, and you never even owned a cow!

What about stocks? If you think the market is going to drop sharply, you want to sell now at today's high prices—and sell with borrowed stock. Most people do not know that they have a good neighbor who is quite able to loan them the stock.

Every stock brokerage house in America possesses millions of shares of stock that they are only too happy to loan you. Where does that stock come from? It is stock "held in street name." In other words, if you buy 100 shares of General Motors and you are not going to hold it to bequeath to your grandchildren, it is more convenient to tell your broker to hold the stock in his name. It is credited to your account, but there is no certificate that has your name on it. The certificate has the name of the brokerage firm on it.

Tucked away amid the fine print of the account application you signed is a clause empowering your broker to loan your stock to anyone who wants to sell it short. Just like your good neighbor, the broker is sitting there with a huge barnful of cows, or millions of shares of stock. He gets a service charge for loaning it.

That is one of the finest services brokers have, and yet they all but keep it a secret because they gag on the word *sell.*

Unlike the fundamentalists, who had the luxury of spending months on an individual report, I was under pressure to produce daily. I worked hard to maintain an original flair in my morning wire. This was generally easy to do because the market is a fascinating, never-ending kaleidoscope of movement. Like snowflakes, no two days on the market are exactly alike.

However, there were a few days when I felt as though I had said everything that could be said. On one such occasion I searched my brain on the train ride in from New Jersey, but I drew a blank. The market had experienced a lifeless session the day before. I had no new buy or sell recommendations.

Somehow I found myself musing upon the infamous statement of Soviet premier Nikita Khrushchev, threatening "We will bury you, not from without but from within." What did he mean by that? I wondered. How could the Russians tear down capitalism from the inside?

When I arrived at my desk at Hutton I was still at a loss for a morning wire subject. It was 7:10 A.M. I had forty-five minutes to produce a full page of single-spaced copy.

Without thinking further I typed a headline: "Are the Russians in the U.S. Stock Market?" The crazy idea just popped into my head. I postulated that the Soviet Union had allocated 3 percent of its defense budget to accumulate shares of the 30 stocks that comprise the Dow Jones Industrial Average. Operating anonymously through Swiss banks, they stealthily accumulated these blue chip securities over a period of five years until their Swiss vaults contained 5 million shares of each Dow stock.

The conclusion of my fanciful scenario was that the Russians would dump their stock all at once, immobilize the U.S. stock market, and bring down the world's capitalistic societies in one brilliant stroke.

Pleased that I had conquered my writer's block, I hustled the copy up to the wire room, and promptly at 8:00 A.M. it was disseminated across the country.

Within minutes I was in Mr. Coleman's office. "What are you talking about?" he ranted. "This is supposed to be a morning wire about realities in the stock market." He waved the wire in the air. "What a harebrained scheme! What do you think you're doing?"

I tried to maintain a solemn demeanor as I endured the reprimand, but in truth I had not had so much fun since I blew up the toilet at the Todd School. My job was secure—I was by then too important to the firm—so I took the tongue-lashing and returned to my desk, assuming that the episode was over.

The following afternoon, shortly after three o'clock, I was hard at work on my closing wire when a man in a crumpled brown suit approached my desk.

"Joseph E. Granville?" he asked.

"Yes."

"I want to speak with you."

I begged off. He was obviously another one of the many market buffs who tried to corner me every day. "I don't have the time right now," I said rather gruffly.

"I must speak with you now," he insisted.

"Well, at least give me a minute to finish my closing wire."

Confident that I had brushed him off, I finished the wire and took it upstairs to the teletype. When I returned to my desk the persistent man was still waiting.

"Look," I said, "it's been a very busy day and I'm tired. Couldn't we talk some other time?" As if to emphasize my point, my telephone rang.

The man then pulled out his wallet and showed me a laminated card with his picture on it. The card was headed: United States Government, Central Intelligence Agency.

"Uh, yes," I stammered. "I'll talk with you, but let's go into the library."

He followed me into our small glass-enclosed research library, and for the first time I noticed that he had a bulky case with him.

"Mr. Granville," he began, "I'm not going to horse around. I have a job to do. You are my current assignment." He pulled a large tape recorder from the case and began to monitor our conversation.

"You are Joseph E. Granville," he said for the record.

"Yes."

"You write the E.F. Hutton morning wire?"

"Yes."

"You suggested in your morning wire yesterday that the Russians could be investing in our stock market?"

"Yes, sir."

He then launched into an incredibly thorough interrogation, asking about my parents, my childhood, my education, and military service. Often he backtracked, asking for the same information from an oblique angle, perhaps seeing if he could cross me up. He grilled me for more than an hour, then left without a comment.

I had nothing to hide and I was totally honest with him. But I was amazed to realize that my flight of fancy had struck a sensitive nerve in Washington. Our government apparently thought that the scenario was feasible.

The next morning Mr. Coleman called me in once more. After leaving me, the CIA man had broken up a partners' meeting to interrogate Mr. Coleman, an action that was not calculated to please him. He was more controlled than on the previous day, however, because he had had time to reflect. I was bringing the firm substantial commissions, and he could not afford to burn me too severely.

"Joe," he reasoned, "fifty thousand copies of your wire are printed every day. You're often quoted on the radio and in newspapers—frequently in the *Wall Street Journal.* People pay attention to what you say, so watch what you tell them! You're not just speaking for yourself, you're speaking for E.F. Hutton."

It may have been the intercession of my friend Gerald Loeb that saved my job that day. He was always in my corner, which set him in ideological opposition to almost everyone else in the office. But even he could not completely quiet Mr. Coleman's wrath. The boss lectured me until I humbly promised to exercise more judgment in my choice of subject matter. "If you don't, Joe, we're going to have to have someone start watching you," he said.

It was the first hint of what would ultimately boot me out of Wall Street. Joe Granville censored? I put the thought out of my mind. I would never allow anyone to leash my tongue.

I was, in fact, ready to speak out about a number of things I had observed on Wall Street. Being on the firing line every day for more than two years, I had learned much about the day-to-day changes in the market. Each day was an entity unto itself, and through observation I had deduced a number of indicators that seemed to forecast the movement of the market on the following day. One of the reasons that technical analysis had remained in its infancy, I realized, was that no one had ever codified its principles into a book.

"I've got a terrific idea for a book," I said to Ruth Aley, the literary agent who had marketed *Everybody's Guide to Stamp Investment*. "It will be a sort of dictionary of market action, a set of rules that anyone can apply to predict the course of the market on a day-to-day basis. It will be aimed primarily at those investors who follow the market every day."

Ruth was impressed with the idea and asked me to write an outline. I did so, and she sold it to Prentice-Hall Publishing Company, presenting me with a $5,000 advance.

I worked every night on the manuscript in my basement office. Carefully I formalized what I had observed about the daily action of the stock market. I pulled no punches, characterizing Wall Street as the antithesis of the market. Fundamental analysts were the targets of my most vitriolic criticisms.

The largest portion of the book was devoted to a series of indicators developed by me and other technicians that, taken as a whole, gave a far more accurate picture of market action than any fundamentalist could ever see. Some of my major indicators were:

The Advance-Decline Indicator. The total number of stocks advancing or declining in price was a better indicator of market action than was the Dow Jones Industrial Average. When advances outnumbered declines, a rally was in the offing. When declines outnumbered advances, a sell-off loomed.

The Rail Indicator. The fifteen stocks that made up the Dow

Jones Rail Average seemed to predict short-term market swings more clearly than the thirty Industrials.

The Leadership Indicator. The daily tally of the fifteen most active stocks showed where buyers and sellers were concentrating their efforts. Two thousand individual stocks might be traded on the Big Board on any given day, yet the most active stocks accounted for about 15 percent of the action. If a preponderance of those stocks rose, then the market was likely to rise on the following day, and vice versa.

The S & P 500 Indicator. Because it is a broader average than the Dow Jones Industrials, Standard & Poor's list of 500 stocks was a more valid measurement of market action. To equate the two averages, the market student had to multiply the gain or loss in the S & P 500 by ten. If the S & P 500 advanced at a greater rate than the Dow Industrials, a market advance was forecast, and vice versa.

The Overdue Indicator. When the market moved in one direction for five or six sessions, it was overdue for a technical turnaround as bargain hunters bought or profit takers sold.

The General Motors Indicator. For some reason the market had a tendency to follow the lead of General Motors. If GM stock rose, a general market rise was likely to follow, and vice versa.

The Closing Indicator. A strong move in either direction during the last hour of trading was likely to spill over into the following day.

The High-Low Indicator. An expanding number of stocks recording new twelve-month highs, or a declining number of new lows, was bullish. Conversely, declining highs and expanding lows were bearish.

Believing that there is safety in numbers, I brought my list to a total of fifty-six daily indicators. Anyone with a newspaper could tote up the balance of the indicators and predict the trend of the following day's market with a high degree of accuracy.

While I created my list of indicators to denote short-term changes, they were also of value in signaling long-term trends. In this context I placed special emphasis upon two indices. One was the High-Low Indicator. If a bull market was legitimate—if the majority of stocks were expanding in price—then, each time the Dow Jones Industrial Average scored a new bull market high, the number of stocks scoring new twelve-month highs should also expand. One of the clearest signals that a bull market was ending occurred when the Dow broke out to a new high but the number of individual new highs was lower than it was at the previous Dow high. It was a sure sign that general market momentum had slowed. The same concept was true in reverse for a bear market. When the Dow scored a new low but the number of individual new lows contracted, a new bull market was indicated.

The other major long-term indicator was the 200-Day Moving Average. By computing the average price of a stock over the past 200 calendar days (approximately 150 trading days) one had a powerful indicator of price trends. Each day the average changed only slightly. The new price was added to the average and the oldest price was dropped. Because it took so much momentum to bring about a major change in the 200-Day Moving Average, such changes were of high significance. This proved to be such a reliable indicator that price chart books such as *Trendline* soon included it as part of their data.

While an individual 200-Day Moving Average was a significant analytical tool for a given stock, it was even more useful when applied to the entire Dow Jones Industrial Average. It was the single best tool I had yet devised to signal major stock market changes. It was a mathematical necessity that the Dow moved above its 200-day line in order to reverse a long downtrend in the line. Such a move almost always signaled the beginning of a new bull market. And vice versa.

A Strategy of Daily Stock Market Timing for Maximum Profit was published in November of 1960 and became an immediate Wall Street bestseller. Bookstores in the financial district sold out each shipment as fast as it could be unpacked. For several weeks the book's sales kept pace with the current best-selling novel, *To Kill a Mockingbird.* The book ultimately went through more than thirty printings and sold over 250,000 copies, for the simple reason that its theories worked. Tens of thousands of investors increased their stock market profits by following my fifty-six daily indicators. In one stroke I brought the art of technical analysis to the attention of countless investors who finally found the way to step from the ranks of the bagholders and join the smart money crowd.

Bob Bleiberg, the editor of *Barron's,* assigned me to write several articles for him. Financial editors at the *Wall Street Journal* and *The New York Times* quoted my opinions with regularity. More and more of Hutton's clients clustered around me every day. On Wall Street, I was suddenly a star.

With my parents and older brother Bill at our house in Yonkers, New York. I was four years old. *(Private Collection)*

As a freshman at Duke University in 1942, hungry for more than just knowledge. I weighed less than 120 pounds that year. *(Private Collection)*

At home in Westport in 1944 with my constant advisor, my mother. *(Private Collection)*

I was only twenty-five when the third edition of my *Price Predictions* was published. *Collier's* magazine ran this photo of me with sheets of uncut rare stamps and a copy of *Stamps* magazine, to which I was a regular contributor. *(Stamps Magazine)*

With Ronald Reagan on the
podium at the Fontainebleau
Hilton in Miami in March of
1979. Neither of us knew that
six months later I would
nearly strangle our future
president to illustrate my Red
Garter story. *(Robin Boatwright)*

A bank trust officer gives
advice. The debut of my
bagholder's costume was the
highlight of this April 1, 1980,
appearance in Indianapolis.
(Michael Fleming)

With David Susskind just before I appeared on his show
in June of 1980. (*Wayne Shapiro*)

A visit with Johnny Carson in his dressing room at Resorts International
Casino. My show was down the street at the Bally's Park Place Casino. At left
is D. L. Smith. (*Ken Catanella*)

Arriving in style at the
Philadelphia stock exchange
in October of 1980.
(*Jules Schick Photography*)

Kissing a stockbroker at the
Philadelphia stock exchange in
October of 1980. This is one field in
which no one has challenged my
expertise. (*Jules Schick Photography*)

One way of answering a question
from the floor during an appearance
in Minneapolis in December of 1980.
If I said it straight, they wouldn't
believe me. (*Arnold Securities*)

WHEN JOSEPH GRANVILLE TALKS...

My January 6, 1981, sell signal triggered a few cartoons, along with everything else. This one ran in the *Los Angeles Times*. (Paul Conrad, © *1981*, Los Angeles Times. *Reprinted with permission*)

Later in the Minneapolis appearance, my stock market shorts answer the question, "How do you follow the market when you're always traveling?" After the show brought down the house, various brokerage firms such as Dean Witter stopped sponsoring me. (*Arnold Securities*)

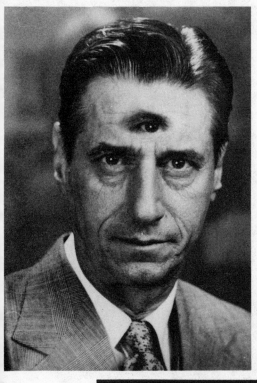

Watching the market. I had this taken after Jack Arnold said he was certain I had a third eye. It hangs on the wall of his office. *(Bob Sherman/Camera 5)*

Another sell signal cartoon, this one from Bill Schorr. The 1981–82 bear market was underway. *(Reprinted by permission: Tribune Media Services, Inc.)*

At a show in Fort Lauderdale in February of 1981, Dr. Granville checks the heart of a bank trust officer. *(Bob Sherman/Camera 5)*

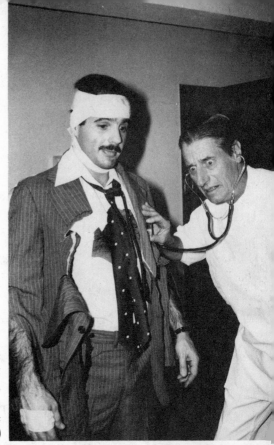

A radio interview in February of 1981 with J. P. McCarthy, on his Detroit-based show. *(Thomas England/People Weekly © 1981 Time Inc.)*

On the road in Las Vegas, dictating a *Market Letter* from my hotel room, in February of 1981. (*Bob Sherman/Camera 5*)

One of my earliest dreams finally comes true in June of 1981 when, as the Doctor of Market Music, I performed in a packed Carnegie Hall. (*Thomas McKinnon*)

With Karen, my third wife, at the Carl Reiner annual tennis benefit in the spring of 1981. *(Jack Rourke Productions)*

Portrait by my wife Karen. She drew this in April of 1982, about a year after we were married.

6.
REVELATION

Notoriety brought ever more hectic days at Hutton. Everyone wanted to stop and chat with me about my *Strategy* book as a means of prying out some inside information. Most of my "tips" were on record in the morning wire, but this did not stop the rumor-hungry Wall Street crowd from speculating about my next moves. I was, indeed, fine-tuning a fresh, exciting theory that would soon revolutionize the art of technical analysis, but I was not yet ready to publicize it. I needed solitude to perfect my method of market forecasting.

Fortunately for me, Hutton moved its headquarters across the street to an upper floor of the new Chase Manhattan Bank Building. With the modern facilities came my own glass-enclosed office and a personal secretary to screen my visitors and telephone calls. Nevertheless, on occasion a persistent caller successfully ran the gauntlet.

A man whom I will identify only as Don was one who charmed his way past my secretary because he exuded an aura of wealth and success. He was so eager to see me and obviously appreciative of my work that I set aside time for him.

"Mr. Granville," he said, "I want to open an account, and I want only you to manage it for me."

"What sort of account did you have in mind?" I asked.

"I want to day trade IBM," he replied.

A day trader! That was my kind of action. If Don believed that

IBM would rise on a given day he would buy one or two thousand shares in the morning and sell in the afternoon. But if he believed IBM would drop in price he would sell short in the morning and cover the sale in the afternoon. Either way he would pay me two commissions every day, one for buying and one for selling.

IBM was a day trader's dream. Its price fluctuated between $500 and $550 a share, generally responding to the predominant direction of the market. Because it was so high-priced it frequently experienced wide swings in the course of a day—as much as $10 to $15 per share. However, its high price also necessitated a sizable investment. Day trading IBM was a game for heavyweights.

I had obtained my broker's license merely as a convenience so that I could transact business for myself and a few relatives and friends. I never planned on earning significant commissions, for my technical analysis work kept me too busy to service many accounts properly.

But Don's proposition was tempting. He wanted me to conduct the trades solely on the basis of my own market judgment. Here was a chance to test all of my theories in the real world and at the same time supplement my income.

"How much money do you wish to place into the account?" I asked.

"One million dollars," he replied.

Here was a man who would be treated to some very special inside information. Attempting to hold my composure, I explained to him that I wanted to use his money to test a bold new hypothesis. He listened with enthusiasm as I detailed what has since become the cornerstone of my market studies, the theory of On-Balance Volume.

Important ideas do not always emerge amid majestic circumstances. The theory of On-Balance Volume caught me, quite literally, with my pants down.

One August morning in 1961 I sat on the toilet in the men's room, away from the hubbub of the research department, musing about the stock market.

For some time I had been uneasy about a built-in problem with all of my indicators. They were based upon price, and price can be the most misleading thing about the stock market. Price is merely the external sign of changes that have already occurred in the levels of supply and demand.

My charts, for example, signaled a major change only when they showed a price breakout. This made it impossible to buy a stock at the very bottom or sell it at the very top. To be sure, the investor could profit greatly by buying *near* the bottom and selling *near* the top, but by definition the practice was always short of the ideal.

All fifty-six of the daily indicators in my *Strategy* book were keyed to price. Furthermore, I had now developed several methods of monitoring long-term trends in addition to my reliance upon the number of individual highs and lows and the 200-Day Moving Average of the Dow.

One of the most reliable methods was to follow the course of the Dow Jones Rail Average and compare it to the performance of the Industrials. Likewise, comparing the Standard & Poor's 500 to the Industrials revealed hidden dramas.

A third, very useful indicator was a running total of the advance-decline line, a simple exercise that reveals much about major market trends. A summary of each day's trading activity includes a total of how many New York Stock Exchange issues advanced in price and how many declined. The number of declines is subtracted from the number of advances, resulting in a plus or minus figure for the day. Each day's figure is then added to or subtracted from the running total.

The key task is to compare these indicators to the performance of the Dow Jones Industrial Average. The most widely followed indicator of any market has to be the least reliable in order for the smart money to bamboozle the bagholders. On the New York Stock Exchange the Dow Jones Industrial Average serves this function, Wall Street constantly pretending that these 30 blue chip issues key the actions of the other 2,000 stocks. In reality, the chief value of the Dow Jones Industrial Average is as a smokescreen for genuine market action. For this reason, and this reason only, it must be closely monitored.

Suppose, for example, that on a given day the Dow Jones Industrial Average reaches a new bull market high of 1,000. On that day the Dow Jones Rail Average, the S & P 500, and the advance-decline line also reach new bull market highs. So far so good. Then, after meandering for a few weeks, the Dow Industrials close at another new high of 1,010. If, on that day, the other indicators stand higher than they were at the previous Dow high of 1,000, the rally is *confirmed*. The bull market is likely to continue.

But suppose that, on the day of the new Dow high of 1,010, the other indicators close somewhat below their levels when the Dow previously peaked at 1,000. In that event the new Dow high is *nonconfirmed*. This is a major sell signal. Technically the bull market is over, even though the Dow Industrials may not indicate this for several months to come.

The reverse is equally true. If a new Dow low is confirmed by new lows in the other indicators, the slide is likely to continue. But if the Dow low is nonconfirmed it produces a major buy signal. The bear market has ended.

These are valuable forecasting tools, yet they are all totally dependent upon the signals of price fluctuations.

But what makes prices rise? More buyers than sellers. What makes prices fall? More sellers than buyers. How could I determine shifts in buying and selling momentum before they showed up in price movements?

I stared at the pattern of hexagonal tiles on the bathroom floor. My eyes glazed over. Out of focus, the tiles seemed to melt together as, inside my head, thoughts crystallized. I mulled over the process that brought this particular tile floor to this particular bathroom. At some point in time whoever designed this new building made a decision about bathroom tiles. Someone else then ordered them from the manufacturer. A production executive scheduled the run; a foreman supervised it. A trucking company arranged for delivery while, at the same time, an accountant billed the contractor.

Throughout the sequence there were innumerable people alerted to the fact that the bathrooms in the Chase Manhattan Bank Building would soon be supplied with this particular tile.

On a larger scale such inside information is highly valuable. If Boeing strikes a deal to supply United Airlines with fifty new jetliners, countless people learn of the impending transaction before the general public is apprised. And a significant number of those insiders are investors.

Technically it is illegal to capitalize on inside information in the stock market, but in practice it is done all the time. The Securities and Exchange Commission is able to intervene only in the most flagrant cases.

I was regularly treated to a classic example of how inside information is used to dupe the investing public. Each month Standard & Poor's selected one particular stock to promote, usually spinning out a comprehensive research report with rosy fundamental predictions.

The identity of the S & P Stock of the Month was supposed to be a guarded secret, but on Wall Street there is no such thing. Near the end of every month one particular stock inexplicably jumped in price as certain anonymous investors silently accumulated it. On the first of the month the S & P Stock of the Month was announced and the public jumped in like lemmings. For a few days the stock rose in price and then began to tumble as the insiders sold out at the inflated, hyped-up price. The smart money won; the bagholders lost.

There were many other examples that convinced me that the market was an entity unto itself, far removed from the realities of the rest of the business world. It was an insider's game. Information that was available to the general public was usually out of date by the time it was publicized. The smart money had already anticipated the favorable or unfavorable news and acted accordingly. I could not escape the conclusion that there had to be some means of identifying the actions of the smart money before they showed up in price fluctuations.

The realization came upon me in an instant, with such force that I sat straight up in the tiny stall.

Volume.

Volume precedes price. If the smart money is accumulating a given stock, that stock must reveal significant changes in its volume patterns. Price will rise only after the volume equation is thrown out of balance by quietly increased demand. Conversely, when heavier, silent selling occurs, supply will overcome demand, and only then will price fall. In either case the alteration in supply and demand must take place before the move in price. Volume is the steam in the boiler that makes the little price choo-choo go up- and downhill.

As quickly as I could, I girded up my loins and scurried back to my office. Instructing my secretary that I was not to be disturbed for any reason, I got sheets of blank paper and retreated into the research library to pore over back issues of the *Wall Street Journal* and formulate a method for monitoring changes in volume patterns.

The knowledge that I had a technical breakthrough was thrilling. I followed the volume and price patterns of the thirty stocks that comprise the Dow Jones Industrials. The volume statistics showed clear patterns of accumulation and distribution that were invariably followed by appropriate price adjustments. Time flew past as I devised a simple method of quantifying the patterns.

Suppose that on a given day U.S. Steel rose $1 to close at $25 per share. Trading was heavy, with 1 million shares of the stock changing hands. On this particular day the demand for U.S. Steel stock was dominant. Supply was inadequate to meet the demand at the opening price of 24 and the result of the day's barter in this seller's market was a 1-point rise in price.

Suppose, further, that the very next day the stock dropped a full point, back to 24. But volume was lighter, only 500,000 shares. On this second day the supply of U.S. Steel stock was dominant. Demand was inadequate to cover the supply at the opening price of 25 and the buyer's market drove the price down 1 point.

Most people who follow U.S. Steel will look in the newspaper and conclude that there is no change in the stock after these two days of trading.

Look at the *volume* figures, however, and you will see that something very significant has occurred. On the first day the stock went up on 1 million shares and on the second day it came down on 500,000 shares. The price is unchanged, but there is a residue of 500,000 shares of net demand for the stock, a residue disguised from a public that watches only price.

I named this residue On-Balance Volume (OBV), and it may be the single most important contribution I will ever make to the art of technical analysis. Anyone who wishes to follow my stock market theories needs to understand what OBV is and how it is calculated, because nearly all of my subsequent theories have evolved from this concept.

By following price, the public sees no change in U.S. Steel. By following OBV, the market student can see clearly that the demand pressure for U.S. Steel during these two days was double that of the supply pressure.

One or two days on Wall Street mean very little, but OBV followed over a period of time proves to be the key to forecasting price moves. One need simply keep a running total of OBV and look for breakouts in the current pattern.

To keep things simple, I did not attempt to segment the trading day. If the price of a stock rose on a given day (no matter how large or small the rise) I assigned all the volume for that day on the plus side. If the price fell, all the volume on that day was assumed to be negative. On a day when price remained unchanged, so did the running total, supply and demand having canceled out one another.

In the example above, U.S. Steel achieves a reading of +1,000,000 on the first day. The second day's negative volume is subtracted from the running total, giving an OBV of +500,000. On the third day, if U.S. Steel rose in price on a volume of 350,000 shares, the running total would be +850,000.

The ideas floated from my head that afternoon. If price could be charted, so could OBV. And if *price breakouts* were critical points of change, *OBV breakouts* were even more critical because they signaled those impending price breakouts.

An OBV breakout, up or down, occurs when the OBV rises above its most recent high point, or drops below its most recent previous low point. Here is a theoretical extension of U.S. Steel's OBV chart:

DAY	PRICE	VOLUME	OBV	BREAKOUT
1	25.00	+1,000,000	+1,000,000	
	24.00	− 500,000	+ 500,000	
3	24.13	+ 350,000	+ 850,000	
4	24.13	NC	+ 850,000	
5	23.88	−1,450,000	− 600,000	DOWN (OBV breaks below its previous low of +500,000)
6	24.00	+ 600,000	0	
7	24.25	+ 450,000	+ 450,000	
8	23.88	− 300,000	+ 150,000	
9	24.00	+ 675,000	+ 825,000	UP (OBV breaks above its previous high of +450,000)

(Continued)

DAY	PRICE	VOLUME	OBV	BREAKOUT
10	23.50	− 800,000	+ 25,000	DOWN (OBV breaks below its previous low of +150,000)
11	23.38	− 300,000	− 275,000	DOWN (extension of the low, forming a cluster of DOWNS)
12	23.75	+ 500,000	+ 225,000	
13	24.00	+ 925,000	+1,150,000	UP (OBV breaks above its previous high of +825,000)

When UP or DOWN designations occur in clusters with no contrary designation in between, the highest UP or lowest DOWN becomes the key figure in the cluster.

Once the stock has recorded four clusters (two UPs and two DOWNs) those peaks and valleys can be charted just like price figures. A chart of the designations for U.S. Steel looks like this:

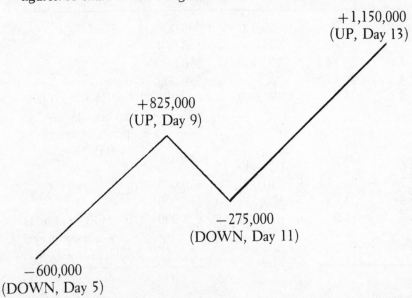

+1,150,000
(UP, Day 13)

+825,000
(UP, Day 9)

−275,000
(DOWN, Day 11)

−600,000
(DOWN, Day 5)

The chart reveals a key pattern of higher UPs and lower DOWNs. Though the price is thus far unchanged at 24, a clear trend of accumulation is evidenced. This pattern is a *rising field trend.* The opposite pattern (lower UPs and lower DOWNs) is a *falling field trend.* Should the OBV chart show no clear trend over four successive clusters, the stock is in a *doubtful field trend.*

As I studied the past performances of the 30 Dow Industrials it became apparent that a field trend was a genuine signal of the current pattern of accumulation or distribution that could be seen weeks or months before any change was reflected in the price of the stock. An OBV chart signaled the proper time to buy or sell any selected stock.

My view of the market would never be the same again. In one stroke I had found the way to peer through the haze of stock prices and read the future.

Busy weeks followed as I worked to apply individual OBV patterns to the process of forecasting the entire market. To accomplish this I created a market index called the Climax Indicator (CLX), which I believed to be the primary volume indicator to predict major market transitions. The CLX is simply the differential between the number of daily upside and downside volume breakouts of the 30 Dow Jones Industrials.

For example, if twelve of the thirty stocks achieve UP designations and six achieve DOWN designations, the CLX for the day stands at +6. A graph of daily CLX readings reveals all the telltale patterns of breakouts shown in the OBV chart of a single stock, the difference being that it indicates the course of the market as a whole.

The CLX is compared to the Dow Jones Industrial Average in the same manner as the plethora of price indicators. To confirm a new Dow high the CLX must better its reading from the previous high point. When the CLX nonconfirms a new Dow high it is a signal that the steam has run out of the choo-choo. Prices may indicate a bull market, but the hidden internal statistics prove that the rally is luring fewer investors into the market. The smart money is taking its profit at the top, dumping stocks. The bull market has ended and a bear market has begun.

When the CLX nonconfirms a new Dow low it indicates the

reverse. Smart money has silently begun to accumulate stocks at bargain prices. Coal is being heaped onto the fire, building steam for a powerful forward lunge. The bear market has ended and a new bull market has begun.

This is Newton's second law of motion applied to the market. That law states that the net force acting on a body is proportional to the mass of the body and to its acceleration; the direction of the force is the same as that of the body's acceleration. The second law of motion is the key to understanding the behavior of moving bodies since it links cause (force) and effect (acceleration) in a definite way. On-Balance Volume either confirms momentum or indicates its loss. It reveals the inner changes of momentum on either the upside or downside that precede all important price movements.

The study of volume, not price, is the key to the actions of the smart money.

Don, my private client, was convinced that my volume studies had solved the 100-year-old enigma of the stock market. He gave me complete freedom to day trade his $1 million IBM account, though he wanted to speak with me at least once a day by telephone to monitor the results. I gave him my home phone number and told him to call me any time, day or night.

Within days I produced dramatic profits for him and spectacular commissions for myself. Even Mr. Coleman was impressed with the turnover of shares that I generated. My OBV figures accurately reflected the current trend for IBM, and my ability to follow the market's gyrations brought handsome rewards. On occasion I bought and sold $1 million worth of IBM as many as four times a day as I saw evidence of changes in market momentum.

Of course my decisions were not always correct, but I was right far more often than I was wrong. On my worst day I lost $18,000 from the account, but on my best day I generated $27,000 in profits. During the first month Don earned more than $50,000, which represented an annual return of 60 percent on his capital.

On top of his profits was the sheer joy he experienced by beating the toughest game in the world.

Somehow I found time for an ever-increasing workload. I now wrote a morning, midday, and closing wire and answered dozens of specific queries each day from Hutton brokers all over the country. I did my volume "homework" religiously, studying the OBV figures, looking for breakouts, following the patterns of the CLX to learn the fine points of my unique new method of monitoring the market. I set to work on another book to announce the OBV concept to the investment world. And on top of it all I monitored the market by the minute, seeking to maximize my client's profit.

Don was so caught up in the stock market game that he was on the phone with me five or six times a day. He called at the office before the opening, checked in several times during the day, and then called me at home, sometimes in the middle of the night.

He never told me what business he was engaged in but I knew that it had exotic overtones. His daily calls were likely to originate from any major American city. But whatever he did and wherever he was, his attention focused more and more on Wall Street.

I got very little sleep. Lunch was a seldom-obtained luxury. My attention was divided among my family's needs, my market wires, my book manuscript, and the constant demands of managing Don's account. I was thoroughly caught up in the madness, but I did not know how long I could continue at that pace.

One morning Don failed to call—the first time he had missed in eleven months. By the end of the day his silence was galling, for I had earned him $25,000 and had no way to report my success.

After three days of silence I ceased trading for him and awaited some sort of instructions.

A week passed with no word. Despite the commissions I was losing, I felt much better. The pressure was off, and I could concentrate on other aspects of my life.

On the eleventh day of silence a Texas law firm called to inform me that Don had died in a plane crash. I closed out the account to his estate. In eleven months, the application of my OBV theories earned him $600,000, but he never lived to enjoy the money.

Reflecting on his fate, I decided that if I was ever lucky enough to amass any kind of fortune, I would luxuriate in it. And now that I had proved to myself that On-Balance Volume worked, I knew that someday I would, indeed, profit greatly from the knowledge.

7.
EXODUS

By December of 1961 CBS newsman Mike Wallace had perfected his now-famous technique of prying information from unwitting interview subjects. Sipping coffee and smoking cigarettes in the waiting room, I watched the television monitor as Wallace plied this art upon novelist Gore Vidal. The interviewer set an easy, relaxed mood, chatting for several minutes about trivial, noncontroversial matters. Only when he saw that Vidal had relaxed did he suddenly shoot out a probing question, goading the colorful, opinionated author into revealing his genuine personality to the camera. Never one to shun controversy, Vidal seemed to relish the verbal thrusts. He gave freely of his eccentric views on politics and contemporary mores.

It was enjoyable to watch these two media professionals at work, and to see the behind-the-scenes activities at a network studio. I took pride in the knowledge that Wallace does not seek out bland guests. He had scheduled two taping sessions this afternoon that would later be broadcast as separate one-hour shows.

After Vidal finished, he and I chatted for fifteen minutes while technicians prepared for the second show. Then I was ushered to an easy chair on the set, a wide grin across my face as I relished my first appearance on national television.

The *Strategy* book, published a year earlier, had generated considerable controversy. For the first time a brokerage house insider had dared to call Wall Street the antithesis of the stock market. A great many Wall Street traditionalists hated me for revealing the inbred nature of the stock market game, but they read my book nonetheless. Appreciative of the turmoil I had caused, Wallace had invited me onto his show.

He began by holding the *Strategy* book up to the camera, a tactic guaranteed to warm an author's heart. Then he asked about my background and my early days at E.F. Hutton. I enjoyed myself thoroughly, recounting many of my Wall Street experiences, some of them funny, some serious, but all contrary to the type of information normally given out by a stock market analyst.

We spent some time discussing my fifty-six daily indicators and how they had proved themselves over the past year.

Wallace had me speaking with ease. I was unafraid of any trick question, for I had nothing to hide.

With no warning, he turned from generalities to specifics. "Joe," he said, "tell me about Standard Oil of New Jersey. Where is it headed?"

Standard Oil of New Jersey, now Exxon, has long been a cornerstone of the Dow Jones Industrial Average. It is true blue, solid American, a stock often bequeathed to widows and orphans in the belief that it will support them forever. At the time it was selling above $70 a share.

With no hesitation I answered, "About forty-one."

Wallace's eyebrows shot up. "Would you repeat that, Joe? Where do you think it's going?"

"Forty-one, Mike."

"Why do you say that?"

"Because that's what its chart tells me. That's what my new studies of this thing I call On-Balance Volume tell me. They tell me it's going to collapse from its current level. It's a sale now, not a buy."

We moved on to other topics, completing a delightful hour before I knew it. I felt satisfied that I had given a clear and exciting exposition of technical analysis. I knew that when the show aired the following week, my star would rise even further at Hutton. Perhaps Mr. Coleman would then take the action that I felt was my certain destiny and make me a partner in the firm.

*　　*　　*

"Bet you a quarter that the phone will ring within ten minutes and Mr. Coleman will want to see me," I said to my secretary when I arrived at work.

It was a glorious morning. The night before, surrounded by my family, I had watched myself on television. I knew that the performance had set me on the road to national prominence. The program had been well publicized, both by CBS and by me, so I knew that every Hutton broker had watched. This morning there was a spring in my step, a twinkle in my eye. When I left the office that afternoon, I would be a partner.

Sure enough, the phone rang shortly after 9:00 A.M. "Mr. Granville, you're right," my secretary said. "Mr. Coleman wants to see you in his office."

"Something very important is about to happen," I announced to her, in one of the most accurate predictions I ever made.

I expected ceremony for the occasion, but I was surprised to see practically every partner in the New York area seated in the room. The chairs were arranged in a semicircle around Mr. Coleman's desk. One empty chair in the middle, directly facing the boss, was evidently reserved for Hutton's rising star.

"Joe," Mr. Coleman growled, "close the door. Sit down."

I eased into the chair, smiled at the morning assemblage, and asked, "Did you all see the show last night?"

Mr. Coleman's face turned red with the effort of restraining himself. He raised his right hand and pointed an elongated forefinger directly at my nose.

"Joe," he said, "who do you think my dinner guest was last night?"

"I don't know, Mr. Coleman."

"None other than the chairman of the board of Standard Oil of New Jersey! We had a lovely dinner, and all through the meal I talked about you. You were the front-runner. You were our bright light at Hutton. We were really looking forward to the show. And then I was so shocked. Joe you never, ever, *ever* go on television and tell the country that one of the cornerstones of our economy is going to collapse. You had some nerve, on national television, to tell us and everyone else in the country that Standard Oil of New Jersey is going to hell in a handbasket."

"Mr. Coleman, he asked me a question," I stammered. "He said, 'Where's Standard Oil of New Jersey going?' "

"You didn't have to tell him so graphically. Couldn't you just say it might go down? Did you have to say *forty-one?*"

"Well, Mr. Coleman, that's what I'm paid to do."

"You're in jeopardy there," he snapped. "We're not paying you to go out and shock the country about the key stocks, the widows' and orphans' stocks. Joe, how could you do this?"

His tirade continued for several minutes before we arrived at his bottom line. Never again would I be allowed to speak with complete freedom. The partners were assigned the rotating duty of reading my material before it went out over the Hutton wire. They had Mr. Coleman's blanket approval to blue-pencil anything with which they did not agree.

Joe Granville was henceforth to be censored.

As I watched stock prices collapse across the board during the bear market of 1962 (Standard Oil of New Jersey dropped to the low 40s), I considered whether or not I had a future with Hutton.

I was on good terms with most of the partners and endured comparatively little editing, but I had to exercise particular caution whenever I was pessimistic about the market. Everyone else at Hutton choked on the word *sell*. And I most certainly could not issue a negative opinion on a stock that the research department was pushing on the basis of fundamentals. I was coerced into elaborating the positives and toning down my outspoken negatives.

In the meantime I came to view Wall Street with an ever more critical eye. Previously I had tended to write off the efforts of the fundamentalists as the acts of blind followers of a false god. I now began to realize that some Wall Street actions are coldly calculated to mislead, confuse, and dupe unsuspecting investors.

For the sake of example, suppose the directors of a firm we'll call the General Tinsel Corporation were concerned because they had too many outstanding debt obligations, upon which they were paying a high rate of interest. It is then that they might rediscover a time-tested method of earning money. They print it. They do not call it money, of course. They call it stock.

Here is how the process works. The chief financial officer of

General Tinsel calls up an investment brokerage house that special-
izes in large transactions. The executive may ask such a firm to
participate in a common and completely legal process known as a
debt-for-equity swap. The executive authorizes the broker to buy up
as much of General Tinsel's outstanding debt as it can up to a given
ceiling, perhaps $20 million.

This first phase of the transaction may take a short period of time
but, before long, the investment broker owns $20 million worth of
General Tinsel's paper debt.

Now General Tinsel orders its printer to conjure up 1 million
shares of fresh, spanking-new common stock, which it swaps for the
$20 million of debt.

To complete the transaction the broker merely pushes the
1 million shares out into the market, usually against a background
of contrived bullishness.

And what happens in the real world? General Tinsel has diluted
its stock, increasing the supply by 1 million shares. The price of
General Tinsel invariably drops because the balance of supply and
demand has been subtly tampered with. But General Tinsel is
happy anyway. It may have to explain its actions to a few irate
investors at the next annual meeting, but chief executive officers
are masters at glossing over such deeds. It is a minor problem, a
small price to pay in return for the ability to pluck $20 million out
of thin air.

The brokerage house, too, is ecstatic over its commissions.

And the bagholders sing the blues.

Early in 1963 Mr. Coleman called me into his office for another
conference. The Wall Street grapevine had informed him that I was
writing another stock market book. That was fine, he said; he liked
the publicity that I garnered for Hutton. But he advised me to "tone
down" some of the references I had made about Wall Street in my
Strategy book. Finally he told me he wanted to review the manuscript prior to publication.

I stammered an excuse. The manuscript was a jumble right now,
I lied. No one could read it in its present form.

Walking back to my desk, I pondered my next move. Prentice-
Hall had advised me that the publication date for *Granville's New*

Key to Stock Market Profits was October 1. It was clear to me that I had to leave Hutton prior to that date.

What would I do? A constant stream of job offers came at me from other brokerage houses, but they were situations no better or worse than my position at Hutton. If I was willing to bow to pressure, I might as well stay where I was. Wherever I worked on Wall Street, I would sooner or later be muzzled.

There was only one answer. I would have to leave Wall Street. The only way I could dispense my advice without bias was to become an independent market analyst.

Polly exploded when I told her of my plan. By this time we had six children to feed—Mary having joined us late in 1961—an expensive home to keep, and less than $3,000 in the bank. Polly thought I was a fool to give up my comfortable salary and throw away a promising career. For a time we were very irritable with one another.

My wife's opposition notwithstanding, in June and July I typed up 500 postcards announcing the creation of the weekly *Granville Market Letter*, available at a subscription rate of $125 per year. I addressed the cards to all my stock market contacts and cached them in a file cabinet.

I leased a $100-a-month, closet-sized office in a ramshackle building across the street from City Hall. Then I rented a post office box. On July 15 I dropped my 500 postcards into the mailbox, marched into Mr. Coleman's office, and tendered my two weeks' notice.

Mr. Coleman offered me more money.

"I'm not interested in money," I replied. I spent the next two weeks briefing my successor, Newton Zinder, who remains today as Hutton's technical analyst.

On August 1, 1963, I left Hutton for good and set up shop in my bare, dingy office. On August 16, the very first *Granville Market Letter* was sent out to my thirty-nine subscribers.

8.
LAMENTATIONS

THE GRANVILLE MARKET LETTER
Volume I, Number 1   August 16, 1963

PURPOSES AND POLICIES

The writer would like to take this opportunity to greet the many subscribers of this new market letter. It is also fitting in this first issue to briefly touch on some of the purposes and policies of the letter which are:

1. *To listen to the market rather than to others.* This stands as the first tenet of market success. The market can only speak in *technical* terms, and thus if this market letter is to serve as an effective listening post, it must by definition be a technical letter.

2. *To stress the technical rather than the fundamental.* Technical does not mean difficult, dull or complex. This word, when pertaining to the stock market, simply denotes such things as tape action, stock price changes, volume changes, the advance-decline line, highs and lows, odd lots, averages, and many other expressions of market language. These things are stressed because there exists a strong tendency for the *technical to precede the fundamental* in terms of giving the earlier warnings to impending changes in market trends . . .

3. *To know that timing is everything* . . . Everybody should become far more conscious of market timing *regardless of his*

current methods. It is only common sense that if a long-term investor wishes to buy 1,000 shares of General Motors and the technical background of the stock market suggests that it could be purchased 5 points cheaper, then that investor owes it to himself to pay attention to the short-term aspects of the market and perhaps save himself $5,000. Market timing is therefore everybody's business . . . and *it is the principal business of this letter.*

4. *To realize that hedging is a waste of time.* Many market letters are masterpieces of hedging (double-talk). This is obviously a disservice to the reader. Theodore Roosevelt had some pretty sound advice which should be followed by market letter writers. He said, "The credit belongs to the man who is actually in the arena; . . . who at the best knows in the end the triumph of high achievement; and who at the worst, if he fails, *at least fails while daring greatly;* so that his place shall never be with those cold and timid souls who know neither defeat nor victory." This letter is going to be right many times and at other times very wrong, but you, the reader, *will always know exactly what this writer thinks of the market.* There will be no hedging.

Perhaps I should repeat that fourth point in every one of my weekly letters. The investor has no difficulty in obtaining market advice from a multitude of analysts, but too often what he receives is a mishmash of maybes. It is a characteristic of advisory services to qualify their opinions so that, if proven wrong, they can always say, "But I said *maybe.*"

The only time I qualify my predictions is when the technical language of the market is ambivalent, which occurs rarely. Most of the time, the market's technical signals are clear, and whenever I read a message in them I state that message without equivocation. This approach is far more valuable to any investor whose money is on the line.

Also clearly stated in my declaration of policy is the fact that I am fallible. Anything can happen. The market is full of capricious twists that call for a constant willingness to learn on the part of the observer. No market analyst can hope to be 100-percent correct. The trick is to be right more often than you are wrong.

These two factors—my outspokenness and my fallibility—have combined to produce strong criticism over the years. In two decades of producing my weekly newsletter, I have been right far more often than I have been wrong, but in either event I am extremely vocal about my opinions. Because a first principle of my theories is that *Wall Street is structured to make you a loser,* whenever I do make an error the fundamentalists are quick to denounce me. It is the price I pay for saying what I believe about the nature of the stock market game.

There is another factor at work in this interchange of criticism: Even though I have been right in the majority of my market predictions, I often *appear* to be wrong for months at a time. There is almost always a lag between a technical forecast and its manifestation. This is inherent in technical analysis because technical tops and bottoms occur before external ones. There is a natural waiting period between my major predictions and their fulfillment, and during this time I can be confident that I will be castigated by my fellow market experts. Here and there will appear stories announcing my death as a market prognosticator.

I shared my cubbyhole of an office with a typewriter, a file cabinet, moldy styrofoam coffee cups, crumpled packs of Marlboros, empty Heineken bottles, yellowing stacks of *Wall Street Journals, Barron's,* and *Horsey's Stock Charts,* and notepads covered with mathematical gambits. I typed and mailed the newsletter myself. I was supremely happy there, because I could now study the harmonious movements of the market free from distracting opinions. I was full of confidence that I would call the future course of the market with near certainty.

I was already on a roll. My morning wire at Hutton had advised my followers to sell out in the spring of 1962. Then I had called the June 1962 bottom, the summer rally that followed, and, to the very day, the Cuban Crisis low of October 1962. That buy signal was still in effect, for I had remained bullish up to the summer of 1963. The Dow Jones Industrial Average rose nearly 170 points during this bull market to a peak of 726.96 on May 31, while I was still at Hutton.

But by the date of my first *Letter,* serious signs of technical weakness had appeared. Though the Dow still hovered around the 720 mark, many other indicators were slumping, most notably the advance-decline line. The most recent rise in the Dow was heavily weighted by large gains in Chrysler, DuPont, and Sears, and my OBV figures indicated that all three might be topping out.

In that first *Letter*, therefore, I predicted that the Dow could register one or two more modest highs, but that these highs would be nonconfirmed as market psychology altered in favor of the bears. I thus achieved the distinction of being totally wrong in my first major independent forecast.

In the next few months the Dow rose more than 70 points to an all-time high of 760.50 on October 29, but this only increased my bearish prognostication. During its rise the market scored a series of nine nonconfirmed new highs. Each time the Dow peaked the advance-decline line sank to a lower level. I was convinced that the Dow had to turn around shortly in the face of such general market deterioration.

As I waited for the impending crash, *Granville's New Key to Stock Market Profits* finally appeared in bookstores and I set off on a round of publicity appearances. This treatise was too esoteric to have the wide appeal of my *Strategy* book, but its sales were steady if not overwhelming. It became the bible of technical analysis for those who saw the wisdom of my new concept of On-Balance Volume.

I was in Chicago, autographing books at Brentano's, when the news reached me that President Kennedy had been shot. I felt the horrible shock, as did all Americans, and my immediate concern was the effect that this tragic event might have on the market. The market cannot foresee such traumatic news, but I still believed the market was poised for a sharp slide and I knew that this event could trigger a precipitous drop. I raced to the nearest brokerage office.

Sure enough, as I watched the board, stock prices toppled. The glamour issues such as IBM, Xerox, and Polaroid dropped as much as $10 per share on every trade. The rest of the market followed their lead. Wall Street hates uncertainty, and panicky investors wanted out of the market until they saw what would happen next. So frantic was the sell-off that the exchange halted trading prematurely, giving everyone a chance to mourn, and to cool off. During that tragic, shortened trading day the Dow lost 21.16 points to close at 711. Brokers called it Black Friday. I was convinced that it was more than a one-day reaction; the bear market was now in full swing.

In the face of my confidence, the Johnson rally began early the next week, extending into a general rise that saw the Dow break through to an increasing series of all-time highs, directly opposed to my prediction.

This was a searching time for me. I knew that On-Balance Volume was successful at predicting the future course of an individual stock, but I had, apparently, an insufficient track record to be able to apply OBV computations to the entire market.

What saved me from failure was the fact that, despite my erroneous prediction concerning the Dow on that rise, I was successful with individual stock recommendations, singling out a group that made many of my subscribers rich. Way back in 1958 Hutton had spurned my prediction of a spectacular rise in gold mining stocks and forbade me to promote them. Now I recommended them to my readers, who scored phenomenal price gains.

As a result of these individual successes, my subscription list grew rapidly. Within months I had cracked the 100 mark and by 1964 I had several hundred subscribers, enough to finance a Florida vacation for the whole family. There was money left over for me to think about putting my own investment cash on the line.

A friend at Hutton agreed to handle an account for me and I churned it frequently for a time, trying to cash in on my own predictions. I did well enough, particularly on the gold stocks. But since I was wrong about the market, I was wrong about too many of my other investments.

A few large losses caused me to rethink my personal investment strategy. Did my own stock portfolio color my judgment? Believing that the market would fall, I held short positions in many stocks. Since I held those positions, I was more inclined to see the evidence of a falling market and ignore any indications of a rising market. Perhaps the bias of ownership was too dangerous.

Just concentrate on the market, I finally said to myself. The market is your love and your joy. Let others make the big money. As long as your income from the love of the market provides for your family, don't create problems for yourself by owning stocks.

I called my broker and told him to close out my account. My final transaction was to cover a short sale of IBM, in which I lost $5,000. Never again would I trade a share of common stock.

So, rather than investing in gold stocks, I put my money into the real thing. I frequented the Nassau Street coin shops, looking for bargains. Soon I accumulated a collection worth more than $15,000, believing that in a few years' time it would produce glorious profits that would be increasingly necessary for the support of my family. Our seventh child, Johanna, was born in the summer of 1964.

The market continued to confound me. It rode a string of advance-decline line nonconfirmations upward, finally setting an all-time record of 881.50 in the Dow on October 20, 1964.

At this point a serious change occurred in the technical picture that taught me a major lesson. After a string of nonconfirmed upward moves, this new Dow high *was* confirmed. The advance-decline line broke through to a new high, as did the Dow Jones Rail Average.

This development brought all the other technicians onto the side of the bulls. Many of them were merely following the principles laid down in my *Strategy* book. Stock market analysts of every stripe were fully optimistic and it was this unanimity of opinion that troubled me deeply. If everyone was optimistic it followed that everyone was fully invested in the market. Where, then, would fresh buying power come from?

I knew how the game was played. A general mood of optimism is the most bearish of all signals. Wall Street must generate maximum belief in the continuance of a bull market in order for the smart money to distribute stocks to the bagholders while prices are at the very top. The best time to be bearish is when everyone else is bullish. If it is obvious, it is obviously wrong. But how could I fly in the face of some of my most basic technical indicators?

Pondering the prevailing mood, I decided to address the question of optimism directly. One of the best quantifiers of investor opinion is the Barron's Confidence Index, which is based upon the ratio of money in high-paying, high-risk, bonds to that in lower-paying, lower-risk bonds. Simply put, when investors are confident about the economy they will opt for high yield at high risk, and vice versa.

It was common knowledge among technical analysts that the Barron's Confidence Index tended to lead the market by two months. If the Confidence Index rose, the market should be rising two months hence. But when I traced the history of the Confidence

Index I discovered an overlooked phenomenon. Whenever the Confidence Index shot up to a dramatic high peak, as it had done now, it actually gave a reverse signal—a lack of confidence—and was followed by a bear market.

I theorized that what happened was that the smart money, when pessimistic, got out of the bond market altogether, leaving only the overconfident bagholders to distort the indicator.

But if the Confidence Index was flashing a paradoxical sell signal, how could the new Dow high be confirmed by so many other indicators? It suddenly became apparent to me that as technical analysis grew in popularity the rules would necessarily change.

My own successes at Hutton, as well as my books, greatly increased the popularity of technical analysis and spawned many imitators. Everyone on Wall Street knew that technicians followed the advance-decline line and the Rail Average. Knowing this, the smart money could manipulate these indicators to give a false reading. I realized that if I was to maintain my success as a technical analyst I must constantly search for fresh indicators to outfox Wall Street. Technical analysis must never be regarded as a science. It is an art; its validity is in direct proportion to the skill of the practitioner.

Having called the market wrong for more than a year, I now swung fully against the tide of Wall Street opinion. In my October 23 *Letter,* acknowledging that I had missed the 1963–64 bull market, I predicted its demise:

> Recent changes in some of the technical indicators heap fresh fuel on the glowing bonfires of roaring confidence, the most notable of these changes being the breakthrough in the advance-decline line, the new high in the rails and industrials so soon after a "crisis" and the maintained high short interest. The very idea that these signs proclaim a new lease on life for the market sets the stage for the next sequential move, THE MOVE TO OVER CONFIDENCE.
>
> The big question now is how long the rise in the Dow Jones Industrial Average will persist during this sequence of over confidence. It might last long enough to provide some whirlwind trading gains, this only being true because the last stair-

case leading to the steeple is the steepest BUT THE BIG DANGER IS IT MAY BE THE SHORTEST IN TERMS OF THE TIME REQUIRED TO ASCEND IT.

I predicted that the Dow would top out at 935 and then begin to plunge. Fortunately for the success of my *Letter,* this second major prediction would prove correct.

But it was agonizing to await the outcome of this forecast. I did not know how long the successes of the gold mining stocks would carry me. I knew that I must soon be visibly in gear with the market or my subscribers would not bother to renew.

I was not easy to live with for the next six months. The market rose, the market fell, the market remained essentially unchanged for six months. I grew short-tempered with Polly and the kids.

Eventually the Dow pushed to an all-time high of 939.62 on May 14, 1965, fulfilling the first portion of my prediction. This was accompanied by an extremely weak Climax Indicator reading of only +1, revealing that the Dow rise was highly selective. In addition, the Rail Average was well under its high and the number of individual new highs was drastically down. This finally alerted a few other technicians to the impending slide, but my correct analysis of the Confidence Index had allowed me to proclaim it six months in advance.

The Dow dropped nearly 100 points—to 840.59—in only six weeks, fulfilling the second half of my prediction in a flash. At that point, fresh strength in the advance-decline line, the Dow Rails, the individual stock highs, and the CLX turned me bullish once more, just as majority sentiment turned bearish. This time my subscribers benefited from an advance that took the Dow to another all-time high of 995.15 on February 11, 1966.

Now, of course, Wall Street was once more fully bullish, looking for the Dow to smash the 1000 mark. That alone should have alerted me to the fact that the market was ready to turn around and slide. But sometimes too much knowledge is as dangerous as too little. I happened upon the fact that the market had *never* reached a major bull market top in the calendar month of February. Therefore, I concluded, the current bullish swing was destined to continue at least until March and I so advised my readers.

Oh, the market is a jealous god! She will continually punish you until you listen only to her. The fact that the market had never peaked in February was not a technical message but a cyclical one. Technically the market was weak but, alas, so was my judgment. February 1966 taught me a truism: *The market is capable of doing anything.*

The Dow dropped nearly 85 points by March 5 and once more I became a difficult, quick-tempered husband and father.

Only a few weeks later we celebrated the birth of our eighth child, John. Now that I had so convincingly proved the Navy doctors wrong Polly and I decided that eight was enough. What a severe bout of malaria could not accomplish, a few well-placed snips of a surgeon's scissors could. Polly and I turned from the task of creating children to the more exacting job of raising them.

I managed to call a 43-point bounce in the Dow in April. Then, seeing a highly speculative bubble burst on the American Stock Exchange, I turned cautious, pulling my subscribers out of most stocks, putting others on hold. The Dow dropped downward to 852.83 on July 25, when I issued a major sell signal, advising the liquidation of all stocks.

"I think that anybody who remains in this market from this point on is tempting the fates and pressing his luck," I wrote in my *Letter*. "This is not Joe Granville talking. It is the market. It is General Motors, the advance-decline line, the volume indicators, and the charts."

I recommended that IBM be sold short at its current price of $344 per share. The Dow then set off on a three-month plunge to 744.32 and IBM dropped to 289.

It was at this point that I devised my facetious Cartoon Indicator, based upon the observation that cartoons often mark milestones in public psychology. The August 1966 *New Yorker* featured a memorable cartoon that coincided with a climactic market event. The "hot" stock of the entire year was Xerox. Early in the year Gerald Tsai had formed the Manhattan Fund, announcing that a cornerstone of its holdings would be Xerox. When a mutual fund plunges heavily into a given stock it is normally a kiss of death, mutual fund managers tending to be among the most fundamental of all stock market analysts. But Xerox weathered the general bearishness of the market that year, remaining well above $200 a share.

Then came the *New Yorker* cartoon depicting a man on his deathbed, gasping out final instructions to his wife: "Sell General Motors, sell IBM, sell Polaroid, but don't you dare sell Xerox!"

Perhaps the cartoon touched upon an unseen nerve, for Xerox dropped from 250 to 125 in the next six weeks, proof that there are no sacred cows in a bear market and further proof that the opinions of mutual fund managers carry equal weight with those of cartoonists.

Now, outwardly, I was a portrait of happiness. In full gear with the market, I found more and more subscriptions pouring into my post office box. But inwardly I was agitated and vaguely restless. At first I blamed Governor Nelson Rockefeller, who seemed to increase the taxes on my business daily. Polly and I talked about this problem and decided that there was no compelling reason for me to commute to Manhattan. As long as I had a daily copy of the *Wall Street Journal* I could read the market from the North Pole. So I closed the tiny office in New York and for a short time worked from another cubbyhole in Newark.

Polly was restless, too, tired of New Jersey's smog, freezing winters, screaming traffic, and rising crime rate. Finally we realized that if I did not have to work in New York, neither did I have to work in New Jersey. Our thoughts turned to the sunshine of Florida, where we had enjoyed respite from the northern winter. After corresponding with a number of my Florida subscribers, soliciting their opinions of the proper environment in which to raise and educate eight children, we made a decision to liquidate everything and move south.

We sold the house in Ramsey for a large profit and, late in 1966, with nearly $100,000 in cash assets, we went house hunting in Florida. Our destination was Ormond Beach, just north of Daytona Beach, because we had learned a curious fact. An aging John D. Rockefeller had directed his doctors to search out for him the healthiest environment in the United States. When their studies concluded that Ormond Beach was the spot, Rockefeller built an estate there known as the Casements, where he spent the last twenty winters of his life.

Polly and I found a large rancher on North Beach Street that seemed ideal for our needs. There was sufficient room to add on so that each of our children could eventually have a private bedroom. The enormous back lawn edged on the Halifax River and featured a private dock and boat house. Although the house had far more lawn than I could mow in a single day (a task I had always despised), it was otherwise perfect. We wrote out a check for $49,000, the entire purchase price.

The market fluctuates because it mirrors life. Just as the human body must exhale as well as inhale, so too the soul must expire as well as inspire. The pattern was not, at first, outwardly apparent, but the years after I left Hutton found my life in a falling field trend. I was a human bear market headed straight for the bottom. The question was whether this onslaught of adversity would break my spirit or cause me to rethink the basic principles of my life and learn from my mistakes.

A bear market cannot begin unless a bull market ends. It is at such a juncture that the greatest number of observers are duped. New highs cannot be reached unless the vast majority of people are optimistic. So it was with me. I did not foresee the numerous problems that lay just beneath the surface of my life.

Immediately upon our relocation to Florida the Dow turned against me, rallying fiercely, rising 120 points in the face of my bearish warnings. IBM skyrocketed all the way up to 433, putting my short sellers in a posture for severe losses. Some were wiped out. Nevertheless the Climax Indicator continued to signal the market as technically weak. I could not alter my bearish outlook in the face of supportive evidence, yet the market continued to prove me wrong.

For months I agonized. The Dow trended upward, gaining another 79 points to close at 943.08 on August 9. IBM ran from 433 to 687, proclaiming a two-for-one split, and continued to rise even as I doggedly and mistakenly recommended it as a short sale to my disgruntled suscribers.

Malaise set in. I spent more time at Billy's Tap Room and at Riviera Country Club and less time analyzing the market. Each week my *Letter* shouted out what I perceived to be technical warnings and each week the market flaunted its superiority at me. I wondered how long I could remain in business without getting into gear with this damnable market.

A year and a half passed, during which I was hell to live with. Polly immersed herself in church work to escape dealing with my frustrations. The kids turned into bronzed sun worshippers. I saw less of my family and more of my misery. Subscriptions trailed off and we had to dip deeply into our savings.

It was mid-1968 before the market turned my way, keyed by a catastrophe.

On the night of June 4, 1968, moments after celebrating his triumph in the California presidential primary, Senator Robert F. Kennedy was gunned down by an assassin. This event was the third in a grisly trilogy of shootings—following those of John F. Kennedy and Dr. Martin Luther King, Jr.—and affected the equation of collective national optimism and pessimism more so than the presidential murder five years before.

"This has been known to happen many times in stock market history," I wrote in my June 12 *Letter*. "An event will take place which will precipitate an emotional break in a rising trend. The sudden change may have no economic significance and stock prices may attempt a quick recovery following the event. However, the event does cast some sort of a shadow and it is subtly followed by a shift in market psychology which in turn is followed by a market downturn. The downturn will be fed by developments of economic significance but the timing of the downturn will tend to coincide with the occurrence of the emotional event. One can say that the market momentum or rhythm was seriously disturbed on June 5th."

That very week the number of new highs peaked, the first sign of a technical deterioration that would not show up in the Dow for months to come. The final top came on December 3 when the Dow peaked at 985.21. Three days later my *Letter* warned subscribers that a new bear market had finally begun, based on the solid evidence of ten important indicators. The Dow high was nonconfirmed by the advance-decline lines of both the New York Stock Exchange and the American Stock Exchange, the number of new highs and new lows on both exchanges, the Dow Rail Average, the Standard

& Poor's 500, General Motors, the prices of gold stocks, and the OBV figures on ten specially chosen high-priced "swingers," such as IBM, Xerox, and Polaroid. Further, the Climax Indicator reading on the new Dow high was an extremely bearish +1. This was the most complete evidence of a bull market climax that I had yet accumulated. If it did not signal a new bear market, I might as well throw myself under a truck. I owe my continued existence to the accuracy of this prediction.

A lifelong Republican myself, I believed that President-elect Richard Nixon was a strong leader who would implement the principles of the party and bring the United States back to a position of world respect. But I also believed that he would first have to weather a recession and deal with an international monetary crisis.

A cornerstone of Nixon's platform was a tight money policy designed to bring inflation under control. I remembered Nixon as a man who played his cards brilliantly and believed that he would carry through on this promise, and that boded ill for the market. Tight money meant high interest rates and a general business slowdown.

I warned my subscribers: "The year 1969 may replace 1929 as the grand example of historic economic collapse."

Nevertheless, I once again advised my readers to invest in gold and silver stocks, believing that they were strong enough to buck the general market trend. During any monetary crisis, investors move away from national currencies and into gold and silver.

The potential of the precious metals was unique. The United States was still attempting to keep the price of gold fixed at $35 an ounce, a ridiculous posture since the price had risen to over $40 on the London market. Consider what this meant to gold mining companies. Assume that it cost a mining company $34 to produce an ounce of gold—about average at that time, although prices fluctuated. At a fixed price of $35 an ounce that was hardly worth the effort and required a government subsidy. But as the price edged up on world markets, the gold mining business would become ever more profitable.

Historically, the price of gold had not often fluctuated, but a chart of gold prices showed a classic flatbase breakout that signaled a meteoric rise. Silver appeared to be just as strong.

Soon after Nixon's inauguration the Dow finally agreed with my bearish assessment, quickly dropping 85 points. It staged a short springtime rally and then resumed its slide.

Growing international concern about the world's monetary system led to an idea for a working vacation, which was long overdue. Polly and I decided to take the family to Europe for the summer, where I could report on numerous international issues and where we might rediscover those traits we had formerly found attractive in one another. We flew to Luxembourg, rented a Volkswagen microbus, and toured through Metz, Nancy, Basel, Berne, Lausanne, and Montreux before we arrived in Chateau d'Oex, Switzerland, 12,000 feet up in the Alps. A summer's rent on a chalet was only $600.

The Swiss countryside was so serenely beautiful that I tried hard to settle into a pleasant summer routine and relearn the pleasures of family life. Each afternoon I walked down to a kiosk near the railroad station to buy a Paris edition of the *International Herald Tribune.* The paper arrived shortly after lunch, but the vendor was a devotee of the aggravating European custom of the siesta. I was always his first customer when he reopened at 2:00 P.M., anxiously awaiting the news of the previous day's stock market action.

The slim paper carried only the barest of market statistics at a time when critical economic dramas were being played out. U.S. banks boosted the prime rate to an unprecedented 8½ percent. The U.S. and British bond markets collapsed. The Tokyo Stock Exchange recorded its greatest-ever one-day drop. The Dow Jones Industrial Average fell nearly 100 points under the bull market high of December 3. I worried that I might miss out on some important development.

Since I had so little market information available I tried to bring an international flavor to the newsletter. I discussed problems with the British pound, the European banking system, the reaction to the French election victory of Georges Pompidou over Charles de Gaulle, and European attitudes toward the Vietnam war—I used any idea I could to fill up six pages of paper. At the end of each week I placed an overseas call to a secretarial service in Florida that typed and mailed the newsletter.

This haphazard arrangement was an immediate disaster. When the first copy of my newsletter arrived by mail I grew very disturbed. The secretaries in Florida had absolutely no knowledge of the market. The supposedly sophisticated *Granville Market Letter* exhibited some of the most inane typographical errors I could imagine. The advance-decline line became the *advanced-*decline line. I referred to an *excelerating* price rise trend. I noted that a tax surcharge failed to *curve* inflation. Odd lot transactions became odd *loc* transactions. The German mark became the German *March*.

The following week my *Letter* sputtered, "We have declined almost 100 points since mid-May, and thus *a vaunce* is to be expected." The last straw was when the stock market became the *rock* market.

The only alternative was to type the letter myself and ship it to Florida by what I hoped would be fast mail. The result was that my subscribers received, one or two days late, a market letter based upon the flimsiest data. But my luck held. Throughout the summer the bear market continued with no major new developments.

I attempted to relax and play the role of the cultured expatriate, but inside I grew increasingly agitated. I was away from the market, my true love. I felt unfaithful.

Though I had envisioned a pleasant interlude with my family, my professional problems made me irritable. I bought concert tickets for Polly and myself to celebrate our nineteenth wedding anniversary on July 11, but that day we had a vociferous fight over some small detail and neither of us wanted the other's company. I threw a change of clothes into a suitcase, grabbed my typewriter and my Eurailpass, and left to cool off for a few days.

I found myself in a hotel room in Geneva, where I angrily pounded out the next edition of my *Letter* and then looked for some means of relaxation. The concierge informed me that the hotel offered bus service to a casino in Divonne Les Bains, France, ten miles across the border.

Soon I was in an Old World fantasyland. The casino was ornate and elaborately appointed, with plush velvet seats and golden trimmings. Formal dress was the rule of the evening. Elegant waiters served drinks and French delicacies to the players. The cashier was happy to honor my traveler's checks. I left $400 at the roulette table that night but enjoyed myself thoroughly. For a time I forgot about the market and my problems with Polly. In my next *Letter* I inserted a tongue-in-cheek comment that capital was recently attracted back into France.

I soon returned to Chateau D'Oex, but Polly and I were both sullen and bored with one another. All I could think of was the pleasant, cultured atmosphere of Divonne Les Bains. Polly did not argue when I found an excuse to go off by myself once again. This time I reserved a room directly at the casino hotel.

While awaiting a train at Geneva, I noticed a book by one of my favorite authors, Ian Fleming, entitled *The Ten Most Thrilling Cities of Europe.* I bought it for the equivalent of fifty cents and perused it eagerly on the way to Divonne Les Bains. The chapter that naturally caught my attention was the one about Monte Carlo.

Here in front of my eyes was Ian Fleming's system for winning at roulette, undoubtedly the method employed by James Bond as he relaxed between assassinations and assignations. It was a simple formula, one that did not require extensive memory or calculation. First, Fleming picked a single method of betting the wheel where the payoff was one to one. This meant he would play black or red, odd or even, for the entire night, never switching off.

The key was money management. On a scrap of paper he wrote the numbers one through six in a vertical column. To calculate the amount of each bet he added the top and bottom numbers in the column; thus the first bet was seven—whether dollars or pounds or francs. If he won, he crossed off the top and bottom numbers in the column, making his next bet also seven (two plus five). If he lost that second bet he added the amount of his loss to the bottom of the column, making this third bet nine (two plus seven). Every time he lost he added one number—the amount of his loss—to the bottom. The genius of the plan was that losses only added *one* number to the column while wins dropped *two* numbers. Since he had a fifty-fifty chance of winning each bet (unless the green zero or double-zero came up) he soon crossed out all numbers in the column, completing a contract for a solid profit.

Arriving in Divonne Les Bains, I hustled to the casino, a pen and notebook in my hand. I purchased a pile of the colorful plastic tiles that the French use for betting chips and tried my luck. It was surprisingly simple. The chips piled up on my side of the table so quickly that I soon moved to a table with a higher minimum bet of twenty francs. The same success followed me there and I graduated to a no-limit table.

Breaking for dinner at eight o'clock, I washed down rich cuisine with drafts of fine wine, celebrating my new pathway to wealth. On the table in front of me was a stack of 100-franc plastic bars, each worth about twenty dollars. Leaving a couple of them behind for the waiter I returned to the casino, reserved a spot for myself in the midnight baccarat game, and sat back down at the roulette table to expand my winnings.

"Monsieur Granville, to the baccarat table, *s'il vous plaît,*" came the announcement at midnight. I scraped together my $2,000 in winnings and headed for the big boys' game.

Baccarat kept me busy until 6:00 A.M. and eroded more than half of my winnings. I was happy, anyway, because I was convinced that I could conjure money from the roulette table whenever I wished. Collapsing into bed, I slept until the casino reopened at 3:00 P.M. the next day.

On this second day I began to see the hook in Fleming's system. On occasion the house encountered a streak of luck that could demolish the player's bankroll before he could recoup. With unlimited capital the player could always win, but such was not my position. I was forced to limit my losses. If the wheel beat me three times in a row I canceled the contract and started fresh. This reduced my winnings but guarded against destitution. For the trip I showed a modest profit.

The rest of the summer found my mind frequently diverted from the market as I sought opportunities to visit a casino. Fleming's system did not make me rich, but it enabled me to play the game with confidence. I frequently wound up an evening several hundred dollars ahead, so long as I avoided the baccarat table.

All too soon it was time to face reality. When I returned to the pleasant suburban home tucked away in a quiet corner of America, far from any casino, I felt an immediate sense of isolation. What was I doing stuck down here away from all the action?

Luckily for me, the market had continued to follow my predictions as I played about Europe, and upon my return I enjoyed even more successes. Reviewing the current status of my technical indicators, I could see no reason to alter my bearish attitude.

The Dow dropped to 770 in December, bounced up 40 points early in January 1970 and then took a hard look at its own reality.

The reality was that the nation's top economists were in total disagreement as to the proper steps for licking runaway inflation. They sounded like a group of doctors arguing about their diagnosis while the patient's condition worsened.

The stock market responds to news in strange ways. It may fall upon hearing good news or it may rise upon hearing bad news. This much is certain: The market always retreats from confusion. Within a month after President Nixon said that if he had any money he would be buying stocks, the Dow dropped 100 points to close at 631.16 on May 26.

The Dow collapsed so quickly that a corrective rally was called for. The Climax Indicator turned upward, accompanied by a decline in the number of stocks making new lows. Increasing public gloom also turned me bullish. I even borrowed a page from the fundamentalist book and proclaimed faith in Nixon's Economic Game Plan.

Now I advised my readers to cover their short sales and buy from a selection of low-priced, thinly capitalized stocks that had the potential of doubling quickly. I called this my list of thirty-nine potential doublers and it proved to be the most popular newsletter item I had yet featured.

Within three months the advance-decline line forged to new intermediate highs and the Dow rose to 745.41, breaking above its 200-Day Moving Average for the first time in more than a year. Now I officially announced the beginning of a new bull market, having put my subscribers back into stocks only a few days after the May 26 bottom.

One of my thirty-nine potential doublers did just that within days of my recommendation; several doubled within months. By the time the bull market was ten months old in March 1971 the Dow had risen 319 points to 950.81 and more than twenty of my potential doublers showed better than 100 percent gains. All but one had risen sharply. My buy recommendation proved to be one of the most profitable opportunities ever offered by any market advisory service. If I could hold to this pattern of success I knew that my *Letter* would make me a millionaire.

I should have been ecstatic. I had called the market with a precision that caused my subscription list to grow to an all-time high of

1,300 as happy disciples told others about the guru in Florida who could enrich their bank balances.

But there was a palpable tension at home between Polly and me that grew like a malignancy. The kids all sensed it and I could feel some of them turning against me, blaming me for much of the unhappiness. I spent more and more time at my little office in the Daytona Beach suburb of Holly Hill.

It was about this time that a younger man, whom I will call Dave, singled me out for friendship. He was an insurance broker with an office down the hall. We shared a common interest in games of skill and chance. Since I did not want to go home, we spent evenings at the office playing Scrabble or chess. Soon we were killing afternoons at the golf course or the pool hall.

At the pool hall I fell in with another crowd who invited me to a friendly poker game, which turned into a tradition that recurred several nights a week. The stakes were low at first, but generally increased in proportion to our liquor intake. There were nights when I won and nights when I lost, but somehow the losses seemed to mount. It was, however, a livelier alternative to evenings at home and I believed that my luck had to change.

Gradually my losses increased. Only later did I realize that my "friends" were passing cards under the table, using hand signals, and betting up the pot for each other so they could lure more and more of my money into the game. At the time, through the haze of my restlessness, I only knew that I was spending far more than I should. On some nights I could count the losses in the thousands.

Already in enough trouble with Polly, I dared not confront her with this fresh evidence of my unconcern for the family. Rather, I took the coward's way out, sneaking checks out of the back of the checkbook to cover my gambling debts.

The house of cards came tumbling down the day the bank called Polly to tell her we were overdrawn. That evening she demanded a full report on our finances.

It was a short discussion. The checkbook was, indeed, overdrawn, cleaned out of nearly $20,000.

"What about the coin collection?" Polly asked.

"I sold that, too," I admitted.

Polly took charge, rightly assuming control of the family finances;

after all, we had eight children to raise. Leona and Blanchard were in college and the others were not far behind. Polly picked up the mail from our post office box and deposited the checks herself, surprised at the increased volume of receipts.

Over the next few months she saved $20,000 over and above our living expenses and placed it in a trust fund for the education of our children. I had no argument with that, but when she put the fund under the management of a pimply-faced junior bank officer, I bristled with anger.

I was reduced to an allowance of $20 a week. Though this was probably a necessary course of action to bring me out of my profligate ways, I grew furious inside. There was no alternative but to take my solace in the market.

"This is the year!" I raved in my first *Letter* of 1972.

This is the year the Dow will, in my opinion, easily vault the magical 1000 level. . . . If I was a Democratic candidate for the Presidency and understood what the stock market technical indicators are saying, I would immediately pull out of the race. The technical indicators are saying that nobody will beat Nixon this year. This should not be construed as political favoritism on my part . . . I am simply reading what the market is saying. The market is saying that Nixon will be re-elected. . . .

Through the early months of the year I became so enamored with the President's leadership that I waxed increasingly eloquent, even as the Dow took aim on the ethereal 1000 mark.

Perhaps the nadir of the *Granville Market Letter* was reached on June 16, 1972, when I wrote:

Like a beautifully thought out game of chess, the Nixon Game Plan has proceeded smoothly and on schedule. Every time over the past two years when it appeared that the Plan was in trouble, the President smashed his critics with a brilliantly executed recovery move and they walked into the trap every time. The opening moves in 1970 were dramatic, topped by still more dramatic moves in the 1971–72 middle game, clearing the board for the critical end game moves. . . . It must be rather obvious that the BEST MOVES, the most effective moves, are

RESERVED for the end game. Therefore we can anticipate such moves and KNOW that they will be made, and made successfully.

Three days later Nixon's burglars broke into the headquarters of the Democratic National Committee at the Watergate. But the nation and the stock market ignored the implications for months. Not for two years would we know the full devastating effects of President Nixon's "best moves."

The world now entered a danger zone. According to various interpretations of the Kondratieff long wave, a stock market crash paralleling that of 1929–30 was possible anytime between 1977 and 1989. The cycle has an average length of 54 years, but the market crash can occur anywhere from 48 to 60 years after the previous one.

What crashes down must first go soaring up, however. Based upon the ramifications of the Kondratieff long wave cycle, I reasoned that the Nixon bull market could be a wild, speculative rally that preceded a major crash.

If so, there were billions of dollars to be made as the rocket shot upward. I visualized Nixon concluding wondrous trade agreements with Russia and China that would send the Dow soaring to 1200.

On October 6, 1972, I predicted that the bull market, already two and a half years old, could continue until the end of 1974. It was a ridiculously bullish posture that would find my personal fate mirroring that of the president. But I glowed with enthusiasm on November 14 when the Dow closed above 1000 for the first time in history, predicting that the next 50-point rise would be a piece of cake. Once we hit 1050, I warned, we might experience a brief pullback before resuming the grand rise.

Shortly after New Year's Day 1973, Polly asked me to chaperone Leona on a London vacation. She gave me an airplane ticket and $150 spending money for the week. This was more cash than I had had in my hands for some time, but I knew it would stretch thin over a week in London, so I managed to pilfer from my own receipts a check from a British subscriber that amounted to about $300.

Unbeknownst to Polly, Leona and I had separate vacations in mind. Leona left me at Heathrow airport and boarded another plane for Tunisia while I headed for the Hilton, cashed my British check, and found the nearest gaming club. Reliving my casino days from my previous European trip was exhilarating. Fleming's roulette system brought a modest accumulation of pounds flowing to my side of the table—for a few days.

Then my small bankroll began to dwindle. Attempting to recoup, I bet more heavily than before. Soon I was nearly broke.

Not trusting myself to venture near another casino, I remained in my room for the next two days reading Margaret Truman's biography of her father. I was hung over, angry with myself, exhausted, worried about Leona, and concerned about Polly's reaction if she ever found out about the escapade. Insofar as the market was concerned, I had blacked out.

If Joe Granville forgot about the market, the market, for its part, forgot about Joe Granville. Almost at the very moment I arrived back in Florida on January 11 the Dow closed at another all-time high of 1051.70, fulfilling my prediction of an easy rise to that level. The new high was totally nonconfirmed by the advance-decline line, the number of new highs and lows, the Rail Average, the Utilities Average, the Standard & Poor's 500, and the Climax Indicator.

Other technical analysts shouted out the warning. Many of them were my own disciples, using the market tools I had created. But something had snapped inside of me. The past few years of gambling, hard drinking, family turmoil, and personal travail threw me into a spin. There was nothing wrong with my theory; only the human element failed. Like Jekyll turning into Hyde, I metamorphosed into that most horrible aberration—the fundamentalist.

I took note of the technical discrepancies, but remained adamant that the bull market had encountered only a minor setback. Nixon had just called an end to phase two of his game plan, removing wage and price controls. I saw this as a tremendous impetus to the business world, an opinion that put me into bed with the nation's economists, who by now echoed my projection of a minimum level of 1200 in the Dow.

Richard Nixon was forced to neglect the details of his game plan as he concentrated on the more basic issue of saving his job. Many Wall Street bears based their gloomy prognostications on the belief that Nixon could not weather the storm of Watergate.

I thought I knew better. My mind harked back to that poker game in the Pacific, shortly after the end of the war, when I watched Lieutenant Commander Richard Nixon pull off such a compelling bluff while holding a mere pair of deuces. I believed he was equal to the pressure, and I came to believe that not only would he beat Watergate, but that his victory would inspire confidence and rekindle the bull market that would precede the great Kondratieff crash.

Basing a market prognostication on such a belief is a trait not of the technician but of the fundamental analyst. Not only did I fall into this fundamental trap, but I was fundamentally wrong in my judgment. I believed what I wanted to believe, coming to my conclusion first and then searching for evidence to support it.

A new personal problem loomed when, shortly after I returned from London, Polly and I opted to sleep apart. I was free to use Blanchard's room, since he was off at college and since it had a separate entrance, but most of the time I chose to sleep on the bare floor of my office. The marriage was finally over, but we were beset with inertia. Neither Polly nor I troubled ourselves to file for a separation.

With more time on my hands, I discovered the local bingo parlors, where I could indulge my passion for gambling on a modest scale. I was fascinated with the numerical probabilities of this simple game of chance and began to study the board for any telltale patterns that might give me the key to regular winnings. I made a number of new friends at the bingo parlors, but still returned at night to my bare floor of a bed in my lonely office.

As I slid downward, so did stock prices, but time after time I proclaimed the drops as mere setbacks in the continuing bull market. These opinions were frequently based upon high Climax Indicator readings despite the fact that the majority of Dow stocks remained in doubtful or falling field trends. Even as my newsletter flashed a continuing series of optimistic headlines, such as NEW RALLY, MAJOR TURN FOR THE BETTER, and DRAMATIC UP-SWING AHEAD, the Dow dove downward to a low of 851.90 on August 22.

I noted with glee that this low was nonconfirmed by the number of stocks recording new lows and ignored other bearish indicators.

My optimism was apparently confirmed as the market headed

back up in the autumn of 1973. By October 26 the Dow had reached 987.05, nearly retracing all of its previous loss. I was right after all! Now I was confident that new subscriptions would flow into the post office box. Polly commandeered most of these business receipts, for she bore the responsibility of raising the children. But if I could expand our income there would be more money to go around. Perhaps I would even lease an apartment for myself. Maybe I could rejoin the country club.

In a quick succession of events Vice President Spiro Agnew resigned and pleaded *nolo contendere* to a felony rap, the Arabs and Israelis went to war, OPEC quadrupled the price of oil, Nixon announced that some of the Oval Office tapes were missing, and the market dropped nearly 200 points in two months.

But I was not to be sidetracked by these unforeseen political aberrations. Believing that the market would rebound with impressive strength, I compounded my error by entering the arena of political forecasting. In my January 11, 1974, *Letter* I wrote:

> Inasmuch as Nixon's popularity has a close correlation with the course of the Dow Jones Industrial Average, the predicted rising market in 1974 suggests a rise in Nixon's popularity. How will this come about? Previous success in foreign affairs will attract the President in that area. His dramatic trips to Moscow and Peking in 1972 topped off by ending the Viet Nam war and bringing our POWs home will offer the same formula for success in 1974. It strongly suggests a trip to Europe to bring home the bacon personally—wrapping up the Arab-Israeli conflict and ending the oil embargo. He would return with a greatly restored image and deflect attention away from Watergate developments. . . . So then, don't let current events so mold your thinking as to think that things can't get better. They are going to get better—an upturn for the market, the President, the country . . . and for you.

I then had the audacity to raise the subscription price of my newsletter from $125 to $150 a year, sure that my subscribers would not balk at the increase. I thought it was a cheap price to pay for the valuable and incisive guidance I was offering.

By now I had convinced myself that Nixon had an ace in the hole, and my theory was supported by some of my cronies at the bingo parlors. Thinking back to how Nixon played poker, I concluded that he was simply sweetening the pot for a hand that he knew to be a winner. He made his stand on Executive Privilege knowing that the issue would go to the Supreme Court amid loud speculations about the contents of the Oval Office tapes. The answer suddenly hit me. Win or lose in the Supreme Court, Nixon would then turn the tapes over to the Special Prosecutor's office. And this was his ace in the hole—the tapes were clean! They would exonerate him and his enemies would be crushed.

I detailed this theory in a newsletter and took the rest of the afternoon off to play golf.

As the Supreme Court pondered the limits of Executive Privilege the market hovered within a narrow range. But when the horrible truth came out a considerable number of expletives had to be deleted from my *Letter*. The Dow began a downswing that continued even after Nixon's resignation in August and was paralleled by the drop in circulation of my newsletter. Only 300 people could be bothered to receive my weekly advice and I had no assurance that they would renew when their subscriptions expired.

I fought to regain sanity. For months I wrestled with the enormity of my error. I pulled volumes of my old newsletters off the shelf and reread my own damning words, searching for clues as to why some of my predictions had been so successful and why I had been such a spectacular failure in 1973 and 1974.

Forgetting about the golf course I filled reams of paper with computations. My faith in On-Balance Volume had never wavered. Volume preceded price and OBV could be used successfully to predict stock market action, and I was determined to discover how.

As I worked, my mind rose out of its extended depression. I could see the issues more clearly now. Plotting the course of the market over many years and comparing it to my OBV figures, I suddenly found the key. I *knew* I had the answer now.

But would anyone listen to Joe Granville anymore?

9.

SONG OF SOLOMON

THE GRANVILLE MARKET LETTER
Volume XII, Number 34   September 6, 1974
IMPORTANT ANNOUNCEMENT

Fourteen years have passed since this writer authored *A Strategy of Daily Stock Market Timing for Maximum Profit.* The market in that period has gone through 4 bull markets and 4 bear markets. All the principles in that book have stood the test of time although the author hasn't, deviating at times in the quest for new indicators and sometimes falling into the very pitfalls others were warned to avoid.

The *Letter* went on to detail my errors and apologize for them. Admitting in cold print that I had called the market wrong for the past two years was one of the most difficult things I ever did, but it was the only way I could begin to regain credibility. Only 300 subscribers were still with me to read the apology and I could not blame them if they issued loud and derisive hoots. I would have to convince them over a period of time that I was once more attuned to the pure technical harmonies of the market. I knew this to be the case, for I was now armed with the most powerful technical tool ever devised. I had just given birth to the Net Field Trend Indicator.

My study of the past performance of the market proved to me that On-Balance Volume was, indeed, the key to calling the future, but

I had not applied it properly. I had placed too much emphasis upon the Climax Indicator and not enough upon the prevailing field trends.

The Climax Indicator, as its name denotes, had originally been conceived to signal major market reversals. But I had failed to see that the CLX tends to disguise significant market patterns. The CLX is the net differential between OBV upside and downside breakouts in the thirty Dow Industrials, but those breakouts vary greatly in quality.

For example, suppose U.S. Steel shows a series of breakouts such as these: −100,000 (DOWN); +200,000 (UP); +150,000 (DOWN); +400,000 (UP). This series of breakouts clearly depicts an upward pattern and is therefore known as a RISING field trend. Note carefully the second DOWN designation of +150,000. It is a *higher* DOWN than the previous DOWN, and such a situation frequently occurs as the price of a stock ebbs and flows in a generally upward direction. Therefore, the +150,000 DOWN is much less significant than the other three designations, yet the CLX assigns it equal weight. Now I could see that the CLX was not the key to major tops and bottoms. Rather, its usefulness was as a *short-term* indicator. I had assigned entirely too much significance to it.

At the same time I had ignored the importance of the field trends. It takes weeks or months of market action to alter a field trend; therefore, field trends are the true gauges of long-term moves.

The Net Field Trend Indicator is simply the differential among the field trends of the 30 Dow Industrials. By assigning a value of +1 to a RISING field trend, 0 to a DOUBTFUL field trend, and −1 to a FALLING field trend, the daily NFI is determined. It has a potential range of +30 to −30.

The NFI does not fluctuate rapidly from plus to minus and back again as the CLX is capable of doing. It moves smoothly from the minus area to the plus area and back again over much longer periods of time. For this reason major changes in the NFI cannot be regarded lightly. While I am always looking for a majority of market indicators to confirm or nonconfirm a major top or bottom, I could see from the past figures that I must stress the NFI in particular.

Early in 1972, for example, the NFI collapsed from +17 to −2 in a matter of weeks. I completely missed this strong evidence that market direction had shifted to the downside, basing my erroneous prediction upon a few strong CLX readings that in reality only represented weak upward blips in a generally falling market.

The CLX is still a valuable tool, but only when studied in context with the NFI. A high CLX reading is far more valid when the NFI is trending upward, and vice versa.

It was this fresh understanding of how to interpret On-Balance Volume that saved me from oblivion. For the next nine years my record of major stock market predictions would be unimpeachable.

Near the end of 1974 public opinion polls showed that nearly half of the American populace believed we were headed for an imminent depression. New York City was bankrupt. Unemployment was at alarming levels, especially in Detroit. Henry Ford II said these were the worst times that he could remember. But the NFI told a different story.

The Dow reached a new bear market low on October 4 at 584.56. It was confirmed by the major technical indicators. The NFI stood at −14, a weak reading but an improvement upon the −19 of a month earlier. This single nonconfirmation caused me to sit up and take notice.

On December 6 the Dow notched another low at 577.60, but the NFI improved slightly to −13. It then began to explode upward, reaching −6 on December 18 and 0 by the end of the month. The Dow Industrials had silently turned around, their field trends shouting out a sharp upward move long before prices rose.

There was no doubt in my mind that this, finally, was the beginning of a new bull market. Throughout December 1974 I made a series of stock recommendations that I was sure would turn a quick profit for anyone who still had the faith to follow me.

The normal waiting period between my pronouncement and the external market action was to be expected, but it was more agonizing than usual this time. I *had* to be right or I might as well close up my business.

And as I waited, life seemed to disintegrate around me. The bank that owned the building where I had worked and lived for two years suddenly notified me that it was taking over the office. I had two weeks to clear out.

My Volkswagen squareback died one night, and I had to abandon it, bequeathing it to the city. I had neither the money to pay the impounding fees nor to repair it and, in addition, I was driving on an expired license and did not relish any confrontation with the local police.

My friend Jon Greaves, an insurance man who had an office in an adjacent building, came to my rescue. He gave me his old, rusted Chevrolet Impala to drive. John's mother owned a small office building nearby and he persuaded her to rent me an office and defer the payments.

I would not have survived this period without Jon, or without the aid of my friend Irene Kennedy, an eighty-five-year-old bingo fanatic who frequently slipped me a crumpled five- or ten-dollar bill to tide me over.

I sold my golf clubs for fifty dollars.

My new office was my new home. Its floor provided a cold, hard bed. Sharing a bathroom with the tenant next door, I mooched whatever I could. One morning I found a note taped to the sink that read, "Why don't you buy the soap once in a while?"

I had no television or radio or phone. I had only the market and the bingo parlor to keep me occupied.

Despite the fact that, for the first time in forty-two years, the President told Congress in his State of the Union message that he had *bad news*, the Dow roared from 577.60 in December 1974 all the way up to 815.08 by April 15, 1975. This activated what I call the 50 Percent Principle and resulted in an important prediction.

The 50 Percent Principle states that whenever a rally retraces more than half the losses sustained in the preceding bear market, then it is likely to recover the entire loss. Conversely, when a slide eats up more than half the gains of the previous bull market, it is likely to fall below the point where that bull market started.

During 1973–74 the Dow had fallen from 1051.70 to 577.60. The halfway point of that drop was 814.65. Therefore, when the Dow surpassed that 50-percent mark on April 15, 1975, it provided the final confirmation that this was not merely a rally in a bear market, but was a bona fide bull market.

However, activation of the 50 Percent Principle generally signals the end of the first important bull market rise, just when the public is beginning to believe in it. It is the point at which the market stops to catch its breath and the farsighted smart money reaps the first fruits of its wisdom. Accordingly, I told my readers, "We're going to take the rest of our fat profits and run."

I issued a series of sell recommendations on stocks that I had promoted in the late months of 1974. The results are shown in the following table:

STOCK	BUYING PRICE	SELLING PRICE	PERCENT PROFIT
American Broadcasting	18.63	21.38	14.7
Boise Cascade	11.50	18.98	65.0
Dr. Pepper	7.13	14.88	98.4
Fleetwood Enterprises	8.88	15.38	73.2
Hershey Foods	10.13	20.13	98.7
Harnischfeger Corporation	22.25	39.50	77.5
National Can	8.75	11.13	27.2

These remarkable profits were achieved in less than six months when the majority of the investing public was horribly pessimistic.

I explained this phenomenon—how stocks can rise during what are seemingly the worst of times—in my March 14 *Letter:*

We are not known as a nation of failures. Among us at all times are people who are blessed with a positive mental attitude, capable of thinking and acting on their own. They do not require a canned analysis of the news. In fact, they can get along very well without the news as far as the stock market is concerned because they are reading the market, not the newspaper. They understand that there is very little correlation between news and the market inasmuch as the news media reports *current* events while the market moves on *future* events. They are amused when they see the media often struggle to explain a market move in terms of current events, trying to make one fit the other. Actually, all news is a market anachronism. In other words, news is for suckers.

On the strength of my renewed market success I was awarded a contract by Prentice-Hall to update my original *Strategy* book. The ideas were so fresh in my mind from studying my mistakes of the past two years that the manuscript flowed from my typewriter in less than five months.

I explained the new emphasis that I placed upon the NFI as a major market indicator, and I stressed, more than ever, the importance of knowing exactly where the market is in its current cycle.

Those cycles were first noted around the turn of the century by Charles H. Dow, one of the owners of the *Wall Street Journal,* and subsequently became known as Dow Theory. Dow Theory was refined and expanded by a series of students, notably S. A. Nelson, William Peter Hamilton, and, following the 1929 crash, Robert Rhea.

The greatest living Dow theorist, Richard Russell, who publishes the *Dow Theory Letters,* characterized the three phases of each bull market in terms of the attitude of the general public versus the attitude of the smart money. He explained that during the first two-thirds of a bull market the general public is fearful, only becoming confident during the final phase. Conversely, public confidence lasts throughout the first two-thirds of the ensuing bear market, and the public only turns fearful in the final phase of the plunge.

What, then, is the smart money doing? The smart money is always bucking the prevailing sentiment. During the first two-thirds of a bull market, while the general public is fearful, the smart money is optimistic and is buying up stocks from bagholders at bargain prices. Only in the final phase of the bull market, when everything looks rosy and the general public is confident, does the smart money begin to grow fearful. At this point the smart money dumps its stocks to the bagholders, gaining maximum profit.

It appears to be a rather simple process but, of course, if it was easy there would be no bagholders and no game to play. The rub is that it is extremely difficult to correctly identify the current market phase.

In my new book I attempted to define the various market phases in relation to the actions of the Net Field Trend Indicator. My model of market action and the correct investor response was thus:

Bull market—phase I. The beginning of a bull market has a clear definition. It is simply the end of a bear market. The technical end of a bear market occurs whenever the Dow Jones Industrial Average reaches a new bear market low in the face of a rising NFI. The NFI usually bottoms out in the range of -17 to -19 and then exhibits upward movements, indicating that the smart money is accumulating stocks at their current depressed price levels. The NFI quickly returns to the plus column and remains there for many months, peaking in the range of $+15$ to $+20$. The first phase of a bull market offers the best opportunity for buying profits. The 50 Percent Principle is generally activated early in bull markets and until the Dow has retraced more than half the loss of the previous bear market, one can be very confident that the market is still in bull phase I.

Bull market—phase II. Six to eight months after the bull market has begun, once most stocks have risen from their undervalued levels, those smart money traders who foresaw the bull market are likely to begin to take some early profits. This pressure will cause a reaction, a technical pullback. A second reaction is likely to occur from twelve to fifteen months after the start of the bull market. Selling pressure is felt at this point from two groups—those who entered the bull market early and those who were at least smart enough to enter late in the first phase. This double pressure produces what appears to be a sharp decline. Careful following of the NFI, however, will show that the obvious pressure on price is not accompanied by enough volume to drop the field trends to the base they established at the end of the bear market. The NFI may drop to the range of -12 to -14, but it will hold steady there. This, then, is the reaction that fools the majority. Many will proclaim it as the end of the bull market even as the smart money plows its profits right back into stocks to take advantage of the sharp rally that will follow, a rally that will once more push the NFI close to the $+20$ mark.

Bull market—phase III. By the time two years have passed the bull market will be losing steam. Lower-priced stocks tend to top out first and thus the advance-decline line turns downward six to nine months prior to the end. The NFI pulls back into minus territory for a time, reaching as low as -11. Then, in one grand final burst, the NFI shoots back up toward the $+20$ mark, topping out three to five weeks prior to the Dow. It is at this point that smart money traders dump their stocks onto the bagholders.

Bear market—phase I. A bear market is in most respects merely the obverse of a bull market. The beginning of a bear market occurs when a bull market ends, when the Dow reaches a new high accompanied by a declining pattern in the NFI. A bear market technically is underway, though the Dow may achieve several additional nonconfirmed new highs. It is on these new highs that the bagholders scream, "GIVE ME THAT STOCK RIGHT HERE AT THE VERY TOP!" and the smart money obliges. Anyone who follows the market from minute to minute can see this phenomenon clearly. When the technical indicators are in place for the beginning of a bear market, any new Dow high will bring an immediate avalanche of selling. Dow highs at this point are flashy, but short-lived. During this first phase the NFI plunges into minus territory and stays there for many months, scoring low readings in the -14 to -16 range as the Dow gives back half of its bull market gains.

Bear market—phase II. This phase is characterized by a sudden sharp upswing that I call the *rally that fools the majority.* It is caused by a combination of smart money short-sellers now covering those sales and the still optimistic bagholders who cannot bring themselves to believe in the reality of the bear market. Technically it is characterized by NFI figures that lag behind the suddenly rallying Dow. The NFI shoots back into low-level plus territory, but only for a few weeks. Typically this rally will fall on its face at the exact point in time when fundamental analysts and government economists are telling everyone that we are not going to have a recession, and the NFI has plunged down as low as -17.

Bear market—phase III. After a few weak rally attempts that bring the NFI up as high as $+8$, the market collapses and the NFI scores extremely low readings approaching -20. By now everyone has been forced to acknowledge that conditions are bad and seem to be getting worse. This is the era when the doomsayers achieve the height of their popularity. Though bear markets recur with almost mathematical regularity, they always seem to generate the belief that the world has collapsed and will never again recover. This is, of course, exactly what the smart money wants the bagholders to believe. The NFI will begin to trend upward even as the Dow scores new lows, alerting the observer to the fact that the smart money has finally begun to accumulate stocks and that the Wall Street game will continue as before.

This is the normal market cycle and it is as old as Wall Street. The cycle typically lasts from four to four and a half years and its timing is a phenomenon widely known and well documented, yet few investors seem to remember it. Prior to 1975 I could count myself among them, but from that moment on I paid much more attention to the classic patterns.

Sylvia Porter was one of the first to note publicly that the market performance bears a curious relationship to the presidential cycle. Bull markets tend to begin in the midst of a presidential term, topping out in a wave of optimism shortly after the election. Bear markets tend to begin near Inauguration Day. So much for confidence in our leaders.

I delivered the manuscript to Prentice-Hall on June 1, 1975, and it was published early the following year with the ponderous title *Granville's New Strategy of Daily Stock Market Timing for Maximum Profit.* It was my most comprehensive achievement to date, but it ushered in a period of increased poverty for me.

The book sold to my disciples, but to few others. Prentice-Hall failed to promote the book with the same vigor that they had applied to my previous works. I had to content myself with the knowledge that my *New Strategy* was a contribution to the art of technical analysis and that someday it would be recognized as one of the most valuable tools devised for forecasting in the stock market.

Now I set off on a tangent that would make my reputation more controversial than ever. No other stock market analyst would dream of proclaiming to the world that he had unlocked the secrets of bingo. But since I spent nearly every evening in this compelling pastime where they paid you cash, it was only natural that I turned my analytical attention to the finer points of the game.

What fascinated me about bingo was its dissociation from human motivation, which made it diametrically opposed to the stock market. There is a market theory that postulates that the ups and downs of price trends are nothing more than random events. This Random Walk Theory is hogwash, for the stock market is merely the reflection of human emotion and human beings cannot act in a random manner. If you want to observe a Random Walk, study the master board at a bingo parlor.

Only a few of the overweight grandmothers and middle-class housewives in the Daytona Beach bingo emporiums knew that they regularly played next to a stock market analyst with a worldwide, albeit controversial, reputation.

A legion of bingo players in the Daytona Beach area were convinced that they were in the presence of a certified weirdo who played only a few bingo cards and occupied himself with charts and tables instead of concentrating fully on the game. But as I studied the erratic action of the bingo numbers, a theory began to take shape that translated into steady winnings for me.

Any observer will agree that bingo numbers occur at random. What most people fail to understand is that random numbers drawn from a universal distribution fall into predictable patterns governed by the laws of probability. A sampling of random numbers will exhibit distinct tendencies:

1) There will be an equal number of numbers ending in *1*s, *2*s, *3*s, *4*s, etc.

2) Odd and even numbers tend to balance.

3) High and low numbers tend to balance.

4) The more numbers that are drawn, the closer their average value will come to the average value of the entire population. The average bingo number is 38; the more numbers drawn, the closer their average will tend to move toward 38.

When a bingo number is called, it is flashed upon a master board. So many devotees jam into the parlors that in most cases twelve numbers or less are sufficient to bring a happy shout from one or more winners. I charted the first twelve numbers and came to the interesting conclusion that, on the average, nine different final digits were represented in those dozen balls.

As I mused upon this phenomenon I realized that there was a statistical basis for it. The first tendency of random distribution is for there to be an equal mix of digit endings. Why is this so? Assume that the first number drawn is 0-74. The population of numbers ending in *4* has now been reduced by one. If the next number is N-33, the population of numbers ending in *3* has also been reduced by one. On the surface this appears to be a slim alteration, but in practice it has a distinct tendency to influence the outcome of the game.

Of course, when dealing with random events, any result is possible in any given game. During an evening of bingo there will be a few games that cause people to murmur about a similarity of numbers drawn, the inference always being that some hanky-panky is going on. This is the odd example, however, and it is far more remote than the varying occurrence of differing final digits.

Accepting the principle of varying final digits, how does one then apply this hidden knowledge to the play of the game? This is easy, for in most cases it is possible to choose your own cards.

Before beginning play for the night you have the opportunity to sift through the available bingo cards and choose which ones you will utilize. This is generally done on the basis of superstition or resignation. In the minutes before play many patrons plunge into the pile of cards searching for their personal lucky numbers, the current date, their husband's birthday, their bust measurement, or some other such idiotic combination of digits. Others, bingo's version of bagholders, grab a handful of cards at random, assuming they are going to lose anyway.

There is a far better method. If most bingo games are won by combinations of differing final digits, why not simply choose cards where the key patterns contain numbers with such differing final digits?

The key positions on any bingo card are the diagonals, because they form the most possible winning combinations. I tested the hypothesis, choosing bingo cards whose eight diagonal numbers all ended in differing digits. Playing only a few cards a night I was not a visible winner, for I did not shout "Bingo!" as often as the people who played multiple cards. But I did something they could never do. I showed a profit! It was modest, to be sure, but I could ill afford a loss.

Not long after I sent my *New Strategy* manuscript off to the publisher I plunged into a fresh project to broadcast my bingo strategies to the world. *How to Win at Bingo* was published in 1977 by Parker Publishing Company. It exposed me to an onslaught of wry criticism from my enemies in the financial world. How could a stock market analyst let himself fall for such notions, they openly wondered?

Wall Street is careful to promote an aura of fiscal responsibility. In some cases this is a true image; some brokers really are serious wearers of gray suits who would never dream of frequenting a casino, race track, or bingo parlor; they are early to rise and early to slumber, resting peacefuly with the inner satisfaction of having attempted to earn money the old-fashioned way; if they drink, it is a drop of sherry before retiring.

But Wall Streeters try to make you believe that the great majority of them behave in such conservative, respectable fashion. The truth is, of course, that in their personal lives Wall Streeters, like doctors, lawyers, politicians, clergymen, and garbage collectors, are no better or worse than the rest of us. Their great personal failing, I believe, is not that so many of them drink, gamble, and carouse, but that they attempt to hide these human foibles from the public. Who's kidding whom?

I believe that one of the major reasons for my success in calling the stock market is what Wall Street might call my "craziness." I am just crazy enough to act out my true feelings and care not one whit whether those actions are derided by the more "respectable" classes of society. This immunity to conventional criticism has helped me to look at the stock market with a very different pair of eyes. What were secrets to the majority of stock market analysts stood out as clear truths to me.

This answers a frequently asked question. If I really have unlocked the secrets of the stock market, why has not everyone followed my lead, effectively undermining my theories?

In some cases they have. Some of my early indicators, such as the Dow Jones Rail Average and the Barron's Confidence Index, became so widely followed that they were no longer valid. But I have no worries that this will become a universal problem, because most people are, and always will be, bagholders.

There are winners and losers in life, and for some unknown reason the majority seem willing to be losers. To win at the stock market game you must be able to act directly contrary to the impulses of human nature. You must buy when everything looks bleak and sell when everything looks fantastic. It is one thing to read those words and nod your head in agreement, but quite another to put it all into practice. Losers do not have the self-discipline to follow my system. To follow me, you must share a measure of my craziness.

Joe Granville bottomed out late in 1974 and had nowhere to go but up. My *New Strategy* and *Bingo* books, though they generated little enthusiasm among the general public, were studied thoroughly by knowledgeable insiders, and that gave me great satisfaction. Most importantly, now that I had worked out the proper significance of the Net Field Trend Indicator, I was confident that I was back in gear with the market.

But, just as in the market the external signs of change lag behind the technical indicators, so the conditions of my life seemed to worsen. What little royalty money the *New Strategy* book earned was already signed over to Polly. I did not fight her on anything; I merely wanted peace in my life. The marriage was a thing of the past to me and I did not have the heart to struggle over the material residue of it. I signed the house, the trust fund, the insurance policies —everything—over to her.

What worried me most about my lack of funds was the ability to get my *Letter* out. During one stretch in the autumn of 1975 I fell behind on the printing bill and failed to put out a *Letter* for five weeks. My subscription list held steady at its bottom of 300. Few people in the investment community knew that I was still alive.

But the market knew. After advising my readers to take their profits on April 25, 1975, and await the normal technical pullback, I once again gave the green light to buy on November 17, calling the next phase of the bull market perfectly. This time I recommended a number of stocks that had risen little in the previous months but now seemed poised to join the general trend.

The Dow closed out 1975—the year that began when President Ford told Congress that he had *bad news* to report—at 852.41, scoring a net gain of 236.17 points for the third-best percentage rise in history.

The rally continued until the Dow peaked at 1011.02 on April 21. Seeing the Net Field Trend Indicator draw a bead on minus territory, I pulled my readers out of most recommended stocks, with the following results:

STOCK	BUYING PRICE	SELLING PRICE	PERCENT PROFIT
Arvin Industries	9.50	12.50	31.6
Avco	5.88	10.13	72.3
Avnet	9.13	17.25	88.9
Carrier	9.63	15.13	57.1
City Investing	8.00	11.13	39.1
Coastal States Gas	7.88	14.75	87.2
Evans Products	4.88	8.88	82.0
Fuqua	4.50	8.75	94.4
GAF	10.88	15.38	41.4

These profits are considerably more impressive when one realizes that they were earned in five months or less.

For the remainder of the year, with the bullish syndrome nearing its second birthday and clearly its third and final phase, I grew very cautious, looking for a characteristic turnaround sometime after the presidential election.

Meanwhile, there was more drama at home. Leona got married. Blanchard and Sally were away at school. My seventeen-year-old son Paul discovered the electric guitar and his constant rocking and rolling threw the rest of the family into turmoil. His high school grades fell into an abyss. Unable to turn him around, Polly suggested that he live with me for a time.

Paul was an easygoing, good-natured Leo, like me, to whom the hassles of life in a small office were unimportant. He was concerned with larger problems, unsure of what to do with this strange phenomenon of life that had been thrust upon him. He sought answers in much the same manner as my mother, by exposing himself to as many points of view as possible.

For a time he came under the spell of an eastern guru, whose icons plastered the walls of the *Granville Market Letter* office. The smell of marijuana smoke wafted about the room. When Paul was not practicing on his guitar or playing chess with me, he was likely to be sitting in a corner with a sheet over his head, meditating.

His habits were not unduly distracting to me. When immersed in market statistics I am oblivious to my environment. What was important was that I enjoyed close family contact for the first time in years.

Despite his penchant for cerebral escape Paul was in many ways more practical than I. He pitched in to make things more comfortable for us, building me a bunk so that I could sleep somewhere other than on the floor.

It was Paul who suggested that I regain control of my finances. "Why don't you open a post office box of your own?" he asked.

"I don't know," I replied. "I just never got around to it. I guess I will." Maybe, after all, there was something to meditation. Why had this simple expedient never occurred to me?

The *Granville Market Letter* moved from a post office box in Ormond Beach to a new one in Holly Hill. With the first income we invested in lawn equipment and Paul set off in his van to supplement our feeble finances by doing yard work. My subscription list remained depressed, but we managed to turn the office into an acceptable bachelors' pad. I came to realize how much I loved this searching, troubled son of mine.

As 1976 drew to a close I watched the market with special care. In my *New Strategy* book I had included long-range predictions covering the years 1976 through 1983, based largely upon the cyclical studies of the Kondratieff long wave. Revising the earlier conclusions that had misguided me during the Nixon years, I theorized that the true method of calculating the years of potential crash action was to measure the time span between peaks in the wholesale commodity price index. Those peaks, detailed by Kondratieff, occurred in 1814, 1864, and 1920. To this we could now add the new peak in February 1974. This gave a more precise reading, a range of fifty to fifty-four years between major market crashes. All that remained was to add that span to 1929. Thus in my *New Strategy* book I forecast a mild bear market in 1977–78, the natural down cycle in the first half of a presidential term, but all bets were off beyond that point. The years 1979 through 1983, I wrote, "represent *the entire critical Kondratieff time span* wherein some maximum trouble might be expected to occur."

I would worry about those years when they arrived. Now I was concerned about the approaching normal bear market.

A September 21, 1976, Dow high of 1014.79 appeared to most technicians to be confirmed, and bullish sentiment was at a peak. A series of extremely optimistic articles in *Business Week* predicted a rosy outbreak of higher corporate earnings in 1977. Most of the key technical indicators reflected great internal strength in the market.

Years earlier I had shown technicians that the Dow Jones Rail Average has a distinct tendency to top out prior to the Industrials. Though this indicator's designation was changed to the Transportation Average in 1970, it was still widely followed, and it, at this point in time, emphatically predicted a continuing bull market. The Transports stood at 221 when the Industrial high of 1014 occurred, and even though the Industrials slipped below 1000, the Transports continued to rise to new highs through the first four months of 1977.

A market analyst must never lose sight of the intricacies of his subject matter. If this were an easy game, everyone would know the proper time to buy and sell, and there would be no more game. Few people took note of the reason the Rails were changed to the Transports: Dow Jones included airline stocks in the average for the first time. The makeup of the group changed radically and there were no guarantees that the average would act as it had in the past.

Henry N. Southworth, reviewing my *New Strategy* book for the British publication *The Chartist,* impressed me with a most astute observation. He contended that in the context of extraordinary times some—perhaps many—technical indicators showed a tendency to give false readings.

Charles Berlitz's book *The Bermuda Triangle* inspired me with an analogy to illustrate Southworth's point. Berlitz noted that when ships and airplanes encountered difficulties in this strange area of the Atlantic, their instruments tended to give them false readings. So it was with the stock market, I reasoned. The market was edging toward the first few critical years of the Kondratieff long-wave cycle. These were not normal times, nor would normal times return for years to come. In abnormal times one might expect normal indicators to malfunction, to give a false reading of confidence just prior to the time when the vehicle stalled out and spun into the ocean.

Such was the case in 1977. The bullish aspect of the Dow Transports proved to be a hook that caught a considerable number of big technical fish. Never had I seen a market situation in which it was more imperative to study a "tree" of indicators. The sapling was too weak to enable an analyst to swing upon a single branch.

A great many conventional technical indicators fueled the general optimism, but they were all based on price. The Net Field Trend Indicator, however, based on volume, dipped into negative territory early in 1977, dropping from +11 to +8 to +3 to −1 to −4 in successive weeks. Recognizing the difference between the internal indicators and the slower external emanations, I did not pull my readers totally out of the market, but I assumed a bearish posture for the year ahead.

And though it was not a time to buy, I drew a hunch from my personal experience and shared it with my readers to save until the next bull market. On April 7, 1977, I wrote:

> Over the years the market has centered attention on a rotating series of hot groups. I have a gut feeling that the next "hot" group in the market is going to be the gambling stocks.

The program chairman of the Market Technicians Association was impressed with my *New Strategy* book and sent me an invitation to be the keynote speaker at his group's May 1977 seminar in the Pocono Mountains of Pennsylvania. It had been years since I had spoken in public, but I always loved it, and here was another chance to tell the investment world that Joe Granville was still kicking. I rushed to the local 7-11 store and pumped quarters into the pay phone, accepting the invitation.

Somehow Paul and I assembled enough cash to pay for my plane fare. I wore my only suit, which I had bought for Leona's wedding the previous year.

There were more than 400 so-called technical analysts at the meeting, including my successor at Hutton, Newton Zinder, and of that number exactly three of us were bearish. One was Abe Cohen, publisher of *Investors Intelligence,* whom I had met years earlier at the New School in New York when I lectured on Bach's "Jesu, Joy of Man's Desiring." I have great respect for Abe's opinions and I listened carefully to him now. Each week his letter rates about seventy different investment advisory services. By compiling data on the number of bulls and bears, Abe devised what he calls the Sentiment Index. At that time the Sentiment Index had an extremely high reading—the great majority of advisors were bullish. This, to Abe, was clearly a major sell signal.

The other bear was Ian Notley, the leading chartist and technician for Dominion Securities in Toronto. It was the first time we had met, and we stayed up most of the night trading philosophies. Ian's bearishness was drawn directly from his stock price charts. He convinced me that night, and I remain convinced today, that he is the top chart reader in the world.

Ironically much of the bullish sentiment at the meeting was keyed to the Kondratieff long-wave cycle. Numerous technicians gave credence to Kondratieff's theories and believed that we were headed for a worldwide depression in the early eighties. But they also believed, as I had in 1973, that in order for a depression to occur the stock market would first have to run up to new heights. The most ardent proponents of this viewpoint circulated flyers at the seminar predicting that during this year of 1977 the Dow would roar upward beyond the 2000 mark.

In the midst of this prevailing sentiment I rose to proclaim that four months earlier we had entered a bear market, albeit a mild one. I used a blackboard to explain my theories of On-Balance Volume and showed them how the Net Field Trend Indicator predicted this bear market in the face of the contrary evidence of most normal technical indicators.

The audience listened, but at the conclusion of the meeting there were still only three bears in the room. After all, even as I spoke, the almighty Dow Jones Transportation Average ran up to a level higher than the one at which it had been at the last top in the Industrial Average.

So I returned to Florida and, once again riding against majority sentiment, advised my readers to go short on the market, betting on the downturn that I could so clearly see coming. During previous downturns I had advised my readers to get out of the market and from time to time had offered a short sale recommendation. But now for the first time I placed special emphasis on short selling. I saw both sides of the game ever more clearly. Turn a bull market upside down and you have a bear market. In either case the vast majority of stocks will make broad price swings in accordance with the general trend, so why not make money on the downside as well as on the upside?

Wall Street discourages short selling because Wall Street is locked into the simpleminded belief that up is good and down is bad. Brokers fear that they will not be able to lure fresh money into a falling market. I have often wondered how much more commission income they could earn if they showed potential investors that enormous profits are possible in a bear market.

But Wall Street is calibrated to take advantage of only half the game. The standard brokerage argument against short selling is this: There is no limit to your losses. In other words, if you buy a stock at 10, the most you can lose is $10 a share if the company goes bankrupt and the stock becomes worthless. But if you short the stock at 10 and it goes against you, it can theoretically rise forever.

However, any smart investor knows to put a stop order on his transaction to limit his losses if he is wrong. If he buys at 10 he can place a stop order at seven. Should the stock drop that low, he will be sold out automatically, limiting his loss to $3 per share. If the stock rises, he may raise his stop order accordingly to guarantee a given level of profits.

If the smart investor shorts a stock at 10, he will do just the opposite. He will place a stop order at 12 or 13, so that if the stock rises to that level his broker automatically covers the short. The investor decides what losses he can afford to incur and guards against further loss. No investor will guess correctly 100 percent of the time. He should always take proper action to limit his liability on those inevitable transactions when the market goes against him. Properly transacted, short selling is no more dangerous than long buying, and it was certainly a profitable strategy in 1977.

One broker who is happy to transact short sales is Jack Arnold, who opened his own discount brokerage firm in Minneapolis in 1977. Arnold Securities, like the few other discount houses, can save its clients more than 50 percent of commission fees because it boasts no research department to offer guidance to investors. While the reduced commissions are a great boon, the lack of a research department is probably even more valuable a service to the investor, who is not bombarded by the fundamental hogwash that slops forth from the traditional Wall Street firm.

From the outset Jack proclaimed to his customers that his firm was heavily oriented to technical analysis. Being a technician himself, Jack naturally read every book he could about technical analysis, and the one that impressed him the most was my *New Strategy* book. Because of this he invited me to journey to Minneapolis and give a market seminar to coincide with his grand opening. The date was set for November 3. I agreed to hold the seminar free of charge, reasoning that it would increase my subscriber list.

Two hundred people crowded into the fifth floor auditorium of the First National Bank Building that afternoon, thanks to much local promotion. Jack had the TV stations and news reporters there.

My bearish posture was no great surprise, for by now the market had pulled most analysts over to my side. The Dow had declined 200 points to settle near the 800 level. My short-selling subscribers had grins on their faces. Most of the audience, however, was astonished that I could document my bearish stance since January, when virtually every other technical analyst had been erroneously bullish.

"Back in January this market was like a train going up a mountain," I said. "All the cars in the front portion of the train are technical indicators, which normally top out ahead of the Dow Industrials prior to a bull market peak. This time, however, the train couldn't make it up the hill in a normal manner. The wheels slipped, the brakes wouldn't hold, and the Dow (the little caboose) led the entire train back down the mountain many times more rapidly than it was able to climb in the previous bull market."

This was a strange aberration of a market, I pointed out. Many of the normal technical indicators malfunctioned. Dow highs had been confirmed by the actions of the advance-decline line and the previously reliable Transportation Average. With such abnormal readings emanating from the traditional indicators, how could anyone have predicted this bear market, I asked rhetorically?

Then I showed them. Using a blackboard I patiently taught the basics of On-Balance Volume. I reviewed the performance of the Net Field Trend Indicator over the last several ups and downs of the market and demonstrated how it had called the present bear market perfectly in the face of a myriad of contrary technical indicators.

"This is because the NFI is based on volume, and most other indicators are based on price," I declared. "And volume tends to precede price."

I spoke for three and a half hours without a break, reducing my voice to a gravelly rasp—a vestige of which has remained with me and become one of my trademarks. Despite my aching throat, I enjoyed once more holding an audience's attention, after so many people had written me off.

Jim Fuller, a reporter for the *Minneapolis Tribune*, described the event:

> It would be easy at first meeting to dismiss Joe Granville as some sort of messianic screwball. He could even be a pushy used-car salesman who became a stock market analyst by walking through the wrong door in a brokerage house while looking for the men's room.
>
> He's a gangly sort of fellow, and his obviously off-the-rack clothing hangs too loosely. He leans at you when he talks, like a man pushing through a gale, and his arms flail awkwardly at times. He speaks in a raspy rush, and there seems to be no way to turn off the flow until he's made his point or told his tale. His eyes stare into yours, demanding your acceptance of his preachments. . . .
>
> The fact is, one decides after awhile, that Granville's style is that of a supremely self-confident but hyperactive man who feels a need to share his wide-ranging insights with a largely benighted world. His intensity, as it turns out, is leavened with humor so that he wears rather better than one would expect. He is great company at table.

I formed lifelong friendships that day with Jack Arnold and his associate, Jerry Mulder. Another of their friends became a close companion of mine. He was a tower of a man named D. L. Smith, a former Los Angeles Laker basketball player who now directs Anchor Investments in Minneapolis. In his six years as a pro athlete D. L. had lived by a motto that I now adopted for my own: "I don't care if they boo or cheer me as long as they make a goddamned noise."

I now set off on a course that would create a tumultuous response, in both boos and cheers. I placed a notice in my *Letter* that I was available for seminars before any interested group.

Invitations poured in, launching me on an odyssey that would see me headline at Caesar's Palace and Carnegie Hall, nearly murder the gallery at the Bob Hope Desert Classic golf tournament, cope with several death threats, stump the panel on "To Tell the Truth," call Phil Donahue a bagholder to his face, get Tom Snyder to admit that I had cost him $25,000, escape a terrorist bomb blast in Munich, preach my market doctrine from the pulpit of the Crystal Cathedral, have my pocket picked by a chimpanzee posing as a bank trust officer, get slipped a Mickey Finn in Atlantic City, walk on water, drop my pants in public, nearly strangle a future U.S. president, provoke a cacophony of hoots on the floor of the New York Stock Exchange, find a glorious, loving wife, and build my business into a $10-million-a-year empire.

10.
ACTS

Her name was Fifi. Local legend held that she had starred at Paris's famous Moulin Rouge before coming here, to the Red Garter in Indianapolis. At any rate, since I had recently downed several shots of straight vodka, she appeared very beautiful to me as she pranced onstage.

My friend Michael "Tiger" Fleming of the Indianapolis office of Shearson Hayden Stone had arranged a ringside table for us. Fifi, seeing us grow more appreciative with each snip of clothing she removed, played up to our boisterous table.

I was exhilarated, having just completed my most spectacular speech to date. I knew the thrill of wild applause and I wanted Fifi to share the same emotion. I sloshed down another vodka and screamed in enthusiasm as she slipped out of her bra.

Fifi undulated toward the front of the stage. Standing directly above us, she reached out and made a "come hither" gesture with her arms. Had I been sober I would have recognized it as a standard crowd pleaser that asked only for a rhetorical response. But I was decidedly unsober and I interpreted the gesture literally, scrambling up onto the stage to join Fifi's act.

Tiger and his friends whooped in delight. Fifi scowled and gently attempted to guide me off the stage, but I merely responded with an attempt to mimic her bumps and grinds.

Fifi finally seemed to realize that she had a new partner and she determined that if I was going to crab her act I would have to adopt her costume.

"Take off zee coat!" she shouted in my ear.

And so I did, tossing it down to Tiger, who was in an ecstasy of laughter.

Fifi bubbled her way to the far end of the stage and back again, whereupon she commanded, "Take off zee shirt."

I pulled off my tie and shirt to the accompaniment of thumping booms from the bass drummer, who had caught the spirit of the impromptu performance.

Swirling and swaying, Fifi made her way around the stage and then returned to call my bluff.

"Take off zee pants!"

And down they came, hurled into the oblivion of the hysterical audience. Then Joe Granville, stock market analyst, wearing only boxer shorts, shoes, and socks, went into a frenzy of bumps and grinds that put even Fifi to shame.

A standing ovation accompanied me back to my table where I sat in seminude splendor, drinking more vodka.

It was minutes before Tiger could stop laughing enough to inform me that every time I did a bump or a grind the slit in my shorts flew wide open, revealing Granville's own technical indicator to the world.

The event epitomized the hysterical course I steered over the next several years. I was caught up in the show, stirred by a bevy of adoring fans to bare myself to the world. It would be many years before I would come to understand that when the drumbeat stops, the dancer is left alone upon the stage, naked.

In the market, the crazy new year of 1978 came in like a bear, and this was a phenomenon guaranteed to turn most technicians into pessimists. Conventional theory states that if the market falls in January it will fall all year along.

I had refined this concept into the following series of five points that, lumped together, constituted my January Indicator: 1) After three days of market action, did the Dow stand higher or lower than the December 31 close? 2) After five days of action, did the Dow stand higher or lower than after the three-day close? 3) By mid-January did the Dow stand higher or lower than the five-day close? 4) At the end of January did the Dow stand higher or lower than the mid-month close? 5) Did the Dow, in January, break the December high or low?

The cumulative answers to these questions gave a reading ranging from +5 to −5, the force of the trend being readily apparent for the year. As January 1978 unfolded, it signaled one of the worst markets on record, the indicators showing this:

1) After three days the Dow had dropped from 831.17 to 804.92;

2) After five days the Dow had dropped to 784.56;

3) After the eleventh of the twenty-one trading days in January the Dow had dropped to 779.02;

4) Downside momentum was so strong it seemed a sure bet that the Dow would end the month at an even lower point:

5) The Dow easily broke the December low of 806.22.

The cumulative reading of the January Indicator, then, was likely to be −5, the worst possible omen for the 1978 market.

By mid-month the Dow had scored a new bear market low that was confirmed by the New York Stock Exchange Composite Average, which measures the price levels of all big board common stocks. The Dow Jones Utility Average broke under the neckline of an important head and shoulders formation. The bond market collapsed. General Motors broke to a series of new bear market lows, fully confirmed by its On-Balance Volume figures. The advance-decline line poised to break to a new bear market low. The number of stocks reaching new fifty-two-week lows incrased dramatically. The Net Field Trend Indicator plunged from −6 to −17 in three weeks.

Everything looked so bad that I began to wonder whether the Kondratieff cycle had been shortened, whether we were already in the great crash predicted by the Russian economist's theories. The fifty-four-year average of that cycle pointed to a crash in 1983, but 1977 was within the early range of possibility.

"The market egg has so deteriorated," I wrote in my January 12 *Letter*, "that Humpty Dumpty cannot be put back together again."

There was, however, one thing that bothered me and caused me to review the data carefully. As the technical situation deteriorated a majority of other anlaysts—fundamental and technical—rushed to the bear side of the equation. The bear market was now obvious. Obviously such a majority had to be wrong.

Sure enough, toward the end of January the CLX recorded a series of nonconfirmations on days when the Dow dropped. The number of stocks reaching new lows decreased, even though the Dow dropped.

In my January 26 *Letter,* in the face of otherwise overwhelming evidence to the contrary, I advised my readers to prepare for a rally. How big a rally I could not yet say.

This was a difficult call. On January 31, the Dow closed at 769.92, completing the January Indicator reading at -5. But on the very next day the Dow rallied to 774.34 and scored a CLX reading of $+10$, the highest in some time. That was short-term bullish. On the other hand, the NFI stood at -19, down two points from the previous week. My mistakes in 1973–74 had taught me to respect the evidence of the NFI as the major indicator of the long trend. But I also knew that it rarely, if ever, dropped below -20. When it dropped that low it had nowhere to go but up. Further, I still had confidence in the CLX as a magnificent short-term indicator.

I have always emphasized the necessity of relying upon a "tree of indicators," rather than swinging from a single branch. The NFI was bearish, but too bearish. This time I was forced to depend upon the CLX, the declining number of individual lows, and the growing popularity of gloomy prognostications.

In my February 2 *Letter,* therefore, I advised my readers to cover their short sales and look for a sharp rally within the context of an overall bear market. I suspected that we were in store for the rally that fools the majority, and in order to fool them, it had to be strong enough to produce significant profits. It was the perfect time to take profits from short sales and earn some quick money on the upside. Once again the market would prove me correct.

Although my unpopular prediction of the previous year's bear market had proved highly accurate, a review of the stocks I had recommended for short sales in 1977 showed only modest gains. Of the seventy-four stocks I selected, twenty-four had risen, one remained unchanged and forty-nine had fallen. On the average, the investor earned a return of 5 percent on these short sales, but that was a misleading figure. Any serious investor would utilize a margin account; that is, he would place only half the necessary money on account, borrowing the other half from his broker. Thus the margin investor's profit on my recommended series of short sales was about 10 percent, less interest and service charges.

Ten percent is only a modest profit percentage for the stock market, but this 10 percent was realized during a period when the Dow Jones Industrial Average *dropped* 300 points. During 1977 Wall Street had continued to sing its moldy refrain of BUY! BUY! BUY! and anyone who had followed those lyrics took a BATH! BATH! BATH! Anyone who was invested in the market from January 24, 1977, through February 2, 1978, would have preferred my course of action.

Now, however, it appeared to most people that I had completely deviated from sanity. The market was so obviously poised to continue its severe drop that my staunchest followers were skeptical. For more than a month my vaunted rally failed to materialize, but I grew more confident because the NFI did, indeed, begin to rise off its bottom.

Early in March I spoke at a meeting of the Technical Securities Analysts Association of San Francisco. That morning the newspapers covered page one with bad news. The dollar was sinking badly against foreign currencies. President Carter contemplated imposing the Taft-Hartley Act to end the current critical coal strike. The majority of analysts in the room had arrived at the belated conclusion that we were in a bear market.

They listened in disbelief when I forecast a minimum 75- to 100-point rise in the Dow over the next six months, but their interest grew as I explained my method of reading the market's internal signals. I showed them On-Balance Volume. Then I showed them how, in the face of an indifferent Dow, the Net Field Trend Indicator had improved steadily throughout February, climbing from −19 to −16 to −13, while at the same time the Climax Indicator appeared to have bottomed out and positioned itself for a rise.

Two days later I participated in an all-day monetary seminar along with Alberto Eogni, economist of the Swiss Bank, and two other independent market letter writers, James Dines and Julian Snyder. All three of these respected financial wizards were bearish on the stock market, faithfully representing the wisdom of the day.

After hearing the dismal projections of the financial experts, one silver-haired woman rose and quietly asked me where I thought the market would go in 1978. "Up, Up and AWAY!" I shouted, jumping from my seat and pointing to the ceiling.

The histrionics brought laughter and applause from the 400 members of the audience. I resolved then and there that in future speeches

I would pay no attention to the conventional rules of decorum. Financial analysts are known for their sedate, conservative, and *boring* speeches. But it was not my style to mumble politely. Rather, I would let my personality loose and to hell with anyone who didn't like it.

I did so a few days later at a Holiday Inn in Westwood, California, where the local office of E.F. Hutton sponsored my seminar. More than 600 people were seated in the large ballroom and another 150 stood in the back, listening to me deliver a sermon on what I perceived to be the new bull market.

Even as I spoke the Dow rose four points and recorded key upside breakouts of +10 on the CLX and −8 on the NFI. The Dow stood at 750.87, only a few points off the bear market bottom. I knew the market had embarked upon a sharp rally, just as I knew that my post office box would be jammed with new subscription orders when I returned home from the successful tour.

I rushed straight from the Daytona Beach airport to the Holly Hill post office. Scores of new orders were there all right, but the checks had been removed from the envelopes. I was furious when I learned that my estranged wife had been allowed access to the box.

This was a disguised blessing, for it brought us, finally, to the point of formal separation. Now alimony and support obligations were legally spelled out. At my current level of income there would be little left over for me, but if I could raise that income I would finally have a cash reserve. And now I could see the way to do just that. I set to work planning additional seminars, convinced that this was the way to better my reputation, and thus my income.

With the technical evidence swinging strongly in my direction, I made major buy recommendations in my *Letter*, concentrating on the airlines, motels and restaurants, and defense contractors. My special pick was Bally Manufacturing, the major supplier of slot machines to gambling casinos.

Then I was off for a triumphant return to Minneapolis, for another seminar sponsored by Arnold Securities. Since my buy signal the Dow had risen from 769.92 to 837.32, a new high for the year on the same day that banks raised their prime rate. Jack Arnold set off an alarm bell as he introduced me to the audience of 400 as "The Clock."

By early May I was flooded with congratulatory telegrams and letters from grateful subscribers who had followed my stock selections in the face of Wall Street "logic." In less than two months they had earned 50-percent profits. And the real swingers, those who dealt in the speculative world of stock options, had doubled or tripled their money.

Before I realized what was happening my life was a whirlwind of travel and excitement. Brokers who hated me with undisguised passion were forced to admit that I was good for business. After a Granville Show they were flooded with new accounts. Despite their reservations about my message, brokers knew that I was money in their pockets.

On stage, where I always wanted to be, I could clown, cavort, and speak my mind without reservation. The best part was that I had a message I believed in and could prove through the simple, elegant concept of On-Balance Volume. I was in tune with the market, and life was exciting.

I no longer cared whom I offended in the staid financial world, for I identified them more clearly as the enemies of the small investor. During a seminar in Milwaukee I took on one of my favorite targets, the bank trust officers.

"Perhaps the most notorious of fundamentalist thinkers are the bank trust officers," I declared. "Being of a fundamental mind, it naturally follows that their thinking is perpetually at odds with what the market is saying. Since volume precedes price, and price precedes fundamentals, bank trust officers bring up the rear, acting woefully too late in every cycle.

"We are forced, therefore, to use the actions of bank trust officers as one of our finest and most reliable market indicators. They sold at the 1974 bottom, bought at the 1976 top, and sold at the 1978 bottom, a perfect record of very expensive contrary opinion."

The combination of my seminars and my correct assessment of market conditions sent my subscription list rocketing upward and, with confidence, I raised the price to $200 a year.

Paul moved out to share an apartment with a friend. With my increased income I was able to move my office to a suite in a new building and hire several secretaries to take care of business as I scurried about the country.

The market rose rapidly that summer with barely a hint of downside action. By early August the Dow stood 120 points higher than it had on the day of my February 2 buy signal. Technical evidence was still strong, but my new Bank Trust Officer Indicator flashed a warning.

"I have just started to notice some bullish comments from various people who were total pessimists in February," I wrote in my August 8 *Letter.*

> This worries me . . . we must not succumb to greed. As the institutional fundamentalists and bank trust officers begin to voice their confidence in this market in the weeks and months ahead we are going to let them have all the stocks they turned their backs on last February. After all, somebody has to hold the bag, and they have already proven over and over again that they are the world's expert bagholders.

Selling a dozen of my recommended stocks in the face of extreme technical strength clouded only by the emergence of fundamental support for the rally, my subscribers earned the following profits in a five-month period:

STOCK	BUYING PRICE	SELLING PRICE	PERCENT PROFIT
Abbott Laboratories	29.50	39.00	32.2
American Airlines	9.25	17.75	91.9
Boeing	33.50	73.88	119.0
Delta Airlines	36.88	56.75	53.9
General Dynamics	43.50	85.00	95.4
McDonnell Douglas	24.88	38.75	55.7
Northwest Airlines	23.25	35.88	54.3
Raytheon	34.13	56.25	64.8
Schering Plough	33.25	37.13	11.7
Smithkline	64.88	94.25	45.3
United Airlines	20.63	40.25	95.1
Western Airlines	7.25	14.13	94.9

Only one week later the Net Field Trend Indicator exhibited a disturbing sign. In that week the NFI rose from +12 to +13, a peak for the five-month rally. On the surface that appeared to be bullish, but I always attempt to look beneath the surface. What bothered me was that several of the Dow stocks, notably International Harvester and United Technologies, had recently scored *lower* UP designations. If they next scored lower DOWN designations their field trends would reverse abruptly from rising to falling. Each stock that did so would lower the NFI by two full points.

Other signals bothered me. On August 3 the Dow rose more than four points on an explosion of trading activity that set a new all-time volume record on the New York Stock Exchange. Abe Cohen of *Investors Intelligence* warned me that his Sentiment Index showed that 67.1 percent of the market advisory services had turned bullish, and I hate to be on the side of the majority. The number of new individual highs topped out. Perhaps worst of all, the notoriously fundamental mutual fund managers had now entered the market, betting heavily on a continuation of the rise.

"Those who are traditionally wrong on important market bottoms now have the reins of the market at the top—and that of course tells me that we are at or very near the top," my August 22 *Letter* warned. "So the calls go out now to trim sail, sell into strength, take profits . . . I could be a month early and 20 points from the top but I am not going to push my luck. It is *always* better to be on the early side of the ledger than the late side."

I dropped another dozen stocks from my recommended portfolio, again with impressive results:

STOCK	BUYING PRICE	SELLING PRICE	PERCENT PROFIT
Bally Manufacturing	20.63	43.25	109.6
Caesars World	10.88	28.88	165.4
Dean Witter Reynolds	13.38	15.75	17.7
Del Webb	20.50	24.00	17.1
Dennys	27.75	32.50	17.1
Hilton Hotels	39.63	59.50	50.1
E.F. Hutton	14.75	22.25	50.8
Merrill Lynch	17.25	22.25	29.0
MGM	35.00	42.75	22.1
Playboy	18.00	23.25	28.9
Shearson Hayden Stone	8.00	13.63	70.4

The performance of the gambling stocks, notably Caesars World and Bally Manufacturing, gave me great satisfaction, for I had predicted the growing popularity of the pastime long ago and alerted my subscribers to look for a meteoric rise in gambling-associated stocks.

But now Wall Street had fallen in love with them also. Argus Research, a fundamentalist group, issued a favorable long-term study of the gambling stocks and that had to be the kiss of death, so I published a series of short-sale recommendations with Caesars and Bally heading the list.

The Dow stood at 897.00 when I issued the sell signal and it remained in the high 800s for weeks. Nevertheless, the NFI performed as I had foreseen, dropping from its peak of +13 to +9 and +6 in successive weeks. In light of that deterioration I pulled my subscribers out of all long positions. The remaining seventeen stocks in the portfolio I had recommended back in February and March showed only small profits and, in a few cases, small losses. This taught me a basic lesson—one must play the market all the way. I should have advised the sale of all stocks at one time, not allowing any to participate in the hidden general deterioration. It is either a time to buy or a time to sell, but never a time to play the market both ways.

On September 9 I was in Fort Wayne, Indiana, for a seminar sponsored by the local office of Paine Webber Jackson & Curtis. At the edge of the stage was a piano and it was only natural for me to ham it up a bit. I played "Jesu, Joy of Man's Desiring" and illustrated how the progression of its notes followed the laws of harmony, physics, and stock charts. The theme from Beethoven's Fifth Symphony exhibited similar patterns.

"Now I will show you how a bank trust officer would play," I announced. I lifted my hands high above the keyboard and sustained a long, dramatic pause. Suddenly my fingers smashed into the keys creating a cataclysmic eruption of dissonance. I held the sour chord for several seconds before dropping my forehead onto the keyboard to complete the caricature.

The audience loved the performance, and from that point forward I required my sponsors to provide a piano for all my shows.

The Dow had not yet followed my sell signal, remaining slightly above the 900 level, but the NFI was in a downward zigzag and I was confident that soon the market would prove my bearish forecast to be correct. During a seminar in Indianapolis on September 11, when someone commented that various economic indicators and optimistic news items ran counter to my current prediction, I launched into a tirade against fundamental analysis.

"I am not influenced by anything outside of the market," I proclaimed. "The dollar was making new lows in February 1978, a headlined story all over the world. The Dow was at 769. The dollar was still making new lows—much lower lows—with the Dow at 900 six months later. What did the dollar have to do with the stock market?

"NOTHING!" I screamed.

"Interest rates have risen fifty percent this year in the money market," I continued, "and the Dow has climbed from 769 to 900. What do interest rates have to do with the stock market?

"NOTHING!

"The price of gold soared to an all-time high of $216 an ounce and the Dow climbed from 769 to 900. What does the price of gold have to do with the stock market?

"NOTHING!

"The president's popularity has sunk to an all-time low. The Dow has climbed from 769 to 900. What has the president to do with the stock market?

"NOTHING!"

The market always does its best to confound bagholders, I insisted. It sends out a series of false signals that I call hooks. A hook is designed to catch a fish and to catch a lot of fish you need a lot of hooks. At the present time there were five hooks dangling in front of the fish.

Hook #1 was the Dow itself, making a new bull market high of 907.74 on September 8.

Hook #2 was the bellwether stock of IBM breaking above 300.

Hook #3 was the new high made by the Dow Jones Transportation Average.

Hook #4 was a new high in the advance-decline line.

Hook #5 was the fundamentalist acceptance of the gambling stocks as the current "hot" group.

In the face of all these hooks the NFI fell to +3, clearly on a plunging trend.

There is almost always a major news hook that also comes into play, I said. I predicted that we would soon hear some great piece of encouraging news that would prove to be the final piece of bait to hook all the suckers just before the market began to plunge (this turned out to be the Camp David peace agreement).

There was a legion of skeptics in the audience. One was a man who rose to counter my bearish forecast. He boasted that he had bought September calls on IBM for 280. He was referring to an option contract that gave him the right, on September 22, to purchase IBM stock at $280 a share regardless of the current price. With eleven days to go, IBM stood at $304 and this bagholder was confident of a fantastic profit.

"I promise you," I said, "that on September 22 those IBM calls at 280 will be worthless."

Another skeptic was the financial editor of one of the local newspapers. He derisively advised his readers to wait sixty days before they subscribed to my *Letter*, to see whether my unpopular market prediction came true.

My streak of successes had made me largely immune to such criticism by now, confident that time would prove me correct. Believing that I had given a superb performance, I wanted to celebrate. This was the night that Tiger Fleming took me across the street from the Hyatt ballroom to the Red Garter, where I performed so memorably with Fifi.

My business took off as a result of all my shows despite the warnings of my critics. Occasionally, however, ghosts of the lean years came back to plague me. I was scheduled to present two seminars at the Barbizon Plaza Hotel in New York on September 28. These were advertised in *Barron's* as Granville's triumphant return to New York. Suddenly the state attorney general's office intervened, noting that for several years I had failed to pay the required $100 annual fee for selling my *Letter* to New Yorkers. They called me in for a hearing to show cause why my license should not be suspended.

During the years in question, I had had little or no money to pay these fees, and no one had raised the issue until I became visible and controversial. I combed my subscription list for the names of attorneys. At the appointed hour I appeared before the attorney general with fourteen loyal defense attorneys, all supporting my case free of charge. After little debate, the attorney general was convinced that I was a bona fide market analyst and reinstated me as soon as I paid the back fees.

Money was no longer a problem. My bank balance increased with each successful prediction. New orders came in from Indianapolis when, on September 22, IBM dropped below 280, fulfilling the dramatic forecast I had made.

The best was yet to come. October 11 found the Dow edging back up over the 900 level amid continuing cries of euphoria from Wall Street and the financial press. That day found me scurrying from California to Kansas City for the 100th anniversary of the brokerage house of B.C. Christopher and Company. I took the opportunity, with the Dow threatening a new high, to forecast an "October massacre" that brought me a considerable amount of scornful press.

The Dow dropped four points the next day, then jumped ahead a single point to close out the week at 897.09. Meanwhile, I headed back to California where I had seminars scheduled for Tuesday, Wednesday, and Thursday.

On Monday the Dow dropped 22 points.

On Tuesday, as I spoke at a luncheon of the Technical Securities Analysts Association of San Francisco, the Dow dropped 9 more points.

On Wednesday, as I gave a two-hour performance at the Registry Hotel in Irvine, the Dow dropped 6 more points.

On Thursday, the Dow dropped 14 more points to complete a 55-point loss since my prediction, one week earlier, of an October massacre. My old friends at E.F. Hutton had signed me up for a seminar that night at the Holiday Inn in Westwood, and all day long they ran spots on the Los Angeles television stations promoting the appearance of the man who had called the October massacre.

Two thousand people attempted to crowd into a ballroom that seated 600. Latecomers were jammed into a rowdy mass outside the door. The question on everyone's mind was, How had I been able to call the October massacre when everyone else was bullish?

"If you want to know anything about the market," I said, "you study the market. You are not going to get the answer from any newspaper or stockbroker, or from any other source. If you are hurting in this market, ask yourself honestly who contributed to your dilemma. One thing I am positive about. You can't blame it on the market.

"The market is the best friend you ever had. It, and it alone, is the only source that can give you the right information. All other sources mislead you.

"But are those sources going to give you your money back? Of course not. Only the market can give you your money back."

Just as I warmed to my subject, I noticed three uniformed firemen pushing their way to the front. One of them came onstage, grabbed the microphone out of my hand and announced that we were breaking the local fire code and the crowded ballroom would be cleared immediately.

The main entranceway was clogged with people still trying to get in, and a near-riot ensued as the firemen herded the audience out through a back door into an alley.

Caught in the crowd, I found myself jostled outside also, where I was bombarded with questions.

"I subscribe to a technical analysis service," one man shouted. "How come they didn't call this market right?"

"Millions of people play the piano," I replied. "And they are all looking at the same music. Most play very poorly, some play fairly well, some are quite accomplished. But there are very few virtuosos."

This impromptu seminar in the alley lasted for several minutes until someone announced that the ballroom had been rearranged with the proper limited number of seats. This started a fresh stampede back inside. Meanwhile, someone opened the main doors and more investors elbowed their way in. The two groups collided with cursing and shouting, but somehow the authorities managed to close the doors when the limit of 600 people was reached. I continued my speech even though riotous sounds emanated from the disappointed horde outside.

I vowed that from now on I would exert more control on the

seminar planning. Reservations were required at future seminars and they were carefully limited to the proper numbers. If my market success continued—and I was sure it would—I could only get more popular.

The October massacre heated up. The NFI fell to −1 and −8 in successive weeks, the Dow following it right on down to 806.05.

All around the country, bagholders were singing the blues, particularly those who had followed the advice of the Indianapolis financial editor to wait six weeks to see if I was correct.

Whenever there is such a precipitous drop in the market it results in an onslaught of margin calls. For example, if you buy $1,000 worth of stock on a 50-percent margin you need only put up $500. The broker will loan you the rest since he holds your stock in his vault for collateral. But if the bottom falls out of your stock it lowers the value of your collateral and the broker must force you to put up more money. If you don't he will sell your stock.

This results in a vicious circle. Investors receiving margin calls must often sell out, adding to the downside pressure, increasing the velocity of the slide, and creating still more margin calls.

October 1978 found most brokerage houses issuing thousands of margin calls to their clients, but there was a notable exception. Jack Arnold of Arnold Securities told me he had to issue only one margin call and that was to a client who refused to sell out Eastern Airlines even after Jack mailed him a copy of my August 22 *Letter.* The reason that the rest of Jack's clients were safe was that he advised them to follow me without question.

The October massacre was a lucrative event for my subscribers. Of the thirty-nine stocks I had recommended as short sales early in September, thirty-eight plunged, most of them dramatically. The Dow dropped well below the 800 level, kicking out the popular support for a bull market. Now everyone began to wonder just how far down we would go.

THE GRANVILLE MARKET LETTER
Volume XVI, Number 42   November 21, 1978
COVER SHORT SALES
Always remember that timing precedes *amplitude.* That means that *when* the market is telling me to cover short sales it is always done *regardless* of where the Dow Jones Industrial

Average happens to be. I never let *price* influence me, only market timing. The market is now telling me that *the time to cover short sales is at hand.*

The most telling evidence was that the NFI bottomed out at −11 on November 14, the very day that the Dow hit a new bear market low of 795.26. On each of the next three days the NFI gained one point to rise back up to −8. It was an early indication of a rally and I found several other confirming indicators. On the day of the Dow bottom the CLX scored a nonconfirmation of −14, three points higher than the −17 reading of one week earlier. The number of new individual stock lows bottomed at 583 on October 30, but was only at 139 on November 14. And Abe Cohen's Sentiment Index indicated that 55 percent of the advisory services had finally turned bearish.

I had no alternative but to advise my readers to cover all their short sales, having benefited from a 93-point drop in the Dow in only three months. Not quite ready to issue a complete buy signal, I recommended only one purchase. Bally Manufacturing, my favorite gambling stock, was poised to move upward once again. Early in the year I had recommended purchasing Bally at 20⅝, advising its sale six months later at 43¼.

It had continued to rise for a short time after that and my subscribers had to console themselves with the wisdom of Jesse Livermore who, when asked how he made a fortune in the stock market, replied, "I always make the mistake of selling too early."

Once Bally had risen to 57 I recommended it as a short sale on September 6. Now at 33⅞, I advised my subscribers to cover the short for a 45-percent profit in less than three months and once again buy the stock. "We capitalized on Bally all the way up and all the way down," I said. "Now we are ready to catch the upmove again."

To some of my readers it appeared that I had turned on a dime, moving from 100 percent bearish to 100 percent bullish at a moment's notice. There was some truth to the argument, because I do believe in playing the market all the way—whichever way that happens to be at the moment. But I had indicated all along that the Dow would probably turn upward late in 1978 or early 1979, and when the evidence was clear, I had no choice but to follow the market.

My readers received the word several days after the market gave its signal, since there was a natural time lag in writing, printing, and mailing my *Letter*.

But, as my following increased, more and more of my subscribers pleaded for faster notice. This gave rise to the Granville Early Warning Service. For an additional $500 per year a subscriber could now receive immediate telegraphic warning of my major market signals. Hundreds of people signed up immediately and one of my first bits of advice telegraphed to them was to plunge once again into the gambling stocks. Those who did so immediately earned far more than the cost of their subscription.

Less than one week after my buy signal, I staged a seminar in Fort Lauderdale sponsored by Shearson Hayden Stone.

Here I related a story that became a basic part of my repertoire. It detailed my meeting the previous year with a famous economist, a future high government official.

We had a chance to spend some time alone together, and he asked me to explain my theory of market forecasting. As it happened, we were in a conference room where there was a blackboard. So I took him over to the blackboard to illustrate to him what the stock market is. Because he was an economist, I remembered to speak in only the simplest language. I picked up a piece of chalk, showed it to him and said, "This is a piece of chalk."

"Oh," he said.

Then I took the chalk and rubbed a tiny spot onto the center of the blackboard. "That spot," I said, "is the market."

He said, "Oh."

Then I drew a huge circle that covered the entire blackboard, centered on the tiny dot. "Now out here on the edges of the circle, far away from the market, are lots of things," I said. I drew a small X-mark on the perimeter. "These are interest rates." I drew more X-marks. "These are things like the unemployment rate, the Gross National Product, company earnings and dividends, the national debt, housing starts, and auto sales."

"Oh, oh, oh," he said.

"These are all the things that economists study," I said, "but do you see how far away they are from the market? Ecnomists only see these things on the outside of the circle. They never see the dot in the center that is the market."

"Oh," he said, staring at all the X-marks on the perimeter of the circle. I left him alone in the room then, and I don't think he has spotted the market yet.

Dick Loftus from Blair, Nebraska, helped me introduce and promote the new Granville Chart and Cassette Service. Every three months a subscriber to this service received a large wall chart that depicted the progress of the Dow, the NFI, and the CLX, with space for him to fill in new figures for the next three months. Included was a one-hour tape cassette with my analysis of market action during the previous quarter.

All told, the *Granville Market Letter* grossed $500,000 in 1978.

After a seminar in Memphis on December 12 I flew to Atlanta, seated next to a Connecticut man who supervised an investment group. He asked me what to buy. "Put as much money as you can into Bally Manufacturing," I told him.

The market lagged behind my bullish prediction well into the early months of 1979, hooking the bagholders into selling more and more of their stock at bargain prices. The Dow fluctuated between 795 and 840. A new Harris Survey reported that 62 percent of all Americans felt that a recession was on the way. The Shah was deposed and Iran was thrown into turmoil. No one seemed to know what would happen to oil prices.

Still the Dow hovered, and most people thought that nothing happened in the market. Most people, of course, are losers. Bally Manufacturing doubled its price in these months. Resorts International went from 31⅞ to 51⅜. All the gambling stocks showed spectacular gains and none of my subscribers complained that the Dow remained flat.

The technical indicators pointed strongly upward despite the lagging Dow. I was so confident that, on February 27, speaking to the Chicago Board of Trade Option Market Makers, I predicted that the Dow would rise to 950 by May 1. Market maker Kenny Weiss replied, "If it does, I'll kiss your ass in downtown Chicago." We made it a formal bet.

Early in March I was invited to be one of the speakers at a

three-day Investment Strategy Seminar at the Fountainebleau Hilton in Miami. The podium was full of fundamentalists and the audience was packed with bagholders. The fundamentalist speakers spread a predictable doctrine of gloom and doom. Bob Bleiberg, the editor of *Barron's,* recommended to one and all that for a thorough understanding of the stock market they must read the bible of the industry, Graham & Dodd's *Fundamental Analysis.*

"For a thorough understanding of the stock market," I yelled when it was my turn to speak, "I recommend that you do *not* read Graham & Dodd's *Fundamental Analysis.* "

The biggest laugh came from my good friend Dick Graham, a nephew of Benjamin Graham, one of the co-authors of the fundamental bible. Dick had by that time renounced fundamentalist theory altogether and was a pure technician.

During one point in the panel discussion Louis Rukeyser, the host of Public Television's *Wall Street Week,* asked me for a prediction on gold prices for the following year.

"What has that got to do with the market?" I shot back. Then I told the story of the circle, the dot, and the *X*s, concluding that the price of gold has "NOTHING!" to do with the stock market.

Ralph Goldman, the sponsor of the event, thought enough of my speech to ask me to host the formal banquet that night, where the honored guest was to be Republican presidential hopeful Ronald Reagan. Louis Rukeyser introduced me to the evening crowd and I spent several minutes entertaining on the piano. To the accompaniment of bawdy music I told the story of how Fifi and I won the 1978 Red Garter Star Performers' Award in Indianapolis. "So you see," I concluded, "everything is on record. Joe Granville hides nothing from the world."

Reagan doubled up with laughter.

Jack Arnold and D. L. Smith met me in Palm Springs, California, for a needed vacation and we found ourselves in an informal golf tournament. As luck would have it, I played way over my head and sank a sixty-foot putt on the eighteenth hole to win the match.

Afterward in the bar we shared drinks with the club pro. Jokingly I asked him how I could get into the Bob Hope Desert Classic.

"Simple," he replied. "Just contribute five thousands dollars to the Eisenhower Medical Center and prove that you have an eighteen handicap."

I could come up with the money, but the eighteen handicap was well out of my range and, for the moment, I dismissed the idea.

A few days later, back in Holly Hill, my secretary brought me a letter from the investment manager in Connecticut to whom I had recommended Bally Manufacturing while sharing a flight to Atlanta. The quick bit of advice had more than doubled his money and he wanted to show his gratitude. A check for $5,000 was included in the letter.

I called him immediately and told him that I could not accept cash for my advice. My critics would roast me. "But there is one thing you could do," I said. "If you rewrite the check to the Eisenhower Medical Center, you will put me into the Bob Hope Desert Classic."

He loved the idea. I temporarily forgot about the requirement of the eighteen handicap.

While in Palm Springs I had met a sexy lady astrologer. On my way to a seminar in Honolulu I stopped off to spend a few days with her. She met my plane and drove me to her home, where I lay down on the sofa for a nap before taking her out to dinner. I was so exhausted from my schedule that I slept for seven hours. By the time I awoke it was too late to go out. So we ate at home and talked into the wee hours about astrology. She informed me that the stars predicted a new spate of earthquakes in California.

The next day we drove out to a quaint club in the desert where I found a piano to clown around with for a few hours. My friend bought me a gold charm on a long chain and told me that if I wore it around my neck it would bring me luck.

For the Honolulu show I wore a white suit with white shoes. With the gold medallion dangling from my neck I looked like a maharajah. My message to these investors was simple. "Gambling and oils, oils and gambling."

I reported on the trip in my March 20 *Letter*, one which shows evidence that the combination of elation and exhaustion was beginning to wear at my senses:

Nursing my failing voice, I spent two days in the California desert with my astrologer before taking the last leg of the trip to the islands. This is all necessary because I have to be absolutely sure that I can keep my date with destiny in Chicago on or about May 1st, the Dow reaching 950 by the appointed time. I have the technical evidence. I was simply seeking other confirmations from diverse sources. One of those sources was supplied by my good friend Jahleel Woodbridge who had sent me my own personal biorhythm chart prior to the Kenny Weiss Challenge. That chart showed my super highs occurring during the last week of April. Nothing else could bring me to a level of elation at that time other than Dow 950, so I had to conclude from that source that the target will be hit on schedule. My astrologer tells me that I can do no wrong and so I now have my triple confirmation; the technical, my biorhythm, and the stars. So, my dear people, *continue to accumulate stocks.* Traffic will be stopped on the corner of State and Madison in downtown Chicago on May 1st as Kenny Weiss does what has so effectively been foreordained. A reenactment on *Wall Street Week* might be planned, so don't go away.

As might be expected, my critics railed at me for the above harangue. What has astrology got to do with the stock market? My answer would be: more than interest rates, the price of gold, and all the economic reports ever to gush forth from the Wharton School of Business.

But let's make two things clear. Yes, I believe in astrology. So did Kepler. So did Shakespeare, Einstein, and many others.

And no, I do not base my market forecasts upon astrology. If I see astrological evidence that confirms my technical analysis, I am intrigued. But my market forecasts are based upon the market and only the market.

Houston, Austin, Dallas, and Kansas City followed in quick succession. At the Aztec Inn in Tucson I was inspired with an idea for my most unique entrance ever. To get to the ballroom where the show was held I had to walk around the swimming pool and enter a side door near the stage. I hired workmen to paint a long plank light green and install it across the width of the pool at water level. From the ballroom at night the plank was invisible. At the appointed hour the lights dimmed in the ballroom so that the pool outside shone with attention-getting briliance. Dressed in a sparkling white suit I emerged from behind a palm tree and strolled slowly toward the ballroom, and approached the microphone, declaring in a steady, calm voice, "And now you know!"

Berkeley, Palo Alto, Newport Beach, Santa Barbara, and Los Angeles were next on my itinerary. The crowds grew larger, often numbering in the thousands.

At one of the California stops I was interviewed by a newspaper financial editor. Reviewing some of my past successes, I mentioned profits my subscribers had made by going short on selected stocks. I grew suspicious when the editor stopped taking notes.

"What is a short sale?" I asked him suddenly.

"I don't know," he confessed.

I terminated the interview immediately. Later I learned that he had been promoted to the financial section ten months earlier after reporting on the bowling scores for the sports pages.

A few days later I was in Minneapolis for a state securities examination. After the test at the University of Minnesota I had a seminar twenty minutes later, barely having time to dress and get on stage. The seminar began six minutes late and I told my audience they could blame the commissioner of securities and the state for questioning my ability in this business and requiring me to take a test that was totally irrelevant.

"While I was cramming for this test I learned that a bank trust officer can do just about anything he wants to with *your* money," I said. "How archaic some of our laws are! People like me have to be tightly regulated but bank trust officers and newspaper financial editors are not subjected to examinations by the state. [Journalists] are the very people who should be more closely regulated. They have caused untold damage with their reporting. If they had to be financially responsible for the losses they have caused their readers, they would sure think twice before they wrote such damaging stories."

More and more people recognized me at airports and frequently asked why my luggage, a gift from Jack Arnold, proclaimed JOSEPH E. GRANVILLE—NOT US.

"It means," I replied, "that you will never catch us holding the bag."

Wherever I went, someone wanted a prognostication about his favorite stock. On a call-in radio show in San Francisco one man wanted to know if I thought Bally Manufacturing and Caesar's World were going to drop in price.

"All those gambling stocks will continue to skyrocket," I said. "Why do you want them to go down?"

"I'm short in both stocks," he lamented.

"Who would do a terrible thing like that to you?" I asked.

"My broker."

Then I gave him my standard advice, freely dispensed to all proven bagholders. "Change brokers," I said.

In Tucson a man rushed up to me and asked me what Scott Paper was going to do in the next two weeks. That sort of question comes from an options player. I have always stressed that I do not make recommendations on stock options. Those are quick-turnover, high-risk gambles that can rise or fall dramatically in days. They often bear no relationship to the clear, longer-term market trends.

"Scott Paper," I told him, "is going to perform its normal function on you and wipe you out."

May 1 came and went with the Dow at 855.51, nearly 100 points beneath the prediction that would have forced Kenny Weiss to make a portion of my anatomy celebrated in Chicago. I shrugged that one off. You can't always be right in the short term.

May 18 found me on *Wall Street Week* for the first time. The first question fired at me by Louis Rukeyser was what happened to my prediction of Dow 950 by May 1?

"Projections do not make you money," I replied. "The important point is not that the Dow is 100 points below my May 1 projection, but that it is 56 points above the bottom, the point when I told my readers to buy stocks. We put people into the market at important bottoms and take them out at important tops."

After a meandering conversation, he tried to catch me with another tack. "Joe, how could you be short on Bally Manufacturing at 40 and like it at 70?"

"Those were two different markets," I answered. "I first recommended Bally at 16 on March 8, 1978, while doing a seminar at the

Holiday Inn in Westwood, California. My talk was tape recorded and thoroughly documented. I also recommended all the other gambling stocks at that time. We carried those stocks all the way up to late August 1978, selling out a few days before the market peak of September 8th. I then recommended them all as short sales. On the way down we were still short on Bally and covered it at 33⅞. I then called the immediate purchase of Bally. Now it's at 70 and I still like it because I think it's going up to 100. The point is, we play the market on both sides. When the market tells us it is going up, we are long in stocks. When the market tells us it is going down, we are short in stocks."

A champion of the conservative Wall Street philosophies that are also so dear to the hearts of bagholders, Rukeyser enjoys getting a guest to stick his neck out. Later, if the prediction fails, Rukeyser invites the victim back to the show and challenges him to defend his error. As a show host, he enjoys the comparative luxury of not having to stick out his own neck.

But life goes on. Louis Rukeyser will continue to have a successful show and I will continue to succeed at making money for my subscribers.

My astrologer had piqued my curiosity about the future of that portion of California that lies west of the San Andreas fault. I obtained a chart that depicted the Richter Scale readings of recent California quakes and found an interesting pattern. Always looking for publicity, I used this material during an August 2 press conference in Philadelphia, prior to a pair of seminars in Cherry Hill, New Jersey. It started me off on a quick flurry of dramatic predictions.

At the press conference I explained that I read the Richter Scale chart just like a stock market chart. "I predict a near-term upside breakout on the Richter Scale chart," I said. I was widely quoted in the newspapers by derisive writers. Four days later on August 6, northern California suffered its most severe earthquake in twenty years.

On August 7 I was a guest on the Frank Ford radio talk show, which began at 9:00 A.M., an hour before the market opened. "What will the Dow Jones Industrial Average do today?" Frank asked me.

"It will close up more than ten points," I replied. That day the Dow closed up 11.26, one of its best recent rallies.

On the next night, August 8, the Cherry Hill Inn was packed full of listeners. One of them asked, "Will the government come to the aid of Chrysler and save them from bankruptcy?"

"Do your homework," I said. "Every time Chrysler has been threatened with bankruptcy the stock has been a good buy."

The very next day the government announced that it would bail out Chrysler and the stock closed up sharply.

That night, August 9, a questioner in another packed audience asked me what the market would do the next day.

"It will have a very strong closing," I said.

The next morning the Dow opened down 5 points and hovered in negative territory most of the day. But a late afternoon rally pushed it up 8.78 points on the day.

Some of the press dubbed my performance "The Philadelphia Miracle." It was no miracle, however. Nor was it a succession of lucky guesses. It was a triumph of pure technical analysis.

That success brought increased enrollment for the First Granville Cruise, scheduled to leave Miami on August 24 to journey to the Bahamas, during which time I would explain my full theories to the participants. This turned into a disaster, however, when the travel agent absconded with our deposit money and failed to reserve a ship for us. My staff and I scrambled to arrange private plane rides and hotel suites for everyone in the Bahamas. We finally pulled off the seminars, but they were exhausting.

One particularly good thing came out of this fiasco. I had a long breakfast with Wayne Shapiro, director of the options trading department for the First of Michigan brokerage house in Detroit. We became fast friends. Since then Wayne has been my source for daily market information, giving me the pertinent statistics over the telephone about fifteen minutes after the closing, no matter where I happen to be.

Wayne mentioned his friendship with Dr. Ed Thorp, the head of the mathematics department at the University of California at Irvine who years earlier had devised the card-counting method for winning at blackjack. Ed was so successful at it that he was forever banned from all casinos; so he wrote a book about his system that has caused many casinos to change their procedures, using multiple decks to throw off the calculations of the card counters.

I told Wayne that I would love to meet Ed Thorp some day.

By late September the Dow had climbed into the 880s and the wisdom of my November buy signal was fully apparent. There were some very strong technical indicators at work to push the market higher, but also a few warning signs. In particular the NFI had dropped from +14 to +6. It showed signs of rising back up, but I knew it needed close attention.

This was a difficult assignment. I wrote my September 21 *Letter* a few days early, for I was due in London for a seminar on the 18th. At the end of the *Letter* I advised my subscribers that I would skip the next week's issue. "If there is any important change in the market, we would of course put out a letter to let you know," I concluded.

Immediately I left Florida for a flight to New York, where I caught the Concorde to London. On September 18 I presented a public seminar sponsored by Bache Halsey Stuart Shields, and bemoaned the fact that the London Stock Exchange does not list *volume* data on its transactions. It merely reports the current prices of stocks. It is impossible to apply On-Balance Volume to the London Stock Market, so I advised British investors to put their money into the U.S. market where they could get a clear picture of the action.

Later that day I spoke to a smaller group of Arabian sheiks and other high-powered investors at the Bache office, and checked the reports coming in from the U.S., where the Dow had dropped 7 points to close at 874.15. I did my "homework" right there in the office and fretted when I saw the NFI drop to +2.

The Dow regained two points the following day, Wednesday, and on Thursday shot up 17 points to a new bull market high of 893.69. The NFI stood only at +4, the CLX at +14.

On Friday I was at the Bache office in Geneva, where I spoke to another select group of clients, keeping one eye on the U.S. market. The Dow opened up strongly and continued its rise throughout the first half of the session. It gave back all the gains in the afternoon, however, scoring a paltry rise of 0.25 for the day. The closing figure of 893.94 was the second consecutive rally high. But the NFI remained at a disappointing +4 and the CLX *dropped* to +9.

That was enough for me. I got on the phone to my office.

GRANVILLE EARLY WARNING #16 SEPTEMBER 23, 1979 (DOW 893.94) INTERMEDIATE TOP AT HAND. STOP ALL NEW BUYING. TAKE PROFITS ON ALL RECENT SHARP GAINS. BEST LOOKING SHORT CANDIDATES ARE: AMERICAN CHARTER COMPANY, HONEYWELL AND LEVI STRAUSS.

It was a new market, one now oriented to the downside. My subscribers had benefited from a climb of 89.89 points in the Dow, and now it was time to play the game in reverse. My scoresheet of recommended stocks was led by the gambling issues, in particular Bally Manufacturing and Resorts International, both of which had more than doubled in value.

Since I was known as the Father of the Gambling Stocks it was only natural that I was invited to give a show September 27 at the Superstar Theatre at Resorts International Hotel and Casino in Atlantic City. The theater was filled with 1,800 people and hundreds more had to be turned away, the stock market being an even more popular form of gambling than blackjack.

During the intermission I was backstage fortifying myself with a supply of vodka and tonic when the casino's chief of security approached me with a worried expression. He told me that the switchboard operators had reported a persistent caller who wanted to know my exit route from the casino, my flight number out of Atlantic City, and various personal details.

That knowledge toned down my second-half performance a bit that night. I have always been controversial, but more enemies tend to surface when I turn bearish. So many people still believe that up is good and down is bad; they are brainwashed into believing that a prediction of a falling stock market is un-American.

After my show an armed guard escorted me up to my VIP suite and stood watch in the hall all night. The following day a guard drove me to the Philadelphia airport for a flight to Dallas. There, another armed escort whisked me off to a top-floor suite at the Loews Anatole Hotel. Fifteen minutes later the chief of police arrived with two plainclothes detectives to arrange security precautions for the weekend.

They had more than Granville to worry about. I was in Dallas for an Investment Strategy Seminar featuring Morgan Maxfield, an

investment advisor from Kansas City; famed doomsayer Howard
Ruff; Bob Bleiberg, editor of *Barron's;* Louis Rukeyser; my friend
Paul Erdman, author of *The Crash of '79;* pollster George Gallup,
Jr.; Dr. Edward Teller, father of the H-bomb; and the man who was
by then the serious front-running Republican presidential candidate,
Ronald Reagan.

In addition to my participation in various seminars, I was to be
master of ceremonies for the evening banquet. Prior to that gala, at
a private reception, I was conversing with Dr. Teller and his wife
when he happened to say, "You know, anyone who flies as much as
you do is exposed to three times the radiation of the average person."

I mentioned that fact in my introductory remarks at the banquet.
"And now you know my secret of predicting the stock market," I
quipped.

Knowing that this was to be a major event, I had contracted with
a private firm to videotape the show for my own records. Accordingly, I played up to the four cameras they had operating. With Dr.
Teller on one side of me and Ronald Reagan on the other, I
launched into some of my more popular, humorous stock market
stories.

To illustrate a point about life and death I related the contrived
story of an old Humphrey Bogart movie.

"Bogie was in the death house at San Quentin for a murder he
did not commit," I began. "He was due to go to the gas chamber.
However, he knew who the real murderer was and he was determined to break out of the pen and catch up with the real murderer
and extract a confession from him and thus save his own neck. In
the movies it is easy to get out of San Quentin—the scene simply
changes."

To my right I heard a chuckle from Ronald Reagan, who knew
the truth in my statement.

"So then," I continued, "Bogie is on the outside and he catches
up with the real murderer. What he doesn't know is that the real
murderer is dying."

When I am speaking I get totally involved in my subject matter.
Stories come flying out of my mouth while my hands gesticulate
wildly to illustrate my words. Completely unaware of what I was
doing, I turned to my right, placed my hands around Ronald Reagan's neck and began to choke him.

"Bogie puts his hands around the neck of the murderer and, as he chokes him, the murderer tells Bogie that he is dying," I screamed, looking out at the audience, unaware that the next President of the United States was red-faced and gasping for air. I could feel his fingers clutching at my hands. I liked that; it added to the strength of the illustration.

"Bogie then says that famous line, 'If you die I'll kill you!' "

I released my grip on Reagan and continued with my speech, unaware until later how comical the scene was and how embarrassing it could be to a presidential candidate. I went to bed ecstatic that I had captured a moment like that on camera.

The next morning at breakfast the director of the television crew informed me that they had missed the scene. All four cameras, he said, had malfunctioned at the same time.

If you believe that one, I know thousands of stockbrokers who would love to talk to you.

Heady success had made me oblivious to a great truth. Nothing travels in a straight line. My personal fortunes had been on a meteoric rise for so long that I forgot that life, like the market, has a downside.

The Dow dropped a few points shortly after my sell signal, and my recommended short sales dropped an average of 4½ points in less than two weeks. The NFI skidded to zero. AND DOWN WE GO headlined my October 5 *Letter.*

In four more sessions the Dow lost 50 points to close at 849.32 on October 10. I could not imagine greater happiness. I completed a seminar that day in Atlanta and headed for home.

I found my son Blanchard waiting for me at the Daytona Beach Airport. From the look on his face I knew that something was horribly wrong.

11.
PSALMS

"Paul," Blanchard simply said.

Not Paul. Not my guitar-strumming, pot-smoking, meditating, searching son Paul. He deserved more than twenty-one years to find meaning to his life.

But it was true. He was found in the house that he shared with his roommate, a plastic bag tied around his head. I was speechless, shocked, saddened beyond tears. I would have traded all my triumphs for the opportunity to bring him back. But he was gone. The finality of it crushed me.

Somehow the coroner managed to rule Paul's death a suicide, a determination that I will never accept. Paul had his problems, but he also had a curiosity about life that would never allow him to surrender. Polly and I later learned that on the day of his death Paul had a vociferous argument with one of his friends, but the coroner refused to reopen the case.

It was a broker, as he drove me to the airport after a show, who quoted to me from Isaiah: "God's ways are not man's ways."

Paul's death played upon my mind, turning me philosophical. It was a blessing that I had a busy travel schedule in the weeks following the tragedy. One can find solace by plunging into work.

All over the country friends came up after speeches to offer their condolences. Friends are nice to have when the times are fun and easy, but they are more important when deep sadness strikes. That has been the greatest boon to my wanderings—the chance to cement so many fine friendships.

But now I was ever more conscious of the fact that I was alone. That one *special* friend was not in my life. There was no one with whom I could really share the pain of Paul's death.

I could only hope that my son had found peace in his new plane of existence. Still, I was plagued with the question, Why?

"God's ways are not man's ways."

There it was. We cannot know Why but we can accept the fact that personal tragedy is a necessary part of a great Plan. I turned to the pages of the Bible for solace, mourning like David: "O my son Absalom, O Absalom, my son, my son!"

A wealth of stock market analogies leaped out at me from the Bible. For two decades I had been a voice crying in the financial wilderness, warning of the institutionalized duplicity that is rampant on Wall Street. There is a legion of brokers and analysts who misguide the public out of their own ignorance. They mean well, and there is always hope that they can be converted to technical analysis. But what concerned me more was the core of Wall Street power mongers who deliberately and intentionally preach false doctrine, lie to the public, and manipulate the market with the clear aim of bilking the gullible out of their money.

"God's ways are not man's ways," Isaiah had proclaimed. It was ever clearer to me that the only way to beat Wall Street at its own game was to act opposite to the dictates of human nature. Wall Street was the epitome of human nature. The worst faults of humanity were basic to Wall Street. If the market was the opposite of Wall Street, I reasoned, then the market followed God's ways. It followed the natural harmonies created by the Supreme Composer.

Bible stories and quotations found their way into my speeches. One of my favorites came from the book of Mark. It was about the wise man who built his house on rock and the foolish man who built his house on sand. The rock of the market was technical analysis; the sand was fundamental analysis.

To me, Matthew 6:23,24 was a statement to those who would mislead the public in order to gain great profits:

But if thine eye be evil, thy whole body shall be full of darkness. If therefore the light that is in thee be darkness, how great is that darkness! No man can serve two masters, for either he will hate the one, and love the other; or else he will hold to the one and despise the other. Ye cannot serve God and mammon.

Advice to the investor fed up with the dubious wisdom of Wall Street came from Matthew 5:29.

And if thy right eye offend thee, pluck it out and cast it from thee; for it is profitable for thee that one of thy members should perish, and not that thy whole body should be cast into hell.

Reporters began referring to me as the stock market evangelist, the preacher, the prophet of profits, St. Joseph. The degree of popular misunderstanding of the stock market appalled me and I burned with a greater desire than ever to clear the beguiling money-changers out of the temple.

The audience picked up the cue, and often asked me questions about religion. One of the most frequent was "What denomination are you?"

"Have you ever tried to drink the label on a bottle of wine?" was my reply. "It doesn't taste very good, does it? It is what is in the bottle that counts. What is in my bottle is called *truth* and you can put any label on it that you want to."

Ever since the security scare in Atlantic City I had paid more attention to the faces in my audience. Paul's death magnified my personal caution. I was not—am not—afraid to die. I believe death is merely a doorway to another existence. But neither do I believe in flaunting one's luck.

My concern deepened when I noticed the same man in the audience at different seminars around the country. I watched nervously when he finally approached me after one speech.

"Mr. Granville," he said, "I've been following you around."

"I know," I said. "Why?"

"I have a monetary stake in keeping you alive. I'm worried about you. You smoke too much. You smoke constantly on stage. It is imperative that you give up smoking. I'm a doctor and I know what I'm talking about."

I saw that his right hand shook when he spoke, as if affected with palsy. Suddenly I knew what his problem was. "You're an options player, right?" I asked.

"Yes."

"That's why your right hand is always shaking." I pulled a pack of Marlboros out of my pocket and pointed to the warning: The Surgeon General Has Determined That Cigarette Smoking Is Dangerous to Your Health. "The Surgeon General missed a bet," I said. "I have determined that more people die every year from option trading than from cigarette smoking. Worry kills more people than anything else."

I told him the story about Sir Winston Churchill's being warned by thirty-four different doctors that if he did not give up his awful habit of starting each day with a glass of cognac and a big, black, ugly-smelling Italian stogie, it would kill him. In fact, I said, Sir Winston outlived thirty-one of those thirty-four doctors until his disgusting habits killed him at the age of ninety-one.

The doctor walked away from me shaking his head in disapproval. I doubted that he would ever be able to kick his own dangerous habit of playing options.

Life goes on for the living. I played Houston, New Orleans, Chicago, and Los Angeles in quick succession and the market seemed to be moving faster than I was. By October 19, less than one month after my sell signal, the Dow had plunged 85 points. My short sale recommendations were instant winners. The NFI dropped to −12 and it all happened so quickly that it made bears out of everyone!

I put my subscribers on hold for two weeks. It was too soon to buy, too late to sell short. The NFI remained at −12 for eleven straight days as the Dow churned in the low 800s and terrorists took over the U.S. embassy in Tehran and initiated the long hostage crisis that threatened to spur global war. The Detroit auto makers reported declining sales, General Motors trimmed its dividend, and the prime rate rose to an astronomical 15.5 percent. What a perfect time to buy stocks.

The technical indicators performed beautifully. The NFI dropped to −20, on the surface a very bearish omen, but this extremely negative figure is about as low as the NFI has ever plunged. It had to be the bottom, because it could go no lower. The CLX scored an apparently bearish −21 reading, but for the very same reason that figure was bullish. The market was telling me that it was oversold and had to rise from this point. How high and how long did not concern me.

The new Dow low of 796.67 on November 7 was nonconfirmed by the Dow Transports and Utilities and the Standard & Poor 500. Abe Cohen's Sentiment Index showed that a majority of analysts had turned bearish. The number of individual lows on November 7 was only 156, far less than the 344 scored on October 22. Taken as a whole, it was a classic buy signal from the market.

"Now the psychology among the majority has shifted," I warned an audience in Portland, Oregon, on November 7. "We've had a 92-point decline and that has produced a whole new generation of bears and you hear projections of Dow 650 by Christmas. You can bet your life that won't happen. On the contrary, the market could be rallying like hell by Christmas. Rather than preparing for a horrendous plunge now, the market will undergo one final decline this year and the big buy signal will probably occur this month. A new low is almost certain to be accompanied by a very obvious piece of bearish news. I don't know what shape or form it will take but it will certainly grab the headline. So, expect one final horror story."

A man in the audience asked, "How close are we to the bottom?"

"Damn close," I replied.

To say anything more would be to rob the pockets of the people who paid me $500 a year for the Granville Early Warning Service. Even as I spoke, my office was sending out the telegrams:

GRANVILLE EARLY WARNING #17 NOVEMBER 7, 1979 (DOW 796.67) COVER ALL SHORT SALES. THE MARKET HAS TURNED BULLISH. BEST LOOKING BUYS ARE IN THE GAMBLING STOCKS, ESPECIALLY BALLY. MORE INFORMATION WILL BE IN THE NEXT MARKET LETTER.

Over the next weeks the news grew steadily worse. The hostage crisis appeared to be settling in for a long stay. The final piece of horrible news that I had predicted was the Russian invasion of Afghanistan. There were additional terrorist outbreaks in Saudi Arabia and Pakistan. Housing starts plummeted. But on November 21 the market gave the lie to all this bearish news. In the morning it broke under the November 7 low but rallied sharply in the afternoon to close at 807.42. The NFI rose quickly off its bottom to −11.

"How marvelous is the language of the market!" I proclaimed in my *Letter* of November 30.

I was so sure of success that I raised the subscription price of the *Letter* to $250 a year, a pittance in the face of the profits my readers earned.

Nowhere in America, at this time, was there more gloom than in Detroit. Economists always watch Motown carefully—it is one of their favorite X-marks on the perimeter of the circle that is so distant from the market—believing that Detroit always leads the economy into and out of recession. I was in Detroit on December 6 when the Chrysler Corporation announced that it was going to close its Dodge main plant. The Dow stood at 828.41 and Chrysler stock was 5⅞. Chrysler faced imminent bankruptcy.

But I knew differently. The OBV figures for Chrysler stock showed that it had recently moved into a rising field trend. Someone, somewhere, knew something. They were exploiting the bad news to accumulate Chrysler stock at a depressed price.

The general market situation was rapidly improving also. The NFI continued to skyrocket, reaching zero; it was a full 20 points higher than it had been one month earlier.

Armed with this evidence, I appeared on a local television show that morning, held up a newspaper headlining the close of the Dodge main plant, and proclaimed, "I bet my *life* that Chrysler will be saved!" No one believed me.

Within two weeks Congress passed and President Carter signed emergency legislation to keep Chrysler in business. The stock soared as the most active issue of the day and I received a grateful letter from Chrysler chairman Lee Iacocca congratulating me on the courage to make the prediction.

It continually amazed me that everyone was so surprised at the accuracy of my forecasts. Years earlier I had published a complete theoretical description of my work. There were no secrets about On-Balance Volume. Everything was on record. By now I had spoken to many tens of thousands of people. I had appeared on television and radio dozens of times. Hundreds of newspaper and magazine articles detailed my theories. More than 10,000 people received my newsletter every week. Still, only a small minority actually believed and acted upon my theories. And only a small minority ever would. Winners are a very exclusive club.

One problem is the circle of resistance that lies between the investor and the market. The market says one thing but most market advisors say the opposite. Where the average investor clashes head on with this circle of resistance is when he talks to his broker. Most brokers will try their hardest to talk you out of following the market —because they are not following the market. If your broker tries to talk you out of following the market, then you need a new broker. It is that simple. Once you know how the game is played, a broker should become only an order taker, and nothing more.

The year ended on a high note. *The Granville Market Letter* multiplied its receipts fivefold in 1979, taking in $2.5 million.

With the Dow in the low 800s but the NFI climbing well into positive territory, I took a few weeks' respite from my show schedule to prepare for what I hoped would be one of the great events of my life. Mike O'Sullivan, the pro at Oceanside Country Club in Ormond Beach, tried to help me sharpen my golf game. It was a hopeless task, and I have to admit that Mike was generous in certifying the fact that I had an eighteen handicap.

For the enlightenment of the non-golfer, an eighteen handicap means that, on the average, you should be able to shoot eighteen over par. For example, on a par seventy-two golf course, your average score would be ninety. Double that handicap and you are in my territory.

Nevertheless, with a certified eighteen handicap in my pocket, I took off for Palm Springs, California, for my appearance in the Bob Hope Desert Classic, January 7–12, 1980.

This one is unique among golf tournaments. Three amateurs play as a group with one professional. The lowest score of any member of the foursome is the team score for any given hole. On the first day I played with pro Bob Mann at Bermuda Dunes Country Club.

Having partied into the wee hours the night before, I barely made it to the first tee on time. The loudspeaker was calling my name when I ran up. There was a large gallery even though the course was bathed in a cold drizzle. I shivered in my short-sleeved shirt as I teed up my ball.

I hit what is known in some golfing circles as an elephant's ass, meaning that it was high and it stunk. The ball went nearly straight up in the air and plopped down into the middle of the fairway about half as far as Bob Mann's beautiful drive. I thanked the stars that I had not shanked the ball into the gallery and set off down the fairway for my second shot. This went skidding off to the right, into the six-inch rough. At this point, knowing that my score would not be the lowest of the group on this first hole, I picked up my ball, muttering to the other players that my game was slightly off that day. Rain stopped us on the thirteenth hole and by then I had picked up my ball thirteen times.

I resolved to do better the second day at La Quinta Country Club. The pro in our group was John Schroeder. The weather was much improved, but not so my golf game. Again I found myself in the embarrassing position of picking up my ball long before we reached the green. But I did not abandon hope. I knew that I would enjoy a moment of glory sometime before the end of the tournament. I could feel Destiny, looking over my shoulder, telling me to keep my head down and my left arm straight.

My chance came on the final hole. The eighteenth was a long 400-yard par four. By some error of coordination I smacked a gorgeous drive straight down the middle of the fairway more than halfway to the green. I grabbed a three-wood for my second shot and this, too, went screaming straight down the fairway toward the center of the green. But then it lost steam and trickled into a sand trap. It was the first time in the tournament that I had come so close to the green in two shots.

Naturally there was a large gallery at this finishing hole, complete with television cameras. Bob Hope was there to watch the action. Spurred on, I strode toward the green with as triumphant a flourish as Palmer or Nicklaus. Schroeder's ball was on the green in two, looking good for a par. That meant that I could go for broke, trying to sink my bunker shot for a magnificent birdie three.

I called for my sand wedge. I stepped into the deep bunker, then walked up to the green and over to the flag, pacing off the distance.

A cameraman came over with a handheld TV camera and stepped into the pit with me. I waited until he focused in on my shot. Casually I took a few practice swings, almost cracking the cameraman on the head. Finally I was ready.

I was so excited about watching the trajectory of the shot that I lifted my head early, pulling up my arms. The wedge missed the sand completely, catching the ball sharply and sending it screaming on a line drive straight across the green at what seemed like the speed of light.

Cries of "Fore!" screamed out. Spectators hit the deck. The ball sped over their heads and crashed into the scorer's tent, missing his skull by inches.

Red-faced, I apologized to the scorer and let Schroeder finish out the hole for our team.

Later a man came up to me and told me he was a subscriber.

"I'm glad to see you're such a lousy golfer," he said. "If you were good I would assume that you were spending too much time on the golf course."

The average investor, being as bumbling with his money as I am with a seven iron, is too parochial in his choice of investment vehicles. When I am in Detroit, everyone wants to know about auto stocks. In Chicago they want to know about commodities. Gambling stocks head the list of interest in Atlantic City. In Los Angeles they want to know about the entertainment stocks. Investors must broaden their horizons; stocks do not know where they live. The important fact about a stock is not the physical location of the company; it is whether it is about to make a broad price swing in either direction.

Never did I see a greater example of this parochialism than in Toronto where I appeared on January 24. Gold! was all anyone wanted to talk about.

I was the original gold bug, as I mentioned earlier. I advised investing in the gold mining stocks way back in 1958, when the U.S. government had the price fixed at $35 an ounce and held it there for years to come. Once the artificial ceiling was lifted gold took off, as I had forecast. On the very day of this Toronto appearance gold broke to a new top at the astronomical price of $875 an ounce.

At the height of this euphoria I did five separate newspaper interviews, four local television shows, and a spot on the "CBS Evening News," always proclaiming the same message that I told the Toronto investors that night. I begged them to sell their gold at $875 an ounce. "Your gold," I proclaimed, "will turn to dross."

The very next day, with optimism at its pinnacle, the price of gold began to plunge. Bagholders, seeing modest drops in price, rushed in to buy after it was too late, yelling, "Give me that gold right at the top of its price!" Within weeks the price fell more than $300 an ounce.

The rise and fall of gold was an example of one of the simplest of all market mechanisms to spot and predict. Anyone who can read a price chart can (and a few others did) make the same prediction. The price chart of gold showed an unmistakable, drastic, parabolic curve.

There is nothing more dramatic than a parabolic curve. It rises from a flatbase, slowly at first, then ever more rapidly until the final burst of the explosion sends the price curve up at almost a ninety-degree angle. The profit potential on the upside of a parabolic curve is maximum—and also extremely dangerous. Timing is everything, for there is no gentle retreat from a parabolic curve. It graphically depicts a totally overbought position.

There is a simple human reason behind the fact that a parabolic rise cannot continue. The price of gold rose because there was far more demand than supply. As the price rose higher it became more and more profitable for various mining companies to actively seek more gold to feed the enormous demand. It was only a matter of time, then, before the greed of the suppliers outstripped the greed of the demanders. Suddenly there was a worldwide gold glut.

The big danger of jumping in near the end of a parabolic rise is that what goes up so fast comes down even faster. It takes two and a half hours to walk to the top of the Empire State Building but if you jump over the wall you will hit the pavement in eight and a half seconds.

After my buy signal on November 7 the Dow rose from 796.67 to 875.85 by January 31, allowing my subscribers to benefit from 79 upward points. Now, however, several indicators signaled caution.

First and foremost, the NFI, which rose from −20 to +6 on the general rally, fell back into minus territory and hovered around −6. This was coupled by lower rises in CLX readings whenever the Dow rose, and lower CLX readings whenever the Dow fell—a clear declining curve. This was not serious deterioration yet, but at least a short-term decline was indicated, and I would predict it to keep intact my record of near perfection that now stretched over the past five years. I called my office and that night the following telegram went out from Holly Hill:

GRANVILLE EARLY WARNING #18 JANUARY 31, 1980 (DOW 875.85) SHORT TERM TOP HAS OCCURRED. NO SPECIFIC SHORT SALES RECOMMENDED. 30 TO 60 POINT DECLINE POSSIBLE FROM TOP. TAKE PROFITS IN STOCKS WITH THE SHARPEST RUN UPS. HOLD ALL DEPRESSED STOCKS.

In my *Letter* of February 4 I explained to my readers:

This is NOT a major top or an important intermediate top. It is a point of upward interruption in a continuing bull market. The market breathes as you know, inhaling and exhaling. The technical indicators have said that this is the time for a normal exhalation.

And I was right, even though the market did not respond immediately. It inhaled another 28 points before its lungs burst and my short-selling subscribers cashed in on a 116-point drop in less than three months.

My seminar schedule was exhausting, but I thrived on it. The irony of it was that most of the seminars were sponsored by brokerage firms who hated my basic message. But after a seminar all a broker had to say was, "Granville loves it," and take the order.

Everywhere I went the crowds grew larger. I believe that much of this had to do with the energy I brought to a normally dull enterprise; but undoubtedly most of the reason behind my growing popularity was the simple and unmistakable fact that I was right. I had called the market with precision since the end of 1974 and along the way had astounded observers with accurate predictions of individual stocks, political changes, and widely divergent phenomena.

I was doing a radio show in Palm Beach, Florida, on February 25 when I predicted an imminent California earthquake. Later in that very hour our show was interrupted by an Associated Press bulletin of an earthquake in Southern California measuring 5.1 on the Richter Scale. It was the sixth time in the last six months that I had correctly predicted a California quake, and it was the sort of success that magnified my reputation.

The wisdom of playing both sides of the game was more and more apparent to my subscribers. Here is the complete scorecard of my recommended short sales between February 11, 1980, and March 31, 1980:

STOCK	SHORT-SALE PRICE	COVERED PRICE	PERCENT PROFIT
Allied Chemical	59.50	43.00	27.7
Amerada Hess	56.75	41.00	27.8
American South African	51.25	37.13	27.6
Asarco	52.63	26.00	50.6
Boeing	67.50	54.50	19.3
Burlington Northern	79.38	55.00	30.7
Cities Service	101.25	86.25	14.8
Exxon	64.13	55.38	13.6
Mesa Petroleum	68.13	45.38	33.4
Mobil	79.50	65.50	12.6
Natomas	44.13	32.00	27.5
Santa Fe Industries	66.50	55.25	16.9
Southern Pacific	45.13	32.88	27.1
Standard Oil of California	72.50	64.25	11.4
Texaco	38.88	33.00	15.1
Union Pacific	91.50	79.75	12.8

Once again this list assumes 100-percent cash coverage of the short sale. The worst investment on the list was Standard Oil of California, which produced 11.4 percent profit in thirty-nine days—

an annual rate of 106.7 percent. The best investment on the list, Asarco, produced a 50.6 percent return for an annualized rate of 473.6 percent. And the investor working on a 50-percent margin could earn double the rate of return. No wonder my subscribers were becoming fanatical.

As the crowds cheered me and the market followed my predictions, I began to feel invincible. But I was totally unprepared for what happened next.

On April Fool's Day, 1980, I came on stage in Indianapolis to the tune of my new theme song, "Bagholder Blues," especially recorded for me in Nashville. I wore a bagholder's apron, its pockets stuffed with all-day suckers for my friends, the bank trust officers, and I carried with me a ventriloquist's dummy to represent brokers who follow the advice of their fundamentalist research departments.

I felt especially good because I believed that the market might have bottomed out on March 27 and 28 and that a major buy signal was just around the corner.

I had only three weeks to wait. On April 19 I spoke at a meeting in Montreal on the same program with Alan Greenspan, an economic adviser to Ronald Reagan. He stated that we had entered upon a recession that was going to be much more severe and last much longer than most people thought. The next day I stopped off in Boston and bought a copy of *The New York Times*. The headline story reported that President Carter had publicly acknowledged that the U.S. was in a recession.

But the market did not care, so neither did I. On April 21 the Dow dropped to a bear market low of 759.13. On the same day, however, the NFI stood at −7, up a full 13 points since the March bottom. The CLX stood at −11, up 11 points since the March bottom. The new Dow low was further nonconfirmed by the Transportation Average, the New York Stock Exchange Composite Index, the Standard & Poor's 500, and the advance-decline line. Accordingly, telegrams went out that night:

GRANVILLE EARLY WARNING #19 APRIL 21, 1980 (DOW 759. 13) COVER YOUR SHORT SALES. MARKET TO TURN UP.

The market opened up sharply the next morning, a bit of a surprise to the fundamentalists who were locked into a recessionist thinking. As the Dow shot up steadily throughout the day various newsmen reported that the reason for the rally was Granville's buy signal. In that one day the Dow gained 30.72 points!

Suddenly I seemed to have the power to move the market on my own. I was proud of the influence my words now carried, but I had no illusions. The market would not have reacted so positively if it had not been poised to rise. Further, I knew that my influence could only be transitory. All my subscribers would have acted within one or two days of my signal. The rest would be up to the market.

And even though my buy signal generally brought favorable press, I wondered what would have happened in the opposite case. What if I had uttered that horrible word "Sell!" and the market immediately crashed?

That night brought a crowd of 1,200 people to an auditorium in Syracuse, New York, to see the man who had the power to move the market. It was one of my most satisfying evenings.

Two days later during a seminar in Fort Lauderdale, one of the "expert" members of a roundtable implied that I was merely on a lucky streak.

"There is no such thing as a lucky streak in the market," I replied. "I say this humbly: If one had to guess all the major turning points since 1974 the odds against total accuracy would be up in the billions. There is only one way it can be done, and that is to understand the language of the market itself. I didn't call all those tops and bottoms, the market did."

Over the next week President Carter sent in a group of crack U.S. combat troops to rescue the Iranian hostages and the exercise failed miserably. Secretary of State Cyrus Vance resigned. And the Dow climbed nearly 30 more points.

The Economy and Business section of *Time,* on May 26, carried stories headlined: A MORE SEVERE SLUMP and DETROIT'S WORSENING PLIGHT and the Dow jumped another 40 points for a gain of more than 100 since my buy signal less than six weeks earlier.

The legend was growing that whomever I touched would become rich, and this caused an occasional problem. After a Denver show, as I was in the lobby shaking hands and answering a barrage of questions, one woman sneaked up behind me and snipped a two-inch hole out of the back of my $500 tuxedo jacket.

Everybody wanted to see me, talk to me, touch me. On one level it was the sort of attention I had always craved. There were frequent opportunities for sexual dalliance. But in truth I was a lonely man, at the top of my profession but with no shoulder to lean on.

In May of 1980, my divorce from Polly became official.

I took off for much of the summer of 1980, spending the time at my new condominium in Palm Springs, California. Of course I continued to produce my *Letter,* but I only accepted media invitations that would bring me national exposure.

Reporters from *Time* and *Financial World* interviewed me, the latter publication characterizing me as a Pied Piper leading little old ladies, clinging to their life savings, over a financial cliff.

I appeared on "The David Susskind Show." When I declared that interest rates had "NOTHING!" to do with the stock market, Susskind said, "Joe, you're just wrong."

A resurrected version of the quiz show, "To Tell the Truth," invited me to appear as the man who could predict earthquakes. We stumped the panel.

Several times that summer I drove my gold Mercedes to Las Vegas to break up the monotony. I played golf. Occasionally I found female company. Mostly I was bored and lonely.

Sometimes a little thing happened to cheer me and make me feel as though everything was worthwhile. I received a letter from an investor who had consistently lost money in the market for ten years. He subscribed to my *Letter* in January and six months later had recouped his entire losses of the previous decade.

The Dow continued to skyrocket upward, reaching 950 by mid-summer. At each intermediate stop along the way more and more analysts called for a technical pullback, but I remained silent. My volume indicators showed consistent strength.

I was amused to see how much influence I now had in the investment community. Some analysts even stopped predicting when the market would turn around and started predicting when Granville would send out a sell signal.

But Granville did not send out a sell signal all that summer. Rather, he sent out himself. Slamming into a heavy autumn schedule, I did three shows in Florida and two in Georgia before heading for a series of European seminars sponsored by Bache Halsey Stuart Shields.

Due to a mixup at the new Atlanta airport I arrived in London some hours before my luggage and had to perform at the Cafe Royale in rumpled clothes, drinking my morning coffee during my speech.

It was the first day of the Iran-Iraq War and many investors were worried about the international ramifications. "What does a war have to do with the stock market?" I asked. "NOTHING!" The *Telegraph* called me an "exotic species." The *Guardian* labeled me "the top fortune teller of the United States." And the sedate *Times* said I was a "self-propelled publicity machine, brash and sometimes tasteless comedian, a self-styled nut."

It was good to be back on the road again, garnering all this praise.

Two days later in Frankfurt I was engaged in a formal debate with Andre Kostolany, who had written an article about me for a German financial magazine. He called me an alchemist, a fortune teller, and a crystal ball gazer, one who gives buy and sell signals purely by intuition. He said that, like a racetrack tout, I had to pick many horses in order to be right a few times and thereby gain followers from the lucky ones who followed the right tip. He then *boasted* that in fifty-five years of fundamental analysis he had been right 51 percent of the time!

I did not speak directly against his tirade. I merely pointed out that the Dow had fallen 12 points the previous day and many analysts had called it the beginning of a major downturn in the market. I then said that I was going to make a statement hardly certain on the basis of intuition, but solidly based on the following market evidence:

1) The 12-point drop of the previous day was heavily weighted by losses in only seven of the 30 Dow Industrials;

2) The Transports fell only fractionally;

3) The S&P 500, the NYSE Composite, and other broad indices did not fall as greatly as the Dow did;

4) The number of new individual highs expanded on the Dow decline; and

5) We never get a sell signal on a down day.

"Based on that evidence," I said, "my statement is this: The Dow Jones Industrial Average will close up on the day."

While awaiting the delayed market news from America my hosts treated me to a nine-course dinner, at Erno's Bistro, consisting of wild rice on caviar, raw goose liver with homemade santeone gelée, mousse of tomatoes with lobster, soup de mer with oysters, fresh salmon, Williams Christ sherbet, fresh pork shoulder, cheeses and wild strawberries—all washed down with Champagne Perrier-Jouet and an assortment of French wines.

Finally the news came in. The Dow was down in the morning but rallied sharply in the afternoon to close up 2.73 points. It was a modest rise, to be sure, but its import could not be lost upon those who had to gauge my effectiveness against that of the analyst who bragged that he was right 51 percent of the time.

To celebrate, I spent the night at the casino in Bad Homburg playing roulette. I had come a long way from the Daytona Beach bingo parlors.

After my show in Munich on September 26 my host invited me to the Oktoberfest. I had a great time drinking beer from huge steins and ogling the muscular fräuleins who served it. Late in the evening, when I was ready to leave, I told my host that I would take a cab from the north gate of the Pauli Girl Pavilion.

He walked with me toward the gate. As we approached within thirty yards we could see that this exit was crowded with revelers, so we veered off toward the east gate. Just as we passed a stone wall a powerful terrorist bomb detonated. It had been planted in a trash can near the north gate. Had we not changed course we would surely have been numbered among the many who were killed and maimed that night.

It was a relief to catch a plane back home the next day.

I predicted in several interviews that the Philadelphia Phillies would win the 1980 World Series in six games. After the first five games it was Phillies 3, Royals 2. More than 1,000 people turned up for a show in Hartford on the night of that sixth game and I brashly thanked them for coming out on the night of the final contest. The Phillies did win that night, fulfilling my prophecy.

I made another prediction that night. I produced a hand grenade and pretended to pull the pin. "My next major market signal will be a sell signal," I proclaimed, "and it will create a new all-time daily volume record on the New York Stock Exchange."

Then I launched into one of my tirades against Wall Street. "Since the April twenty-first bottom I have never read so much pure garbage in the financial press," I complained. "Economists bearish on the market, bank trust officers bearish on the market, advisory letters telling you to remain in cash. . . . It goes on and on and not one of them is simply following what the market is saying. They are their own best documentation that they don't know how to read the market."

One man rose to ask why I was rarely quoted in the *Wall Street Journal.* My answer was simple: "Because I am a winner."

Patiently I taught the assemblage a simple method for accurately predicting the market. "The *Wall Street Journal* can be one of your most important indicators," I advised. "The first rule is to turn to the inside back page. Most people, doing the obvious, look at the front page first. In fact, the only page to look at is the inside back page. The rest of the paper has nothing to do with stock market timing.

"On the inside back page columnists such as Charles Elia or Victor Hillery quote people each day regarding their market thinking. When you see an economist quoted, or a bank trust officer, the probabilities favor the market doing the very opposite of what that person thinks."

For a Newark show I appeared dressed as Moses to present to my audience the Four Commandments of Investing:

I. Thou shalt play market swings in both directions. Buy stocks at market bottoms and sell them at market tops; sell stocks short at market tops and cover them at market bottoms.

II. Thou shalt select a sampling of stocks. For example, choose five or ten stocks spread over various industries. If one or two stocks go against the general market trend, the others will keep you ahead.

III. Remember to hold all long purchases or short sales for the entire length of the swing.

IV. Honor market tops and bottoms by subscribing to the *Granville Market Letter.* Get that extra edge by subscribing to the Granville Early Warning Service.

After shows in Boston and in Charleston, West Virginia, I headed out to the West Coast for several appearances. The first of these was arranged by my friend Bob Rotstan, a superb technically oriented broker from the E.F. Hutton office in Newport Beach, California. My drawing power was such that 4,000 people signed up for the show. When Bob could not find a local hall big enough to accommodate everyone, he rented Dr. Robert Schuller's Crystal Cathedral in Garden Grove, where the nationally televised "Hour of Power" originates.

I had a lengthy visit with Dr. Schuller in his private office before speaking that night. He gave me a copy of his latest book, *The Peak to Peak Principle*, and inscribed it: "Your visit is historic—the first public lecture in the Crystal Cathedral."

This turned out to be a prophecy. My show was the first of many secular events staged there, an action that ultimately brought Dr. Schuller into conflict with the Internal Revenue Service over the validity of his tax-exempt status.

Perusing Dr. Schuller's book, I found an interesting message that coincided with mine. "If you've been listening to losers," he wrote, "you'll probably be angry if a winner starts talking, because it may be a judgment upon what you have been doing. Losers get angry with winners! Negative people can't stand positive people."

Thirty days earlier I had spoken at Bally's Park Place Casino in Atlantic City and now I was in a cathedral. It was a giant step, but truth plays on all stages. It was fitting and proper that the truth of the market be taught right there at the Crystal Cathedral because the market follows every principle laid down in the Good Book.

Two evenings later, at a show in San Francisco, a silver-haired woman who must have been in her seventies rose from the audience and asked one of the most memorable questions ever thrown at me. Perhaps she was a plant—I don't know. Her question caught everyone off guard.

"Would you explain the Climax Indicator to me?" she requested. "My sister gave me your book and said it would tell me all about the Climax Indicator, but I could not understand it. I thought it would tell me when I would have a climax!"

Several minutes later when the audience settled down and I regained my composure, I explained that the Climax Indicator had originally been envisioned as a tool to call major market tops and bottoms. Thus it was given its exotic name. Then I pointed out that my undue reliance on the CLX at the expense of the field trends was what caused me to err so badly in 1973–74. Since that time I had used the CLX more for the indication of short-term swings, rather than climaxes.

For my November 25 show in Niagara Falls, Wayne Shapiro, his wife Barbara, and their six-year-old daughter Jennifer drove over from Detroit. Barbara had fashioned Jennifer a bagholder's bag out of back issues of the *Wall Street Journal* and the little girl opened the show by singing "Bagholder Blues" to the audience of 1,500 people.

It was a time for celebration, for the Dow had climbed upward more than 240 points from my April buy signal to touch the magical 1,000 mark on November 20. The high was confirmed by the NFI, the CLX, and a great majority of other indicators, so I did not worry. This bull market had not yet seen its top.

Over the next few weeks the market subsided, dropping back to the 908 level, but the technical indicators still clearly signaled a coming upsurge. This was the last great buying opportunity in the current market.

Dan Dorfman, the nationally known syndicated business columnist, did not see things this way. He believed that a new bear market was underway and wrote a column chastising me for not issuing a sell signal. He apparently thought that his best shot was to call me a clown.

What Dorfman and so many other Wall Street traditionalists failed to understand is that I am a clown by design and with purpose. It is a documented fact that people remember three times more of what they hear when they are entertained instead of lectured to.

People sleep through seminars, lectures, forums, and speeches offered by most financial experts, but nobody ever slept through a Granville show.

Dorfman and his ilk conveniently forget that this clown compiled the best track record of stock market forecasting ever before seen. Would you rather follow a clown with that kind of record or go broke following a Wall Streeter in a pinstriped suit?

Dorfman's comments made me so mad I decided to become even more of a clown. A few days later I was scheduled to return to Minneapolis for another show sponsored by Arnold Securities. I have a warm spot in my heart for Jack Arnold, who launched the first Granville Show and since that time has followed my market calls faithfully, making his clients rich. So I wanted this show to be special and I searched for a unique prop. By showtime I was ready.

Three thousand people packed the ballroom at the Radisson Hotel and were entertained by a jazz band prior to my entrance. D. L. Smith acted as my bodyguard as I entered in the costume of a bagholder in an oversized overcoat with a mask on my face. During the first portion of my show I removed my outer garments to reveal my conventional tuxedo.

Fifteen minutes earlier the prime rate had been raised to an all-time high of 21 percent, and one person in the audience asked me, in light of this particularly bearish news, what the stock market would do that day. "It will close up," I predicted (it rose 6.51 points).

The highlight came in the second act, however, when someone posed the type of leading question for which I had been waiting.

A woman asked, "How are you able to watch the market when you are constantly on the road giving shows?"

"I carry the market with me," I announced. "Watch!"

Quickly I dropped my tuxedo pants to reveal a pair of boxer shorts imprinted with stock quotations. I pointed to various spots on the underwear and named stocks, finally approaching my crotch where I cried delightedly, "And here's Hughes Tool!"

And so another incredible year ended. Gross receipts for the *Granville Market Letter* were $6 million.

The Dow closed out 1980 at 963.99, a rise of 204.86 since my April buy signal. My first *Letter* of the new year was entitled STRAIGHT UP:

"It takes moxie to use a title like this one," I wrote.

To be effective, you have to totally trust the market and repeat without hedging the exact words of the market language. *That language is stating that the next 50 points up in the Dow will be a piece of cake.*

12.
JUDGES

GRANVILLE EARLY WARNING #20 JANUARY 6, 1981 (DOW 1004.69) SELL EVERYTHING. MARKET TOP HAS BEEN REACHED. GO SHORT ON STOCKS HAVING SHARPEST ADVANCES SINCE APRIL.

Only three days after my *Letter* stated that the next 50-point rise in the Dow was "a piece of cake," that prediction came true. The advance took place so quickly that I was dazzled. My January 3rd *Letter* was actually written on New Year's Day, based upon information as of the December 31 closing when the Dow was at 963.99. On Friday, January 2d, the Dow climbed 13.79 points; on Monday it added another 14.88 points. The following day, January 6, it reached an intra-day high of 1013.13, almost exactly 50 points higher than when I wrote the prediction. Later in the day it fell back to 1004.69.

That new Dow high was nonconfirmed by the Net Field Trend Indicator, the Climax Indicator, the number of new individual highs on both the New York Stock Exchange and the American Stock Exchange, the advance-decline lines of both exchanges, the Dow Transportation Average, the NYSE Composite Index, the S & P 500, and the General Motors Indicator.

There were three cover stories that day to hide the end of the bull market. One was the obviously bullish beginning of the January Indicator figures, widely followed by technicians. The second was a drop in interest rates. The third was the imminent presidency of

Ronald Reagan, highly extolled in the *Wall Street Journal* as a boon to the market.

The staff in Holly Hill worked into the wee hours, flashing the sell signal across the world. The Early Warning Service now used the telephone, resorting to cables only when an individual could not be reached immediately.

Some wealthy subscribers were contacted during breakfast in posh European hotels; others on Caribbean beaches. One was pulled from the tables at a Las Vegas casino in order to pay attention to the bigger crap shoot on Wall Street. A surgeon delayed an operation until he could get through to his broker. At least one subscriber was tracked by his answering service to the apartment of his mistress.

By 10:00 A.M. on January 7 they were all poised for their assault on Wall Street.

To fundamentalist brokers it seemed as if the floodgates of hell had ruptured. Many of the Dow stocks opened late. Floor specialists had far too many sell orders to match their few buy orders. I sat in my office that morning and watched the market plunge, knowing that from this day forward my name would be anathema. I had issued sell signals many times before and my smaller band of followers quietly took their profits, sold short, and profited from the coming bear market. My influence was not highly visible to the world in those years. Wall Street did not appreciate my sell signals, but did not criticize me in the popular press lest they enhance my following.

All of that had changed on April 22, 1980, when my Early Warning had sent the market skyrocketing. Then, of course, I had uttered the magic word "Buy!" and Wall Street was delighted. But I had known that the next call would be different. Few brokers would see a major sell signal as a positive development. Up is good, down is bad; they are locked into the belief. For eight months I had lived with the knowledge that the impending sell signal would detonate not only the market, but also a tidal wave of derogation and paranoia.

Since I had refused to get out of the kitchen, so to speak, I had to brace myself for the heat.

At the end of the day on Wednesday, January 7, the Dow was down 23.80 points. Fulfilling my prediction of a few months earlier, my sell signal created a new all-time trading record. Volume on the New York Stock Exchange totaled 92.9 million shares; counting the regional exchanges more than 100 million shares changed hands.

The entire world heard of Joe Granville that day, and few of the media commentaries were flattering. It was as though I had predicted the end of the world. What has the stock market to do with Judgment Day?

On January 8 the Dow lost another 15.19 points. The outcry was bitter and nervous. How could one man dare to pit his wisdom against the collective intelligence of the investment community? How could one man be allowed to wield such power in the nation's —no, the world's—economic life? *Newsweek* estimated that I influenced, in that one day of January 7, $1 trillion of capital investment worldwide. *Time* said that when it came to moving the market I had four times the power of the Federal Reserve Board.

Having only short memories and failing to understand the time lag between a technical call and its outward manifestation, however, the nation's financial wizards breathed easier as the market soon regained nearly the entire two-day loss. Analysts were convinced that the immediate rebound demonstrated the inherent strength of the system to counter the irresponsible ravings of a guru who based his predictions on mere caprice. Wall Street decided that it was time to silence Joe Granville.

Only too happy to sponsor my shows when I was bullish, several of the large brokerage houses now had second thoughts. I had many shows scheduled for the immediate future, but longer-term bookings fell off. "I found out one thing he does to make points in the show is drop his pants," one brokerage house executive told *Time*. "That's not the kind of thing we want to be associated with." That same executive made no reference to the fact that my track record of market calls caught his own fundamental analysts with *their* pants down.

Phil Donahue invited me onto his show with one stipulation: he wanted me to offer a list of stocks to buy. I would not comply—it was not a time to buy anything—and Donahue relented. On the show I discussed the Kondratieff long-wave cycle, and I declared that this beginning bear market could see the Dow drop all the way down to 700.

Donahue became irate. "How can you tell me that the market is going to plunge now? We've got a new president who will be inaugurated tomorrow with a grand economic plan. The hostages are coming home from Iran tomorrow. And the market is going to fall?"

"That's right," I said.

"You're crazy," Donahue proclaimed.

"And you," I retorted, "are a bagholder."

Never had I garnered more severe and unfair criticism from the press. In the January 26 issue of *Newsweek,* a Nobel Prize–winning economist lumped me together with a number of bagholding market advisors whom, he claimed, had no batting average in calling market tops and bottoms.

Another "expert," quoted in the *Wall Street Journal,* said that he could not point to one thing that would push the market lower. That same expert was bearish during the entire 245-point rise in the Dow from April 21, 1980, to January 6, 1981. Yet he is classified as an "expert" and is qualified to criticize my advice.

The first Granville Show after the sell signal was scheduled for February 5 in Detroit at the huge Masonic Temple. Eight thousand people signed up. Numerous death threats had been received, so the Detroit police force, backed up by Pinkertons, provided maximum security for me.

During the intermission one of the Pinkerton guards spotted a man who had worked his way past the security net. He was walking toward my dressing room with a mysterious bulge in his right pocket. The guard accosted him, twisted his right arm behind his back, and hustled him out to the lobby. There, he discovered that the man was a local minister and the bulge was a Bible he wanted me to autograph.

February 19 found me in New York for the first of three appearances on "Tomorrow Coast-to-Coast," hosted by Tom Snyder. When I first met Tom in the makeup room he remarked that my sell signal had cost him $25,000. But he bore me no malice and we became friends.

Tom and I chatted about the stock market but we also digressed onto other topics. I pointed out that the impending spring lineup of the sun, the moon, and the planet Mercury was an ill omen for Southern California. Success making me ever more confident and outrageous, I predicted that a magnitude 8.5 earthquake would hit Southern California on Friday, April 10, at 5:31 A.M., centered twenty-three miles east of Los Angeles.

The Dow hovered around the 950 mark for a time, breathing. Then it rallied back up to 974, to the delight of my critics who failed to follow and understand anything about technical indicators. The market told me not to worry.

I was so overconfident that I declared to an audience in Vancouver, "I'll never make another major mistake in the stock market." A measure of success does strange things to the mind.

Four thousand people packed Caesar's Palace on February 27 for my first appearance in Las Vegas. I wanted this one to be special, for David Brinkley had a television crew there to film footage for his "NBC Magazine." I had planned to introduce my trained chimpanzee (named "Dwarfman" in honor of the syndicated financial columnist) but he fell ill two days before the show. Quickly I arranged for a substitute, a performing chimp named Brandy, to be flown out from the Los Angeles zoo. Her trainer worked with me for several hours before the show.

In one scene we had Brandy climb a stepladder to retrieve a carpet bag, illustrating the typical action of the bagholder who would clutch his stock tenaciously all the way down the ladder. Later I stuffed my pocket with dollar bills and small bits of candy. Brandy came on stage dressed as a bank trust officer and, as I spoke, she raided my pocket for the candies, in the process spewing dollar bills all over the floor.

Brandy was a delight. During the intermission, as I rested out in the sound truck behind the auditorium, she suddenly began to rub my leg. At first I was dubious about her intentions—I do have a few morals—but eventually she found a pack of Marlboros in my pocket, took one out, managed to light it, and sat smoking, calmly awaiting the second act.

My travel schedule, coupled with the ceaseless requests for media interviews, grew ever more frantic and lonely. I flew to Philadelphia for an E.F. Hutton show followed by an appearance on "Wall Street Week" for a grilling by a belligerent Louis Rukeyser. One of the panelists on the show called my sell signal "intellectually dishonest and immoral."

"Nobody saw anything dishonest or immoral in my April 1980 buy signal," I countered. "But now you call me dishonest and immoral simply because I advised everyone to break Wall Street's Ten Commandments: One, Thou shalt not sell; Two, Thou shalt not sell; Three, Thou shalt not sell; et cetera. That is Wall Street's version of immorality. But truth is never immoral."

By March 16 the Dow had climbed back to 1002.79 in a totally nonconfirmed bubble. That night, when the subject of my sell signal came up, I told an audience in St. Petersburg, Florida, that I had never been more certain of a market call.

Then it was on to Houston for a show and a refreshing interlude of golf with Vic Damone.

I had been on the road almost nonstop for three and a half years, logging nearly a million miles in the air. My 185th show was scheduled for Kansas City, sponsored by B.C. Christopher. It was to be held on March 24, a Tuesday, but I arrived in town the previous Friday night. I had done several shows in Kansas City over the years and for some reason this town, in the very heartland of America, attracted me like a magnet.

Since I arrived four days early my sponsors faced the problem of keeping me entertained. On Friday night one of the local brokers took me to a topless club, but this sort of entertainment had lost its appeal. Sex without love was beginning to bore me.

On Saturday, after a round of golf, I was wined and dined at Fanny's Restaurant. Looking around the table all I saw were couples. Lonely and morose, I left before the dessert was served.

On Sunday I was the guest of honor at a cocktail party hosted by Peter Gattermeier of B.C. Christopher. Many of Kansas City's VIPs were there, including Henry Block, the *H* of H & R Block. I parked myself at the piano for the afternoon. Peter came over and reminded me that I was to be his dinner guest that night at the Alameda Hotel.

"I'm not going," I said, "unless I have someone to share the evening with. I'm damn tired of being lonely."

Peter knew the perfect lady for me. Her name was Karen Erickson, a local artist who was one of his clients.

Karen was fashionably late that night, but when she walked into the restaurant our eyes met and there seemed to be an immediate chemical reaction. Fire and earth. A graduate of Stephens College, she possessed not only beauty but class—two qualities lacking in my life. At that moment there was only one thought in my mind: get rid of everyone else at the table.

I turned completely boorish. I pulled a trick photograph out of my wallet that showed a naked toddler with a penis that stretched down to the ground. "This is a picture of me when I was two years old,"

I announced proudly, passing it around the table. The women were shocked, but somehow I could sense that Karen knew what I was up to.

I did my best to insult everyone at the table, save Karen, and they all made polite excuses for leaving early.

Both of us knew that something special was happening between us. We ate dinner, danced, drank, and conversed with ease. Left to ourselves, we discovered that we shared a deep interest in astrology, Tarot cards, and other forms of the mystic arts. She claimed that her fifteen-year-old Siamese cat Charlie was a prescient feline who would someday enter *The Guinness Book of World Records* by setting a longevity mark. In sum, Karen was deliciously unconventional. Karen worked long hours but for the next two days I monopolized her free time.

All too soon it was showtime. I remembered little about what I said or did on that occasion, for my head and heart were with Karen. I had to catch a plane for New Orleans after the show, but I knew that I would soon return to Kansas City.

My euphoria was not to be disturbed by the market. The day after my Kansas City show the Dow hit 1015.22, another nonconfirmed high. I let my critics have the stage, for I believed that the market would soon clobber them.

I did a show in New Orleans, managed one night back in Kansas City to see Karen, played Salt Lake City, and then took a few days off to enjoy the Masters Golf Tournament in Augusta, Georgia. As a spectator.

The press poured on the heat when April 10 passed and my earthquake prediction failed to materialize. Lapses such as this are totally removed from my market prognostications. My earthquake predictions are astrologically based; my market predictions are technically based. The press makes no such distinction and I must admit that I open myself to the allegation of crackpot when I pursue such diversions. But they add to my nonconforming image and perhaps serve the function of keeping my following to manageable proportions. This leads me to another prediction, perhaps my most accurate of all time: Joe Granville will never be able to curb his tongue.

Undaunted by the continuing existence of Los Angeles, I gave shows in Louisville and in Melbourne, Florida, in quick succession. By the time I arrived in Pittsburgh on April 27 for a show the following night, the Dow reached a peak of 1024.05. Wall Street fairly glowed. I was wrong about California and now the market had finally beaten mighty Joe Granville.

Once again this new Dow high was nonconfirmed across the board. Three and a half months had passed since my sell signal and the Dow was still making new nonconfirmed highs. This could only mean one thing—the projected drop would be greater and longer lasting than anyone could imagine. I now fully believed that we were, at long last, on the verge of the great Kondratieff crash.

But my thoughts were not on the market as much as they were on a beautiful woman in Kansas City. I often assume a façade of indifference when the market appears to contradict my forecasts. But I am only human. Despite technical assurances, it is difficult to remain on an emotional high when the external indicators appear to signal my failure. I craved the solace of one who could understand me and get me through these temporarily demoralizing episodes.

I called Karen that night from Pittsburgh. "I love you," I told her. "I love you, too," she replied.

"That does it. Let's get married."

To my everlasting delight, Karen accepted the proposal immediately. I changed my airline booking from Palm Springs to Kansas City.

Karen and I were married May 4 at the Jackson County Courthouse. As we walked down the steps outside after the ceremony the wind caught us, driving my hair wild and almost carrying away Karen's hat. At that moment photographers caught a picture that was reproduced all over the world.

After a short honeymoon in Karen's apartment we set off for Atlantic City for a show at Caesar's Boardwalk Regency Hotel and Casino. The whirlwind tour included a New York luncheon with the *Time* board of editors and a variety of press interviews. *Newsweek* reporter Susan Dentzer interviewed me on the way to the casino for the show.

Caesar's threw a pre-performance cocktail party in our honor, during which I quaffed a number of vodka tonics. That is standard procedure for me, but on this occasion the drinks slammed into my head with unusual force. Perhaps the strain of long hours was catching up with me, I thought, or perhaps this was the effect of the agonizing delay in the predicted market slide. I slipped with relief into a coffin shrouded with ticker tape for a brief rest before pallbearers carried me onstage, a martini in my motionless hand. I lay there as a loudspeaker blared "Bagholder Blues." Then I sat straight up. "I'm rising from the dead," I screamed. "Now get me out of this goddamn thing!"

Ten minutes into the show I found that I could barely speak a coherent sentence. The sponsor rushed onstage with a cup of coffee and ushered me off for a breather.

Many minutes later I felt my head begin to clear from what I now suspected were the effects of a Mickey Finn. Somehow I forced myself back onstage to complete the show in front of a disgusted audience that had thinned out greatly.

The press reported the fiasco with glee. Joe Granville was losing his touch. The market was giving the lie to his predictions, and he was so shaken that he could barely perform anymore.

The Dow attempted many times that spring to rally back up beyond the 1000 level, but each successive spurt was increasingly short-lived. The technical situation deteriorated rapidly; the NFI swung into minus territory.

Misinterpreting the message of the Dow's high-level holding pattern, the bulls were convinced that they had finally ended my streak. Thomas F. Fogarty of E.F. Hutton & Company was quoted in the *Wall Street Journal* of May 28: "Look at what's happening! The airlines are soaring and the oils are stagnating. And technology, consumer and interest-sensitive stocks—the very victims of OPEC-inspired inflation over the past seven years—are under massive accumulation by investment institutions. By next week we could see the short sellers panic and touch off a runaway market on the upside."

Some people put their money where their mouths were. Dan Bott of Kidder Peabody in Newport Beach, California, bet me $1,000 that the Dow would close higher than 1104 before it closed lower than 904. I like Dan, but I am always ready to bet on a sure thing. I accepted his offer immediately.

I did a June 11 show in Hartford, entering the stage with a live iguana named Greenspan. While he was onstage Greenspan happened to thrust out his dewlap, a protective device that is used both for camouflage in the natural world and for enticing the fair sex. I explained the function of Greenspan's dewlap and then characterized the current stock situation as a Dewlap Market—one which camouflaged its real direction and enticed the unsuspecting into its lair. And what happens to the female iguana when she falls for the attraction of the dewlap? The answer is clear.

From Hartford, Karen and I flew directly to San Marcos, Texas, to visit her parents. We were robbed of half of our luggage at the airport but retrieved most of our important papers when Bill Hagen of the First State Bank of Pflugerville spotted someone throwing my attaché case into a trash barrel, the precise location where most Wall Streeters believe my work ought to be.

In mid-June the Dow again crossed the 1000 level, scoring a far lower NFI reading than on its previous high. Similar deterioration was evident in the high-low indicator. "There is absolutely no question in my mind that the market has been forming a major top for many months," I wrote in my June 20 *Letter.* "It is dangerously past the normal cycle and the very longevity of the topping process implies a much more severe corrective process ahead." Despite my public statement Karen knew that I was extremely edgy. I was used to the market lagging behind my predictions, but five months had now passed since my sell signal. Many of my subscribers failed to renew. I longed for the visible vindication of my theories.

June 25 was one of the most memorable days of my life. I was in New York for a very special show that night. During the day I visited the stock exchange, appearing at the railing of the visitor's gallery high above the floor action. I busied myself signing autographs and told other visitors that the market would soon collapse so badly that investors would start jumping out of windows as they did in 1929. On their way down, I predicted, they would cry out, "Thanks, Paine Webber."

One by one brokers hustling around the floor noticed me, heads turned upward, and the activity on the New York Stock Exchange ground to a halt. Even the ticker tape stopped. When I was sure that everyone was watching I slowly turned both thumbs downward. To one side of the floor a murmur of boos began that quickly spread across the exchange until all of the fundamental brokers, immersed in the false belief that up is good and down is bad, built the negative applause into a crescendo of excoriation. I loved it.

On that rainy Friday I played Carnegie Hall to an audience of more that 4,000, using the Steinway concert grand piano. I was brought back for three curtain calls amid a wild, standing ovation. It was a moment that my mother and I had dreamed of since I was a young boy, with the exception that the instrument of my virtuosity was the market, not the Steinway.

My lifelong love affair with candy bars caught up with me that summer when I had all of my teeth extracted. Fitted with a brand-new set of choppers, I flew to London with Karen for a show. Beforehand I was interviewed by a reporter from the _Financial Times_ who was concerned that the London market was beset with fundamental uncertainty. Interest rates and unemployment were at critically high levels. I heightened his concern, warning that the London market, as were all world markets, was headed for a crash.

Onstage that night, just as I warmed up to my topic, my upper set of teeth suddenly flew out and clattered onto the resonant floor of the platform. Most of the 1,000 people in my audience assumed it was just another planned Granville stunt, and it sent the normally staid Britishers into hysterics. Playing up to the crowd, I retrieved my fangs and shoved them back into my mouth upside down. "Now this," I proclaimed with garbled eloquence, "is how a fundamentalist broker talks to you."

Back in Florida with my teeth in, I had the exquisite pleasure of meeting the oldest living market technician. Justin "Josh" Ricker, who had befriended my dad in retirement, was ninety-six years old. He had known Jessie Livermore, Bernard Baruch, and Roger Babson. He learned technical analysis from Frank H. Tubbs, who wrote a Wall Street best-seller in the 1920s. Josh concurred that my January 6 sell signal was 100-percent correct.

After nearly six months of waiting, that fact was finally becoming more apparent to all. The Dow dropped to the 940s despite constant Wall Street predictions of a coming rally.

On August 24 the Dow closed at 900.11 and I called Dan Bott in California to give him the address of the charity where I wanted him to send his $1,000 check. The market had chastised him into becoming a believer. He now informed me that he was convinced the Dow would fall at least another 100 points before it touched bottom. Dan said that his mistake was that his ownership of stocks had blinded him to the clear technical message of the market. Ownership of anything always blinds one to reality. This is why I have maintained my practice of owning no stocks.

By mid-September the Dow had lost another 50 points to the 850 level and Wall Street was predicting support there, just as it had at 980, 960, 930, 900, and 880.

Only a month after our previous trip, Karen and I stopped in London again on our way to a Paris show. I taped a radio interview to be aired during the morning rush hour. With the Financial Times Index of London stocks hovering in the 500 range, I reiterated my prediction of a month earlier that it would soon fall further, perhaps all the way back to the 150 level. Responding to my warning, the Index declined 16.6 points that day, one of its largest drops in months. London newspapers referred to me as "Jack the Ripper," "The Hunchback of Notre Dame," and "Market Wrecker."

During that show I noted that trading action on a Monday often seems to underscore the current market trend. Against the background of current technical weakness, therefore, I said I would not be surprised if Monday, September 28, was a very Blue Monday on all the world exchanges. By now whenever Joe Granville made such a pronouncement the press was quick to pick it up. My forecast made headlines around the world, setting off the predicted slide earlier than I expected. After all, anyone who believed that the market was going to crash on Monday would sell out on Thursday and Friday.

On Thursday I was in Paris for the show that night. Karen and I ate oysters at a restaurant across the street from the Paris Bourse, the French stock exchange, watching doleful brokers come and go. The French market lost the equivalent of 17 points in the Dow that day. The governor of the Bourse allowed me the honor of ringing the closing bell on the very day of a crash that the media said I had caused.

Friday was another jittery day on all the world's markets as investors awaited Granville's Blue Monday. Karen and I traveled home that weekend, one of nervous anticipation.

On Monday the Tokyo stock market recorded its biggest one-day loss in history. London followed suit with the Financial Times Index losing 30 points. British stock values dropped by $6.4 billion. Panic brought about similar sharp drops on stock markets in Hong Kong, Sydney, Zurich, Paris, Singapore, and Frankfurt.

When the New York Stock Exchange opened at 10:00 A.M. the news of events in the worldwide markets had set the stage for a debacle. In the first half-hour of trading the Dow plunged more than 14 points. Then something happened. The big boys took over, determined to silence the Granville mouth with one swift blow. Large institutional investors poured droves of money into the market, creating an afternoon buying spree. Though virtually all the other world markets crashed that day, Blue Monday ended in New York with the Dow up 18.55 points.

Countless hordes of Wall Streeters crowed with glee, claiming that a new bull market was underway.

But it did not appear so to me. The strong rally produced a totally unimpressive +7 on the CLX. The NFI stood at a dismal −15. The high-low list showed 590 stocks making new fifty-two-week lows and only one making a new high. The advance-decline line stood only a whisper above its bear market low. And while the media made hay with the "giant" upside reversal in the Dow, the NASDAQ Index of over-the-counter stocks declined for the day.

It was with confidence, therefore, that I appeared that evening on ABC's "Nightline." Newsman Ted Koppel, whose career is built upon words, seemed to respect the power that my statements carried. I made the public claim that night that the rally in New York represented a concerted effort of Wall Street to discredit me. It was, I predicted, an effort that would ultimately fail. No one-day rally could alter the reality of the encompassing bear market. "The house is still burning down," I declared.

Another "Nightline" guest was an editor of London's *Financial Times.* He lashed out at me for causing the British market to crash.

"Are you aware that I told the readers of your paper in the first week of August that the London market was headed for a crash?" I asked.

He was not.

"You're trying to lay the panic at my feet when I have the documented proof that I smelled smoke in early August six weeks before the English market burned down," I noted. "I didn't cause the crash. I merely sounded the warning."

The editor mumbled his embarrassed apology for not reading his own newspaper.

I call the market to the best of my ability. I got people out of the market in January 1981 only 1.89 percent under the exact Dow peak, yet Wall Streeters crucify me as an irresponsible guru who sabotages the market and upsets investors from New York to London to Paris to Tokyo. When will they learn that no one can make the market do what the market is not positioned to do?

Buoyed by the New York rally, other world markets rebounded from Blue Monday. On Tuesday the Tokyo market registered its largest one-day rise in history. The Nikkei Dow Jones Index, which lost 302.84 points on Blue Monday, stormed ahead the next day to record a 320.56-point gain.

London recovered also, gaining back all but 6 of the 30 points lost on Monday.

Most of the other world exchanges also rallied, with the exception of Singapore, Hong Kong, and Milan. *Time* headlined its story of the event "A Whiff of Panic." The subhead read "But Wall Street has the last laugh."

Monte Gordon, vice-president and director of research at Dreyfus Corporation, chortled, "A couple of more Blue Mondays like that and we'll break through a thousand."

Paul Harvey cackled with glee on his national radio broadcast about a bumper sticker with the legend: JOE GRANVILLE—SHUT UP.

One of the most vitriolic critics was Louis Rukeyser, who head-lined his syndicated column of October 5: "Let's Forget About Joseph Granville."

"Joe was fun for a while," Rukeyser wrote. " . . . even his oleaginous self-promotion had an engaging Barnum-like quality the first nine times around the poop deck.

"What Joe never could do was, alas, the one thing he fooled a lot of innocent people into believing he actually could accomplish: call short-term swings in the stock market. . . . "

When I defend myself against attacks like this, there is a tendency for the exchange to degenerate into a personal feud. It may be more objective, therefore, to allow one of my followers to mount the defense. Never has such a defense been worded more eloquently than that presented by my good friend Wayne Shapiro when he introduced me at a show in Kalamazoo on November 17:

"By far the most vicious attacks on Joe have come from within our own profession. From the fundamental research departments of major Wall Street firms, from financial reporters, like Dan Dorfman and Alan Abelson, from 'Wall Street Week' host Louis Rukeyser, from hordes of economists, bank trust officers, lawyers, accountants, and finally, from other market letter and advisory publishers.

"Ninety-eight percent of the reporting has been negative. Of that ninety-eight percent, one-third has bordered on paranoia.

"Why is this so, you ask?

"Let me give you my theory of why it is so.

"If Joe Granville were really some kind of kook, nary a comment would be made.

"But what if Joe Granville's theories really do work? The entire industry that I'm a part of would be widely shaken up.

"There would be no need, for example, for research departments, there would be no need for Standard & Poor sheets, there would be no need for Value Line, there would be no need for thousands upon thousands of high-priced people currently employed in my business. They would simply be obsolete, redundant. A great charade would be exposed and the reverberation would be devastating and would be worldwide.

" . . . Granville's theories allow him to pick the bottoms or the tops of major markets as well as all market moves of more than 100 points' duration. Ladies and gentlemen, evidence of this can be documented as follows:

"October 1974   Dow 631—He said buy.
"January 24, 1977 Dow 962—He said sell and sell short.
"February 2, 1978 Dow 769—He said cover shorts and buy.
"August 22, 1978   Dow 897—He said sell and sell short.
"November 21, 1978 Dow 797—He said cover shorts and buy.
"September 23, 1979 Dow 893—He said sell and sell short.
"November 7, 1979 Dow 796—He said cover shorts and buy.
"January 31, 1980 Dow 875—He said sell and sell short.
"April 21, 1980   Dow 759—He said cover shorts and buy.
"January 6, 1981   Dow 1004—He said sell and sell short.

"The total traverse of all these moves is 1,385 points in the Dow Jones Industrial Average and this, ladies and gentlemen, is in the form of hard evidence. His market letters are readily available at any library if anybody asks for them.

"It is this record that frightens Wall Street to death. 'My God,' they said, 'what if this guy is for real?' "

Four years and a million miles were enough. After our extended summer tour Karen and I decided to settle into a more relaxed married life. We subleased a condominium in Kansas City's Crown Center and moved there with Karen's prescient Siamese cat Charlie. Soon we added a minature poodle, Granville's Brandy Alexander, a gray tabby named Gamble, and Aristotle the parrot to our menagerie.

Sometimes we stayed up late at night searching through the prophecies of Nostradamus.

Karen cleaned up my act, furnishing my closet with tailored suits and tuxedos that actually fit the contours of my 140-pound body. She threw away my collection of J.C. Penny's short-sleeved dress shirts and supplied me with elegant French cuffs. She washed the grease out of my hair and fashioned me a 1980s style.

Over a period of time we phased out the Florida office and moved the *Granville Market Letter* to Kansas City, where Karen took over the day-to-day management, leaving me free to concentrate on the market statistics that constantly flashed across the screen of our closed circuit TV, mesmerizing Charlie. On days when the market fell Charlie moaned and swished his tail, a delightful downside omen.

There was enough smart money in the world to enable the *Granville Market Letter* to close 1981 with gross income exceeding $10 million. But many of those subscribers anxiously awaited the developments of the new year, as did my critics. At year's end the Dow stood at an even 875.00, down 129.69 points from my sell signal but up 50.99 points since the Blue Monday turnaround.

For months Wall Street and I played a game of cat and mouse as the Dow sank lower. Then in my March 6, 1982, *Letter* I made one of the most consequential of all my predictions. Noting that the Dow had zigzagged lower for more than a year in the face of Wall Street's best efforts to churn out optimism (nearly every day Treasury Secretary Donald Regan, on leave from his post as chairman of Merrill Lynch, proclaimed that recovery was just around the corner), I predicted the event that would bring the last of the bagholders into the market before it really skidded. "The final hook in this market will be the Kaufman Hook," I wrote. Henry Kaufman, an economist for Salomon Brothers, is considered one of the most salient prognosticators of interest rate fluctuations. "He will finally tell you that interest rates are headed importantly lower and you will take that as a market buy signal, forgetting that in the final phase of all important bear markets, interest rates skidded."

My prediction was correct. Within a few months Henry Kaufman would indeed hook investors with my fulfilled forecast. Unfortunately for me, I failed to realize just who was about to be hooked.

Wall Street was so desperate to promote action that, on March 9, the day after the Dow hit a new bear market bottom of 795.46, someone circulated a rumor that Granville had sent out a buy signal. This caused a mild, 8-point rally in the Dow. I cautioned my readers not to fall for hearsay. Any buy signal I sent would be telephoned directly to my Early Warning Service subscribers one hour before market opening; it would never go out during the middle of the day. And if I had issued a genuine buy signal I could envision the Dow reacting with far more enthusiasm, rising as much as 50 points.

During the second quarter of 1982 the Dow attempted a half-hearted rally, but the legitimacy of the rise was belied by a series of twelve nonconfirmations in the CLX reading. In other words, on twelve successive higher Dow readings the CLX was lower. The market appeared to be setting itself up for one of the greatest smashes in history—perhaps a greater fall than the debacle of 1929–30.

My *Letter* continued to offer the same advice it had every week since January 6, 1981: "Sell everything!"

That advice held up well. The Dow forsook its thoughts of a summer rally and turned downward, continuing to fulfill my forecast and continuing to anger millions of bagholders. When I walked into the Farmer's Market in Kansas City one day a man came up to me and asked, "Should I cut your throat now or later?"

"You must have the wrong subject," I replied. "Maybe you should cut your broker's throat."

"I already have, but I'm mad enough to keep cutting throats," he answered.

On August 12, 1982, the Dow dropped to a new bear market low of 776.92. This was accompanied by a Net Field Trend Indicator reading of −10, the lowest figure in several months, but only half as negative as one might expect from such a low Dow. On that same day the Climax Indicator nonconfirmed the Dow low with a −8 reading, a full 13 points higher than one week earlier. The number of individual new lows was only 134, compared to a whopping 590 nearly a year earlier when the Dow had closed at 842.56.

A review of my short-sale recommendations that had been in force for nineteen months showed respectable profits:

STOCK	SHORT-SALE PRICE	COVERED PRICE	PERCENT PROFIT
Aydin Corporation	36.75	29.50	19.7
Boise Cascade	39.13	22.63	42.2
Browning Ferris	30.63	30.00	2.1
Computervision Corporation	32.75	20.38	37.8
Control Data	40.38	22.00	45.5
Cox Broadcasting	38.75	27.63	21.0
Delta Airlines	35.63	25.75	27.7
Digital Equipment	87.50	62.38	28.9
Dupont	48.63	30.63	37.0
Electronic Data Systems	29.25	25.25	27.7
Federal Express	57.50	42.75	25.7
General Instrument	40.38	27.88	45.8
Georgia Pacific	29.38	14.63	50.2
Johnson and Johnson	34.38	38.88	−13.1
Joy Manufacturing	39.38	19.25	51.5
Eli Lilly	64.88	47.50	26.8

(Continued)

STOCK	SHORT-SALE PRICE	COVERED PRICE	PERCENT PROFIT
Macy & Company	30.88	33.13	−7.3
Minnesota Mining & Mfg.	63.13	52.13	17.4
Northwest Industries	51.00	37.00	27.5
Paradyne	28.75	23.63	38.9
PPG Industries	49.25	33.38	32.2
Rolm	37.88	23.13	38.9
Santa Fe Industries	29.88	16.00	46.7
Tandy	38.63	23.25	37.2
Time Incorporated	39.13	26.13	33.2
Warner Communications	56.25	38.13	32.2
Weyerhaeuser	36.88	24.25	43.2

By utilizing margin accounts with Treasury Bills as collateral, the average profits on my short-sale portfolio would have been more than 70 percent.

If I had issued a buy signal!!!

"There is absolutely no way a competent market analyst could be puzzled by the action of the market," I said in my August 14, 1982, *Letter,* shortly before taking off for Minneapolis to play in the first annual Granville Open golf tournament, a local charity event sponsored by Arnold Securities.

The market would quickly swallow my words like a gaping sand trap. Nine years of catching the brass ring on the Wall Street merry-go-round had convinced me that I was infallible. I was on a roll. Instead of playing golf that week I should have been reading three particular passages from a selection of my favorite writings.

I should have reread my very first *Letter* of August 16, 1963, where I wrote: "This Letter is going to be right many times and at other times very wrong . . . "

I should have reread page 215 of my *New Strategy* book, which stated: "Now he consults his market timetable and carefully measures off 48 to 54 months after the previous major bottom seen in the previous bear market. If the market is in the *timing ballpark*, then the smart money trader can confidently know that the bear market has at last ended." In the margin I had penned, months earlier, the notation, "August 1982."

Most importantly I should have reread Proverbs 16:18: "Pride goeth before destruction, and a haughty spirit before a fall."

I was on the golf course in Minneapolis when news reached me that Henry Kaufman of Salomon Brothers had predicted falling interest rates, the market responding with a sharp rise.

There it was, the Kaufman Hook, predicted five months earlier in my March 6 *Letter*. Score another one for Joe Granville, I thought. Elation overcame me when I learned that Kaufman himself had said that the only reason interest rates were coming down was because *the business climate was so bad that loan demand was almost nonexistent.* To me it was clear that the economy was suffering from the malaise so brilliantly predicted by the Kondratieff long wave, and that the bear market would yet see a severely depressed bottom far below Dow 776.92.

Institutional investors did not share my outlook. Biting at the Kaufman Hook, they gobbled up stocks in record numbers, causing a buying panic that sent the Dow soaring over the 900 mark by the end of the month. Daily volume totals easily eclipsed the all-time record set on the day after my January 6, 1981, sell signal. The NFI shot up to +11, gaining 21 points in only thirteen trading days.

Programmed to expect the Kondratieff crash, blinded by my past successes, congratulating myself on the accuracy of my Kaufman Hook prediction, I ignored the warnings of the NFI and the rise in other indicators. Instead, I searched for any bit of evidence to prove that I was still correct.

First and foremost, I pointed out, no bull market in history was ever spawned by institutional money. At normal market bottoms, mutual funds and pension funds tend to be net sellers, bagholders to the end. Therefore, I concluded, this meteoric rise had to be the rally that fools the majority—a giant speculative bubble—that was necessary in order to set up the final, precipitous crash. It was a bull trap of major proportions, locking in billions of dollars of investment capital.

One agonizing month passed. Every trading day I studied the stock tape religiously, awaiting the crash. On down days I jumped about my office like a schoolboy; up days found me sullen and morose. Even if this was a bubble in a bear market it was still more than a 100-point rise and I should have called it. By the end of September, the Dow was barely beneath 900. The NFI rose as high as +17 in mid-month, and had now tailed off to +13. I jumped on this as early evidence of movement to the downside. The advice in my *Letter* remained constant: "Sell all stocks."

Explosive power rocketed the Dow to a runaway rise early in October. The Dow gained 37 points on the sixth and added 21 more points the following day. Gains of 21 points were right behind, the latter cracking the Dow past 1000. On October 13, the average closed at 1015.08.

Still I did not relent. I warned my readers that this most spectacular rally in Wall Street history was a "Bermuda Triangle." I theorized that normal technical indicators, such as the NFI, which stood at a healthy +15, were malfunctioning during this extraordinary aberration.

October 21 brought another Dow high of 1036.98 and an NFI of +16. Yet I had the audacity, in my October 30 *Letter,* to draw a parallel between myself and the Biblical Joseph who correctly interpreted Pharoah's dream. This market, I proclaimed, was like the seven fat cattle who were about to be devoured by seven lean ones.

Wall Street traders continued their buying frenzy. Countless analysts predicted 1100, 1200, even 1300 in the Dow and no one wanted to be left behind. November 3 found the Dow climbing a one-day record of 43 points to close at an all-time high of 1065.49.

The Kaufman Hook had turned out to be the Granville Hook. I could only hope that my short sellers had protected themselves with the proper stop orders. If they had, their profits were realized in the early stages of the rally. If they had not, their profits were now losses. In either case, no one who followed my recommendations had earned a penny from the nearly 300-point rise in the Dow.

No longer could I persist in defining this as a rallying bear market. It was a bona fide bull market, albeit a strange one. I had forgotten that I am a fallible human being. I had forgotten that even great theories may not be perfectly applied. I had forgotten that the market can do anything.

But one thing I still believed with certainty—this rally was far too rapid and spectacular to be healthy. The only historical parallel was the 1929 rally that preceded the Great Crash. A chart of the Dow showed a clear parabolic curve, and there is only one way down from a parabolic. In my twenty-five years of market analysis I have seen various groups of stocks rise on parabolic curves. Missile stocks blasted off the very day I went to work for E.F. Hutton & Company, the day that Russia launched Sputnik. This was followed, over the years, by parabolics that meshed with Wall Street's latest fads: rocket fuels, copying machines, color televisions, bowling, electronics, fried chicken, nursing homes, mobile homes, casinos, gold, silver, home computers, and video games. All of these crazes came to a common end. Once the euphoria ended, all stocks in all of these favored categories suffered a near-total price collapse.

And now, late in 1982, and through 1983, a parabolic curve rose its foreboding head on the charts of the Dow Jones Industrial Average, the Standard & Poor's 500, and the New York Stock Exchange Composite Index of all big-board stocks.

I had missed the greatest rally in stock market history, breaking my nine-year record of near perfection. I could not blame my subscribers for losing faith. On the other hand, I could not escape the conclusion that, when history writes the final chapter, hordes of investors will curse themselves for becoming caught up in the market parabolic.

Inwardly I was incensed at myself for blowing my record of market calls over the past nine years. I fought against reality for a time, conjuring up every excuse that I could find to "prove" that this great stock market rally could not possibly continue.

But continue it did. All the way through 1982 and well into 1983. Karen tried her best to console me. Nobody's perfect, she reminded me. We analyzed the past together, knowing that we must learn from our mistakes. My errors in calling the 1973 market had forced me to restudy my theories and learn the importance of the Net Field Trend Indicator, which served me well for nine years. My error in August 1982 must serve the same purpose; it must remind me that

I am human and vulnerable. It must remind me to listen only to the market, not to Granville.

In August of 1982 I had so locked myself into a long-term prediction that I ignored the short-term technical evidence. I must never again fail to listen for the counterpoint in the market's harmonious music. The humbling events of 1982 did nothing to disprove my market theories. Those theories will last far longer than the mortal who was blessed to discover them. Those theories correctly predicted the great stock market rally of 1982–83. It was only the man who failed.

There is, perhaps, a ten-year Granville cycle. In 1942, as an uninspired youth smashing glass in the Duke chemistry lab, I was aimless and morose. In 1952, having failed to capitalize upon my success as a postage stamp analyst, I struggled over a printing press in order to feed my family. In 1962, after achieving fame and a measure of fortune on Wall Street, I fell into disfavor with my superiors at E.F. Hutton & Company, precipitating the end of my brokerage house career. In 1972, enamored with Richard Nixon and blinded by excessive gambling, I fell into the trap of fundamentalism that nearly destroyed my career. In 1982 I missed the greatest stock market rally in history.

The intervening years in the cycle brought me success, acclaim, and fortune. Perhaps I would rise from the ashes of my 1982 holocaust and set off on another nine years of glory.

By late springtime of 1983, when euphoria was at its height, when stock prices, at least as reflected in the Dow Jones Industrial Average, were at record levels, I finally could see—and document—that this strange bull market was beginning to sicken and die. I noted several incontrovertible points:

1) The spring of 1983 saw a peak of frenzy in the rush of Big Board companies to produce new stock issues. Of course they wanted to pour more stock into a market that was hungry to eat it up at the top of its price cycle. Historically, a bear market has always followed such a peak of new issue activity.

2) At the same time the low-priced stocks rose to an extremely sharp parabolic peak. Once more the historical record is clear. Such a run-up is always followed by a bear market.

3) Throughout 1983 there was feverish activity in stock splits.

Years of maximum stock splits are always followed by bear markets.

4) The year saw a tremendous resurgence in mutual fund deposits as the small investors sought to get in on the tail end of Wall Street's historic action. Charts of mutual fund activity show that such bubbles of interest are always followed by bear markets.

5) Pension fund managers increasingly assigned a greater percentage of their assets to the equities markets. Such love affairs by pension fund managers are always followed by bear markets.

6) During the great rise of 1982–83 brokerage firms hired more new employees than during any comparable period in history. The record clearly shows that all such massive hiring binges are followed by bear markets. Some time ago I had coined the phrase, "They always hire at the top and fire at the bottom."

7) The year 1983 saw the largest number of new stock market advisory services—some 500 of them—registered by the Securities and Exchange Commission. All peaks in such registrations are followed by bear markets.

8) American public companies made some 600 secondary stock distributions in 1983, a record total. This is another classic way to water the supply of stock, and all years of numerous secondary distributions are followed by bear markets.

9) The year also saw a parabolic curve of pernicious and concentrated insider selling. The people in the know were dumping their stock. Every time insider selling is that persistent it is followed by a bear market.

10) I noted a parabolic rise in margin debt, following the same rising curve that brokers' loans exhibited back in 1929. All such bubbles in the use of speculative, borrowed money are followed by bear markets.

11) During the year mutual funds achieved their lowest liquidity position in five years, meaning that they were overloaded with stock and short on cash. That condition is always followed by a bear market.

12) The very same year that brought all these other bearish indications also brought a nine-year peak in merger and acquisition activity. All such peaks are followed by bear markets.

It was a "Dirty Dozen," twelve sets of proof that the bull market ended in the spring of 1983, at least internally. There was nowhere to go but down.

Although much of my readership dwindled away as the market

outwardly continued to give the lie to my bearish predictions, those who remained with me were given no letup in my *Letter*. I wanted my documentation of the coming crash to be total, so I turned all my energies to researching the past and reporting the amazing parallels that leaped out at me from the pages of history. I knew where the market was, and I knew where it was headed. My readers would not be surprised at what was to come. I had documented twelve areas of trouble that—taken singly—were always followed by bear markets. And here we were *hitting on all twelve cylinders at the same time*. The conclusion was inescapable that we were not heading merely into a bear market, but one that would stand out in history as a full-fledged panic and crash!

"Flee for your life!" was the message I repeated all through the remainder of 1983. I said those very words to Ted Koppel on "Nightline," to Pat Buchanan and Tom Braden on "Crossfire," to David Hartman on "Good Morning America," and to hundreds of interviewers from all forms of media. I reiterated the message to an audience of 700 in Zurich, Switzerland in November of 1983.

Few people seemed to believe my message, for I was the discredited Cassandra. I had missed the big rally. Beyond that, no one *wanted* to believe me. They were unable, as usual, to see the possible personal benefits of a huge bear market.

But by February 1984 the tenor of audience reaction had changed. On a ten-day swing through South Africa, widely advertised as a series of lectures entitled "The Crash of 1984," I was heralded as a true prophet. For by that time, the crash was visibly coming to pass.

Technical analysis backed me all the way. Consider this table of the technical aspect of the market at the point of each successive record high closing of the Dow:

DATE	DOW	NFI	CLX	HIGHS/LOWS		A/D LINE
5/ 6/83	1232.59	+16	+18	388	− 2	−77,687
6/16/83	1248.30	+10	+15	306	− 6	−76,287
9/20/83	1249.19	+ 5	+15	76	− 8	−79,367
9/26/83	1260.77	+ 7	+ 5	98	− 5	−78,936
10/10/83	1284.65	+16	+16	75	− 8	−78,765
11/29/83	1287.20	+14	+13	73	−24	−80,714

Here we see that the maximum number of new highs was reached on May 6 while the Dow stood at 1232.59. Thereafter, even though the Dow recorded a number of all-time record peaks, the high/low indicator had pronounced the fact that as far as most stocks were concerned, the bull market was long over.

The important advance/decline line peaked on June 16 and never recovered thereafter.

The performance of both the NFI and CLX were listless when gauged against what Wall Street told us the new Dow highs meant.

And so the spring of 1983 gave the lie to the rising Dow just as the 1929 market had done. Back then, most stocks had peaked out by December 1928 and the final rise in 1929 had been concentrated in a handful of showy blue-chip stocks. We all know what happened next.

The bull market made one more grand attempt to regenerate during the first week of January 1984. I saw it coming, and traders who followed the advice of my *Letter* and my Early Warning Service cashed in on the modest rise, although I warned them ahead of time that it was merely the final blow-off of the bull market. Then, four days before the end of the year, I sent out a bulletin to sell all holdings. I also recommended a very special list of short sales. This time I suggested simply that an aggressive trader go short on all thirty of the Dow Jones Industrials—with no stops. I was certain that we were headed for the BIG slide this time.

For a couple of trading days I took some heat. The Dow rose 16 points on January 4 and 13 points the following day. January 6 saw a near-record close at 1286.64, whereupon the bottom fell out. The Dow, as of February 27, 1984, dropped 106 points nearly straight down.

And it was only the beginning.

EPILOGUE

Looking back over the past 27 years of my stock market experience, what have I learned that will help stock market investors and speculators? First of all, the years have demonstrated that *no information has any value unless it comes directly from the action of the stock market itself.* That, therefore, eliminates corporate earnings, dividends, price/earnings ratios, book values, and all types of news. In other words, *it sets aside the entire fundamental school of thought,* the body of theory and practice principally responsible for most people's losses in the market. The first order of business is thus *to eliminate that entire area as a source of buy and sell signals.* I learned that early in my days at E.F. Hutton from simple observation. Seldom did the stock market move the way Wall Street's research departments thought it would. It would for a while, but when the turns came—in other words, when it mattered the most to investors—fundamental research sadly lagged.

Let us briefly look at those fundamental guideposts and put each of them in their proper perspective. First of all, corporate earnings, the one thing that most people look at. It is the reason brokerage firms have extensive research departments. It didn't take me long to realize that an earnings statement is a statement of something that has happened. It tells you that a corporation earned or lost so much in the latest quarter. In other words, it is a statement of the past. It doesn't tell you a blessed thing about the future. Yet the stock market deals with the future, not the past. It is a game of tomorrows, not yesterdays. Even if one did make an accurate forecast of the next earnings report, it wouldn't tell you how the market was going to respond to those earnings. The key word here is response. A stock market response to anything is a *technical* function, which is the territory of a stock market technician, one who follows the market and nothing else. In a bull market, most stocks go up *regardless* of earnings. Therefore, why become entrapped into following earnings?

Dividends likewise serve to entrap the investor. If a stock selling at 30 pays a $1 annual dividend and the stock falls to 20, then the drop in the price of the stock equates to ten years of dividend income. Assuming the stock does not recover, the investor would have to hold the stock for ten years just in order to break even. When a stock is down, the investor who holds it for income may be less concerned about the stock's price because he is getting that income. Actually, though, he is kidding himself. He is only getting a partial return on his diminished capital. And, to make matters worse, he is taxed each year on his dividend income. Early in my career I viewed dividend payments as a device designed to make the public *hold* their stocks. All bull markets are followed by bear markets; and in a bear market, somebody has to hold the stocks all the way down. Most of those holders are holding for "income."

Price/earnings ratios are also misleading, and yet all fundamentalists follow them. If earnings constituted the determinant of a stock price, then price/earnings ratios would tend to be stable. If a $20 stock showed earnings of $2 a share, then the p/e ratio would stand at 10. A rise in earnings to $4 a share should see the price of the stock doubling to 40 with the p/e ratio remaining at 10. But that is seldom the case. If one examines stock prices and earnings for any given year, one will discover that the p/e ratios jump up and down like Ping-Pong balls. If corporate earnings are not the determinant of stock prices, why follow them?

Book value is the net liquidating value of a stock. Since most companies intend to stay in business, the market price of the stock most of the time has no meaningful relation with the book value. It is used mostly as a tool by brokers as a reason to buy a stock when it is selling below its book value, but there is no guarantee that it can't sell further below its book value.

All these things are reflected in market prices, and thus *one's attention should at all times be on the market and nothing else.* If the technical evidence confirms a bull market, then be bullish. Most stocks are going to move up simply because there will be more buyers than sellers, measured in terms of On-Balance Volume. As suspiciously simple as it sounds, stocks will continue to move up until they don't. In other words, important technical indicators such as the high/low indicator and the advance-decline line will peak out. If a rise in the market remains genuine, then there should be an expanding number of stocks making new highs. When that statement can no longer be made, then the bull market is no longer genuine and is reduced to what is known as a "solitary walk" by the Dow Jones Industrial Average, the average most people watch. When that situation is reflected by a declining advance-decline line, it makes the bull market further suspect. One then would look to the secondary markets, such as the Over-the-Counter market and the American Stock Exchange, to decline in step with the high/low indicator and the advance-decline line. And at that point, one could clearly identify what is known as an "internal" bull market peak. The external, or final peak, is measured in terms of the Dow Jones Industrial Average. Generally, it peaks six to nine months after the internal peak. Once it comes down and breaks under its own trendline, then a new bear market comes out into the open.

The whirlwind 1982–83 rise in the market peaked in the spring of 1983 because at that point there was no further expansion in the number of stocks making new highs. That action was reflected by a peak in the advance-decline line in mid-June 1983, as well as peaks in the Over-the-Counter and American Stock Exchange markets. The Dow was then on its own, tracing out a solitary walk to a bull market high of 1287.20 on November 29, 1983. Failing to close at a new high in early January 1984, the market then collapsed in the face of tremendous Wall Street optimism.

The lesson is clear, and it repeats itself unfailingly on every cycle. If a technical case can be made for weakness at a time of great Wall Street optimism, then those are the greatest of the selling opportunities. Conversely, if a technical case can be made for strength at a time of great Wall Street pessimism, then those are the greatest of the buying opportunities. Markets move exactly opposite to human nature at the great turning points. Since most people are faithful to human nature, it naturally follows that most people faithfully lose money in the stock market. They then become the most avid buyers of stocks while Wall Street is most optimistic (and the technical situation is deteriorating), and the most avid sellers of stocks while Wall Street is most pessimistic (and the technical situation is improving).

Long-term investing is for suckers. Wall Street loves the bull markets, because most people would rather buy than sell, and brokers have a field day. Bear markets are unpopular on the Street because people do not know how to profitably take advantage of them. Wall Street will always announce a bull market but will never announce a bear market. You have to rely on your own technical analysis to tell you when you are going into a bear market. In my twenty-seven years in the stock market business, I have never had anyone come up to me and ask me to suggest something to sell. It is always a request for something to buy. People are oriented to the buy side simply because Wall Street has encouraged them for generations to believe that that is the side to be on. Constant buyers naturally think that bull markets are good and bear markets are bad —and they always will.

So, then, human nature tells people that up is good but down is bad. What the market knows, however, is that up is good and down is good if you have your money in the right place.

Let me demonstrate with an example. You are playing roulette in a casino. Let us say you have a system that tells you to bet on the color red on the next spin of the wheel. Now, suppose the number that comes up is on the red. You are a winner. That is good. Suppose your system now tells you to switch to black on the next spin of the wheel. Now, suppose the number that comes up is on the black. You are a winner. That is good. In both cases the croupier pays you. Now, how could one say that red is good and black is bad? Yet in the stock market, people think up is good and down is bad. Since most prices go down in a bear market, then down is good if you bet on it. Since most people don't bet on a down market, it logically follows that most people do not make money in the stock market.

Right now as you are reading this you are duplicating the principle of the stock market; and if you weren't doing so, you would be dead in four minutes. What do you always do after you inhale? Right.

What do you always do after you exhale? Right. Now, each of these opposing functions is as necessary as the other for sustaining life. How in heaven's name could you say that inhaling is good and exhaling is bad? Bear markets are as necessary and certain as bull markets, and they are *both* good. Simply bet on them when technical analysis calls the major turns.

Some years ago a study* was done that proved that the long-term holding of stocks was not the way to go. It showed the comparative percentage gains for long-term holding, selling out and avoiding bear markets, and playing the bear market as one would play the bull markets. Here were the results:

Results of Alternative Market Strategies (1964–1975)

STRATEGY	AVERAGE ANNUAL GAIN	TOTAL GAIN	$10,000 GROWS TO
Buy and Hold	3.8%	55%	$15,500
Avoiding the Bear Markets	20.4%	769%	$86,874
Long and Short Major Swings Only	31.4%	2,368%	$246,790
Long and Short Every 5% Swing	103.3%	393,660%	$39,376,060

The message is clear: market timing is everything. There is no way to time a market by following corporate earnings, dividends, price/earnings ratios, or book value. One can begin to see why fundamental analysis is the very anathema of technical analysis. It completely blinds one to what is really going on. It is championed in Wall Street because the game requires new generations of buyers to hold the losing stocks.

But we live in an ever-changing world, and technical analysis has

*Norman G. Fosback, *Stock Market Logic* (Ft. Lauderdale: The Institute for Econometric Research, 1977), p. 7.

come a long way since my early days at E.F. Hutton. Many of my early discoveries and contributions have become generic, and new tools are constantly required to measure the impact of a whole new generation of amateur technicians. Back in the 1950s I had a crude device on my desk which was a slow-moving paper ticker tape. The Dow Jones Industrial Average was announced once every hour. A 5-million-share day was a big day. Today a 90-million-share day is termed moderately active, and the advent of 200-million-share days is simply a matter of time. That could reflect only one thing: The public was back in the stock market with both feet in the 1982–84 markets. But this time a whole new array of goodies had been placed on the shelves of the Wall Street candy store. The public was gambling heavily in the option and stock index futures markets. Technical indicators were also changing, some going by the boards as new ones were devised to measure the impact of these new markets. These developments demanded that technology keep pace, and thus stock market software programs sprang up by the dozens in a rapidly overcrowding home computer market. By early 1984, over 9 million people had personal computers, and a large number of these were spitting out stock market signals to their millions of owners.

Here was a new era. Instead of the 3 million shareholders of 1929, we saw the number grow to an all-time record of 42 million shareholders in 1983, with an indirect ownership much greater than that due to pension funds. With the addition of a new generation literally betting billions in the option and futures markets, you have a time bomb. If anything ever happened to make a majority want to sell their stocks at around the same time, the time bomb would explode. The stakes are higher than ever before in history—and at the same time there are far more amateurs involved in the market, too many cooks in the kitchen.

So, one is walking into the marketplace today at a highly charged time in America's financial history, and more than ever it becomes increasingly vital to know whether to bet on red or bet on black. This is one game where there is absolutely no room for emotion. When the stock market affects your emotions, then you are doing something wrong. When you get into a position in which you have to hope and pray that your stocks go up, then you will be encountering what has kept the masses ignorant about the perfect fairness of the market. Yes, prayer can change things, but probably not the prices of your stocks. While you are praying that stock XYZ goes up five points to get you out of a jam, somewhere somebody else is praying just as fervently that stock XYZ does down five points to get him out of a jam. God is fair. He cannot answer your prayers and those of a short seller simultaneously. Instead, He invented the perfect answer: the stock market; and if you follow *it,* then your prayers *will* be answered. Stock XYZ answers simply to the laws of supply and demand, the only things that can change the price of a stock, the principle that led me to discover On-Balance Volume.

Do your own thing. Think as an individual even though the pull of "crowd thinking" seeks to rob you of that individuality. When you find yourself walking with the crowd, go back and do your market homework. It is only that homework that can protect you from making a serious mistake and getting sucked toward the overwhelming majority viewpoint.

Don't expect to be right all the time. Stock market success depends on being right most of the time, not all the time. After being right for practically eight straight years, the longest stretch on record, I fell on my face in August 1982. But, unlike Jesse Livermore, who was wiped out in the stock market between 1930 and 1932, I didn't blow my brains out in a New York hotel. Encountering a blistering wave of anti-Granville criticism, and seeing my business threatened with collapse, I saw that survival demanded immediate steps. I could not watch my business and the market at the same time. Fortunately, my new wife Karen's middle name was survival. With my eyes on the market and hers on the business, survival became revival. It was Karen who brought my business out to Kansas City, Missouri, effecting cost savings, hiring a new staff, helping to man the phones, and setting up all the systems, while I got back into gear with the market by the spring of 1983. It was a valley experience, but it had to lead to new peaks.

Likewise, my August 1982 miss may have turned out to be a great blessing in disguise. History just might record that if I had caught that turn, my sell signal thereafter might have been credited with *causing* a crash. For it is likely that a sell signal following a nearly perfect nine-year record would have been followed by widespread, simultaneous selling.

There is a great lesson here for all market students. One cannot do technical analysis without formulating a scenario. It is very difficult to avoid. I had a scenario following my early 1981 sell signal that encompassed three distinct legs to that bear market, but it only walked on two. By the summer of 1982, I was so sure that there was going to be another leg down that I fell in love with my scenario and took my eye off what the market was doing. It is a temptation to make the market fit one's scenario. If it *does* fit, then retain the scenario. But if it doesn't fit, then change the scenario, rip it up. The market doesn't follow you, you have to follow it. My 1983–84 signals called for a stock market crash, and nothing happened in 1984 to undo my scenario. On the contrary, the January-February 1984 slide was merely the curtain raiser to a repeating 55-year drama. I had been watching a growing number of 1929 parallels carefully since the summer of 1983. In the search for additional ones, I acquired microfilms of the 1929 *Wall Street Journal,* and they provided a plethora of new parallels.

As the year wore on, the parallels proliferated and the stock market acted accordingly. My technical work was flashing major warning signals in the opening months of 1984, in sharp contrast to the January 1984 Wall Street euphoria, which was replete with forecasts of the Dow rising to the 1400–1500 level that year. By the spring of 1984 it was more than apparent that the Dow was not going to return to the earlier 1287.20 closing high of November 29, 1983. The market clearly demonstrated that it had entered the first phase of a major bear market. There was no turning back. Once the first phase of a bear market is clearly documented, it can only progress into later phases. It doesn't revert to a bull market until the bear market has been completed. Inasmuch as the brief 1982–83 market rise had terminated as early as June 1983—probably the shortest bull market in history—I saw the rise as the ending of a major cycle rather than the beginning of a new one. In terms of the popular four-year cycle, the brief 1982–83 rise left room for a longer bear market than usual, with the bottom of the cycle likely to occur in 1986.

The implications were clear. I stated that President Reagan would rue the day he decided to run for re-election. By this time I had literally hundreds of 1929 parallels, and that was statistically beyond luck or coincidence. There couldn't be that much smoke without the fire being just down the road.

Wall Street passed off the 1984 declines as simply normal consolidation in an ongoing bull market. By June of 1984, however, Vartanig G. Vartan of *The New York Times* was stating that 1984 had been a bust for equities and that many people had lost whatever profits they reaped in the bull market.

Thanks to my development of a trading barometer based on On-Balance Volume, I was able to catch every trading swing in the 1983–84 market and returned to the top of the ladder in market timing according to the *Hulbert Financial Digest,* a service based in Washington, D.C., that rates the leading market letters every month. While the majority of analysts were showing portfolio losses in 1984, I was enjoying my finest year in calling the turns in what was considered to be a tough year.

The Dow broke sharply in May and June following a bear market rally, dropping to a bear market low of 1086.90 on June 15. The rally attempts thereafter were unconvincing. The Dow began to head lower again in July.

By this time my extremely bearish prognosis was well known; I would be the last person expected to suddenly call for the biggest rally of the year. I thought through the 1929 pattern very carefully. All the reasons for a crash were existing by May of 1929, but the market turned upward again in June of that year and rallied throughout the summer, peaking on September 3. I reasoned that not all market rallies are followed by a crash, *but all crashes are preceded by a rally.* Evidence was piling up very rapidly that I was going to be right, but something was wrong. I needed the rally that fools the majority, the final high-diving board.

Just when most people were beginning to throw the towel in on a summer rally, my trading barometer flashed a buy signal on July 13. The longer-term implications, however, were very bearish. The purpose of this rally would be to turn everyone bullish at the worst of times. The bulls would be widely believed because the bond market had bottomed in May and June, and Wall Street had been telling everyone for months that a drop in interest rates would launch the second leg of the bull market. In a special bulletin on July 17, I told my followers to close out all their short positions and put out options. The effect was electric. The *Orlando Sentinel* headlined their business page on July 20: THE BULLS ARE OFF AND RUNNING, complete with my picture and a prediction that I saw a 400-point rise coming. The *Toronto Star* also carried a similar article and prediction ascribed to me. Rumors spread rapidly. Of course, I never stated that I saw a 400-point rally coming, but simply that I saw the probabilities for the biggest rally of the year.

All the hooks were there. Interest rates were coming down, and it would soon be August, a month that would remind everyone of the big August 1982 turn. The stage was set, and I was certain that the majority would be effectively hooked on this predicted rally, especially in an election year when the incumbent appeared at that time to be a shoo-in for re-election.

My followers received my July 17 bulletin two days prior to the July 24 Dow low of 1086.57. Thereafter things moved rapidly. I had stated that a move above the 1140 level had to take place to confirm the large rally I expected. That upside breakout occurred on schedule, and the opening days of August erupted with the heaviest volume in stock exchange history. My trading barometer flashed a sell signal on August 3, the very day of the highest volume in history. By the time my followers received my August 6 sell bulletin, they were able to sell into the highs reached on the morning of August 10, the Dow reaching an intra-day high that day of 1253.75.

Most analysts turned very bullish in that August advance. Even the percentage advance was almost identical with that of the bear market rally of 1973, the technical blueprint I was following for this one. Now Wall Street was totally hooked. I had my summer of 1929 parallel.

Due to appear on national television on September 4 in California on Financial News Network's "Money Talk" program, I saw an opportunity to repeat the famous Roger Babson prediction of September 5, 1929. I repeated my prediction that a stock market crash lay ahead. I had the identical technical evidence that Babson had had when he made his famous prediction. Over half of the stocks listed on the New York Stock Exchange had been in a bear market for the previous nine months. That was true in September 1929. It was also true in September 1984. Just as the Babson prediction wasn't taken seriously, nobody took me seriously either. Of course that was the greatest of all the parallels: nobody saw it coming. That was especially true with Election Day just weeks away.

I had stated my case to the best of my ability. All market action after August 10 had shown more concerted downside action and weaker rallies. In my view, we were moving into the fall of 1929.

But it isn't what Granville says, it is what Granville does. My Hulbert record of the previous twelve months demonstrated that I was always the technician, rotating from sell signals to buy signals and back again whenever the market indicated. So, regardless of the major scenario, my followers knew that I had learned the lesson of August 1982. If the crash was not yet to be, my followers knew that they would be back on a buy signal.

In making mistakes in the market, it is one thing to miss a bottom —but don't ever miss a top. When one misses a bottom, one misses future profits. That is mentally painful but it does not cost you your capital. Since only a minority of people ever go short, a missed bottom costs most people only lost profits. On the other hand, if one misses a top, especially a major top preceding a long and severe bear market, then that miss can cost one all or part of one's capital. Looking back and having to make a choice, I would gladly miss August 1982 again and again rather than miss the 1983 top that Wall Street did and never apologized for.

What of the future? Is John Templeton's Dow 3,000 going to be reached in the 1980s, or is there to be a sizable detour that could turn out to be the main highway? I think the nub of the ultimate truth was hit upon in a February 1983 quote from *Horoscope* magazine (most astrology magazines now contain stock market coverage): "Remember, a Dow Jones average of 1600–1700 is the magic number if it is to keep pace with the growth of other economic indicators. According to some leading analysts, we will never again in our lifetimes see the lows of 1982—when the market was considered to be 50 percent or more undervalued." The key word there is the word *never.* Whenever somebody tells you that the stock market will never do this or that, then the odds shift dramatically in favor of that event happening. With all due respect to Mr. Templeton, his long-range viewpoint has far too much company. The decade of the 1980s has been so overpublicized in books talking about the big boom in stocks that contrary opinion would favor looking at those rosy predictions as signaling a major long-term top rather than a stairway to the stars.

There are several certain developments ahead. For one thing, the market is becoming increasingly more volatile, as well it might with 42 million shareholders taking a shorter-term view of things. I think people are just beginning to take a dimmer view of long-term investment. They have been sold a bad bag of goods by Wall Street, which has used the long-term investor as the repository of many a stock gone sour. One only has to flip through the pages of a long-term book of stock charts to see the fate of the long-term investor. There one finds the old high of $75 a share for American Telephone twenty years ago that was never bettered, the high of $113 a share in General Motors back in late 1965 that was never bettered, the old highs in Avon Products, Polaroid, and Xerox in years long past never bettered, and it makes for a growing case against the doctrinaire long-term investor. The technician's credo is love 'em and leave 'em. You don't marry a stock. You have brief love affairs. Too many people marry the stocks they own. The real reason for this is that they eventually get locked in with a paper loss and they rationalize that loss by telling themselves that they are getting income. Unwilling to take a loss, they hold the stocks—in many cases literally till death do them part. Then an heir will hold them still longer because then the stocks will be held for sentimental reasons. That is why some people have had American Telephone in their family for three generations.

The stock market, like a giant casino, is headed toward a twenty-four-hour market. You will soon be able to take a position in New York on the short side and close out your position in Hong Kong, or do it in reverse. The combination of modern technology and instant news eliminates all secrets and almost ruins the old arbitrage game; increasingly, what everybody knows is worthless. Instant news creates a greater number of simultaneous suckers. We don't have the old delays today that enabled the Rothschilds to clean up in London on Napoleon's loss at Waterloo because they were smart enough to employ carrier pigeons to tell them first that peace was at hand. (Peace is bearish and the Rothschilds went short across the board while everyone else was still long.) Today we have the carrier pigeons of technical analysis.

Backgrounds are constantly changing, systems of government come and go, technology is always shifting, but there is one thing that never changes, and that is human nature. Everything that preceded all the English panics of the nineteenth century came into play in the U.S. market in 1983, and that leads up to an important point. You must move contrary to human nature at all times. That is very difficult to do because we are human. But the market demands this, being the exact opposite of human nature. That requires a special, "inhuman" discipline, unrelenting and devoid of emotion.

Whatever the future mechanics of markets—whether totally computerized and stock ownership a number on a computer screen —making money still comes down to human nature and supply and demand. There will always be a search for new indicators as old ones become too widely followed.

Like a giant magnet, the stock market will continually attract the younger generation to it because it looks like an easy living and is glamorous. But the high road won't be via the Harvard Business School or Wharton School of Finance. It will be via technical analysis and the computer. Like all popular fields, it too will become overcrowded. The market always has an answer for such overcrowding. As wars periodically decimate overpopulation, severe bear markets periodically separate the men from the boys.

How can one best prepare for a stock market career? A study of economics is useful only because it teaches one what *not* to pay attention to. One can better understand the Wall Street game and see why it is designed to separate fools from their money. Who missed the 1929 top? The economists. Who missed the 1983 top? The economists. What does economics have to do with the stock market? Nothing. Economics and the stock market operate in two different time worlds, and timing is everything. The technical precedes the fundamental, and that is why economists are always late in their market calls, always loving the market at the worst of times and hating the market at the worst of times.

What about the study of psychology? Yes, definitely yes. The market is people, and anything that deals with the entire study of human nature explains the stock market game.

History? Ah, yes. There is the discipline that reveals the repetitive cycle of human nature. Winners have long memories, and losers have such short memories. He who understands the past is master of the future—a maxim often misappropriated by fundamental analysts who merely look at the past.

In the end, though, there is no substitute for experience. I learned more in the E.F. Hutton boardroom in less than two years by just observing than I did from all the books I will ever read on the stock market. So if you yearn for a stock market career, write well and speak with authority and be willing to walk in any door that serves as an entrance. If you have anything at all, somebody will beat a path to your door.

What books most influenced my thinking? As definitely required reading, read *Memoirs of Extraordinary Popular Delusions* by Charles Mackay (1841), *The Crowd* by Gustave LeBon (1895), *Reminiscences of a Stock Operator* by Edwin LeFevre (1922), *Only Yesterday* by Frederick Lewis Allen (1931), *The Battle for Investment Survival* by Gerald Loeb (1957), and *The Day the Bubble Burst* by Gordon Thomas and Max Morgan-Witts (1979). There are others, of course, but the above are memorable.

Open your mind to everything. A closed mind will never grasp more than a portion of what the stock market has to offer, for the market mirrors the abundance of life itself. But she is a demanding taskmistress. She is jealous and wants all of your time. You benefit by your investing in proportion to the effort you put into it. If it is to be part time, you will get part-time results. Give it your all and you will have the love affair of your life. I gave it my life.

GLOSSARY

Accumulation. Any stock that consistently evidences higher volume on upside days than on downside days is said to be under accumulation. Important price advances are generally preceded by accumulation. The most accurate measurement and evaluation of accumulation is effected by the use of On-Balance Volume.

Advance-Decline Line. The orthodox advance-decline line is a *net differential between the number of stocks advancing each day and the number of stocks declining each day kept on a cumulative basis.* The word orthodox is used here because most people are still not aware of the *volume advance-decline line.* The orthodox advance-decline line is a measurement based on *price,* not volume. The advance-decline line is one of the *major* technical indicators having broad implications concerning the trend of stock prices. A declining advance-decline line implies that one should be far more selective when purchasing stocks and can even rule out purchase of stocks completely when such declines are in definite bearish configuration with other key indicators. A declining A-D line does not necessarily rule against new highs being made by the Dow Jones Industrial Average during the first three phases of a bull market, but such unconfirmed highs spell out developing trouble. The market can usually sustain one or two nonconfirmed new Dow highs for a while, but a third Dow high lacking A-D line confirmation is one of the clearest of all market get-out signals. While the advance-decline line has always peaked ahead of the Dow Jones Industrial Average prior to the start of a bear market, *it is not a definite requirement for the line to reach bottom prior to the Dow at the start of a bull market.* The line was late on the 1962, 1966, 1970, and 1974 bottoms, the Dow having bottomed first.

Bar Chart. Prior to the use of On-Balance Volume, the bar chart was the orthodox method of recording volume with a stock price chart, a series of vertical lines depicting the daily volume. It is still being used and is an entirely unsatisfactory method of showing volume in a technically intelligent manner. Looking at that type of presentation, one can only guess at possible accumulation or distribution trends. This writer maintains that the way to intelligently relate volume to price so as to identify accumulation or distribution is by On-Balance Volume.

Bear Market. True bear markets tend to start "out of the blue" with the majority at a loss to explain the first downswing. Bear market means a declining market. A bear market is related to the bull market that it follows, thereby completing the entire bull-bear cycle, *but it has absolutely no relation to the bull market that follows after that bear market is completed.* That is a new ball game. Bear markets may or may not be accompanied by business recession. Bear market is a *market* term referring specifically to the opposite of a bull market.

Bear Trap. Any *technically unconfirmed* move to the downside encouraging the bulk of the investing and speculating public to be bearish. The most important bear traps terminate bear markets. In any case, they precede strong rallies.

Breakthrough (Breakout). The terms *breakthrough* and *breakout* are interchangeable. They imply that either a stock price or average has moved above a previous high-resistance level or has moved below a previous low-support level. Such breakthroughs imply that the movement will be enhanced in the direction of the breakout in an analogy to the physical principle of bodies in motion. The same terms apply to the more important On-Balance Volume movements through previous support or resistance levels on the demonstration that volume precedes price.

Bull Market. Any rising market might be called a bull market, but that would be a very loose definition. True bull markets imply a sweeping uptrend of many months' duration with three definable phases. Like bear markets, bull markets vary widely in scope and duration. However, *a bull market has no relation to the bear market it follows,* and thus there is little to go on at first in estimating its length or importance. Since the time span between major market tops is a *complete variable,* unlike the more predictable cyclicality of major bottoms, one has to depend heavily on the bull phase characteristics (see bull phases) to estimate the probable duration of a bull market.

Bull Phases. Running in three phases, the first bull phase is characterized by public disbelief in what is happening, disbelief that stock prices can rise importantly in the face of all the obviously bad news and bad fundamentals. The smart money, having turned confident during the third phase of the preceding bear market, is now more confident than ever in the face of the pessimistic public. All through the first bull phase the news is bad, and the public gapes in disbelief as prices climb the wall of worry. When the lagging fundamentals attempt to catch up and the public is told that there is light at the end of the tunnel, eliminating the earlier public disbelief in the rise, then the first bull phase is ending. The ending is technically shown by a topping out in the number of new individual highs, a topping out by the advance-decline line, one Dow stock after another having recorded an On-Balance Volume peak and other deteriorating phenomena. Just when the public confidence is given a shot in the arm and a little belief in the rise begins to replace the widespread pessimism, the market goes into a decline. At this point it is possible to project an approximate duration of the bull market, multiplying the duration of the first bull phase by three and adding the total time span to the last recorded major bottom. The outstanding characteristic of the second bull phase is the decline that fools the majority. The smart money, having taken the first easy profits at the end of the first bull phase, sells out to the public fooled by the shot-in-the-arm burst of confidence. They sit back, awaiting the new buying opportunities on the wide second phase market decline. The public is still generally confused, getting whipsawed on the second phase decline. Fundamentals get obviously stronger and the media helps to blow this up to boom proportions. Bull phase three is at hand. The outstanding characteristic of that phase is the public belief in what is happening. They now take over the bulk of the market buying as the smart money period of confidence comes to an end. When the next decline comes, it usually starts a bear market, but by that time, it would be the last thing the public could believe, thus the disbelief attached to the next phase, the first bear market phase.

Bull Trap. Any *technically unconfirmed* move to the upside encouraging the bulk of the investing and speculating public to be bullish. The most important bull traps terminate bull markets. In any case, they precede important declines.

Buying Climax. A climax implies *an ending.* A buying climax is associated with such a sharp price run-up, with everything so heavily one-sided on the rise, that a move in the opposite direction becomes inevitable. Such a climax may be of the one-day variety ending a very short-term swing, or it could be of intermediate or final significance ending months of advance or even years of advance. All climaxes involve increased volume. While heavy volume is never a concern during the first two phases of a bull market, very heavy volume during the third phase is uninformed public buying, often ending in a buying climax. Beware of such climactic action late in a bull market.

Buy Column. When a stock is up in price at the end of a market trading session, all the volume generated during the session is recorded on the upside and the figure is placed in the BUY column.

Climactic. A term used to describe any movement that smacks of "excess," regardless of whether it is a price movement or a volume movement. Climactic moves are followed by moves in the *opposite* direction.

Climax Indicator. The Climax Indicator is the *net* number of On-Balance Volume breakouts among the thirty Dow Jones Industrial stocks. It either confirms a move in the Dow average or fails to confirm. Nonconfirmations are particularly meaningful at new high and low Dow levels. When the Net Field Trend is down, all high CLX readings of +20 and higher are excellent selling opportunities. When the Net Field Trend is up, all CLX readings of −20 and lower are excellent buying opportunities. It is an essential daily market indicator as well and an important intermediate and longer-range indicator.

Contrary Opinion. Contrary opinion in itself is meaningless. *It depends on whose opinion it is contrary to.* If the public holds a widespread popular opinion about something, then a minority contrary opinion is worth listening to. It is never the other way around because how could the huge public have a *minority* opinion about anything? Contrary opinion is most significant at all major market turning points.

Declining Tops. A pattern of declining tops implies a loss of upside energy and an ultimate decline. Each peak is less than the previous one, showing increasing weakness. The pattern is significant both in terms of price and On-Balance Volume.

Defensive. Anything that tends to remain relatively stable in a declining market is a *defensive* situation. A defensive technique involves the purchase of bonds in a bear market or some stock capable of going counter to the trend, perhaps a gold stock. During a period when high-priced stocks are under attack, it might be said that a move into very low-priced issues moving in a narrow range around their base lines would be a *defensive* measure. The best defense against a falling market is not to be in it.

Distribution. The opposite of accumulation. Distribution occurs when the market is high, accounting for the accommodation of the late bull market stock buyers, allowing the market equation to balance. It is often very subtle and not too easily detected, but the use of On-Balance Volume will clearly reveal its presence every time. Inasmuch as late bull market third-phase public buying usually *generates a lot of volume,* distribution is the heaviest at such times, balancing off the heavy public buying *in the required market equation.* At such times one should ask: *Who is doing the selling to make all this buying possible?* Distribution seeks to camouflage its presence by hiding behind GOOD NEWS.

Divergence. All market forecasts (forecasts made by the market) involve divergence. The high-low indicator is a divergence indicator. The advance-decline line is a divergence indicator. The Climax Indicator is a divergence indicator. In divergence something deviates from the norm, requiring a *market adjustment.*

Dividends. One of the market "hooks" to insure that somebody will be holding stocks in a bear market. In such markets the "dividend" buyer is getting no dividend at all, but merely a *partial return of his own capital,* a return the government considers "income," thus hitting the "dividend" buyer again. Notice how often companies raise their dividend payments at or near market tops, a move that often entraps many to buy at the wrong time.

Dow Jones Industrials. These are the thirty stocks that go to make up the Dow Jones Industrial Average. On-Balance Volume is computed on these stocks each day in order to determine the daily readings of the Climax Indicator. The thirty industrials are as follows:

Allied Corporation	General Foods	Sears Roebuck
Alcoa	General Motors	Standard Oil of
American Brands	Goodyear	California
American Can	INCO	Texaco
American Express	IBM	Union Carbide
American	International	United States Steel
Telephone	Harvester	United
Bethlehem Steel	International Paper	Technologies
DuPont	Merck	Westinghouse
Eastman Kodak	Minnesota Mining	Electric
Exxon	Owens Illnois	Woolworth
General Electric	Proctor & Gamble	

Down Column. When On-Balance Volume is being computed, all the volume on downside days is placed in the DOWN column. This is a cumulative volume total. It is subtracted from the volume in the UP column and the result is the On-Balance Volume.

Field Trend. On-Balance Volume records upside breakouts and downside breakouts. When those breakouts trace out a rising zigzag, there is then a *rising field trend.* When there is no evidence of a rising or falling zigzag in the clusters of breakouts, the field trend is said to be *doubtful.* When the OBV breakouts record a downward zigzag, the field trend is said to be *falling.* The field trend mix of the thirty Dow Jones industrial stocks is very important in determining the true trend of the Dow, comparing the number of stocks in rising field trends as against the number in falling field trends. The field trend is extremely important in determining when to buy or sell an individual stock.

Fifty Percent Principle. Based on the physical principle of a seesaw, the principle states that if a previous decline in the market is more than 50 percent retraced on the next rally, then the market will ultimately retrace the entire decline. Conversely, if a previous advance is more than 50 percent retraced on the next decline, then the market will ultimately retrace the entire advance. It has a very good short-term batting average, but in using it measured against entire bull and bear markets, it is most reliable in the early stages of a bull market when retracing more than 50 percent of the previous bear market. To avoid expensive miscalculations, only stress the halfway penetrations when measured against *completed* bull or bear markets. Such valid better-than-halfway retracements tend to be early in bull markets and late in bear markets.

Flatbase. Some of the greatest percentage gains have stemmed from stocks breaking out from flatbase formations. A flatbase is made up of a long period of price fluctuations in a very narrow range. When accumulation can be detected, the flatbase situation becomes very attractive from the technical standpoint.

Flatbase Breakout. This is the actual price move above the long range of narrow price fluctuations that have traced out the flatbase formation. Such breakouts are always *preceded* by rising On-Balance Volume. The flatbase description also can refer to the On-Balance Volume fluctuations, and an upside breakout from that narrow OBV range either predicts an imminent price breakout or both the OBV and price breakout together. The results of such breakouts can only be bullish.

Floating Supply. This is a term used to describe how much stock is around that is not closely held, stock that is in the trading pool of available supply. The smaller the "float," the more susceptible the stock is to day-to-day supply-and-demand pressures. When the float becomes small enough and the price high enough, then maximum vulnerability to price decline is reached. To estimate the floating supply, subtract the On-Balance Volume from the capitalization. A real squeeze on the price of the stock is seen when *the short interest comes to equal or surpass the floating supply.*

Four-Column Analysis. This is a separation of stock price analysis into *four* charts, a chart of the opening prices, the high prices, the low prices, and the closing prices. The theory here is that no price penetration is necessarily valid unless confirmed by the other three charts. The separate series can be shown in price *columns*, and thus the term *four-column* analysis.

Fundamental Data. Data comprising the entire gamut of economic intelligence—covering such things as the economy, stock earnings and dividends, price/earning ratios, new products, management changes, and the computation of what a stock is worth, among other things. *Most of the time fundamental data is totally irrelevant to the market.* The market never speaks in terms of fundamentals. The market only speaks in *technical* terms. I have never ceased to be amazed at so much stress on the wrong things when it comes to the market. How can fundamental data be important when timing decisions are made when the market doesn't even speak the language? Nine times out of ten the overconcentration on fundamental data has resulted in losses. What the market does to the price of a stock is a *market function,* therefore, a *technical* function. When viewed in this light, the study of fundamental data as a prerequisite to making money in the market doesn't make much sense. Yet some very intelligent people have made the mistake of putting fundamental data ahead of technical data.

Gaps. These are visible separations or skips in either prices, On-Balance Volume, or both. Gaps set up targets for retracement, and it is not wise to ignore them. Gaps occurring early in a price upswing are not as bearish as those showing up in the third phase of the price movement, a definite technical characteristic suggesting the end of the line on the upside.

Logic. It is sometimes said that the market is illogical, not at all acting in a rational manner. Those who accuse it of such illogical moves are trying to relate two different time periods, the past or current events with the future. When something happens the market has not had time to discount, then the market *acts on a current events basis.* Everybody understands the market on such days because *they can relate it to the current events.* That is why the market is so one-sided on such days. Examples would include the Eisenhower heart-attack market of 1955, the Kennedy assassination market of 1963, etc. When the market is viewed in retrospect, *its unerring logic is inescapable.* After all, millions of game players are trying to beat out millions of other game players, always thinking ahead, and only on those rare occasions does the news catch up with the market. Those who accuse the market of being illogical are themselves illogical.

Momentum. This is the *rate* of acceleration in price or volume expansion, best noted by developing gaps in velocity figures or gaps in an On-Balance Volume series. Upside *momentum* is the greatest just short of price maturity, and downside *momentum* tends to reach a peak at or near an important bottom.

Net Differential. This is the difference between volume assigned to the *up* column and volume assigned to the *down* column. Obviously, *net differential* is the same as On-Balance Volume.

Net Field Trend. Major indicator depicting the true volume trend of the thirty Dow Jones industrial stocks. It is simply the difference between the number of Dow stocks in rising field trends and the number of Dow stocks in falling field trends. For the correct interpretation of the daily Climax Indicator readings, one must take the Net Field Trend into consideration.

OBV. This is the abbreviation for On-Balance Volume.

On-Balance. This is the difference between the pluses and the minuses in any situation.

On-Balance Volume. This is OBV, the result reached after subtracting all the volume on the downside from the volume on the upside. Readings can either be positive or negative.

Overbought. Price maturity and the term *overbought* are interchangeable descriptions. An overbought condition is detected when upside gaps show up in the velocity, price, and OBV. All vertical movements imply that a stock is overbought.

Overhead Supply. This is the total amount of shares traded in a stock at higher price levels through which the stock (after a decline) is trying to cut through on the recovery movement. Some chartists call it the *high volume zone*. High volume at higher prices presents a formidable resistance on recovery movements. To put it another way: Too many people are waiting to move out of the stock the minute it returns to the higher levels at which they originally made their purchase. If a stock can cut back through overhead supply, it is a strongly bullish endorsement for a further upswing. Overhead supply can be measured, and when a decline has generated an equal number of shares with the overhead supply, then the decline is either over or just about to be terminated (overhead supply concept).

Oversold. This term is associated with *first-phase* stock price movements. An oversold condition is detected by the presence of downside gaps in price and On-Balance Volume, or price returning to a key support level, or OBV reaching down to fill some gap overlooked on the way up.

Price/Earnings Ratios. A favorite tool of fundamental stock analysis that completely fails to take into account stock supply and demand patterns largely created by psychology. If p/e ratios contributed valid intelligence in making market decisions, then they would tend to be stable. Earnings would move up, the price of the stock would go up, and the p/e ratio would essentially remain the same. Instead, what happens? Earnings go up, the price of the stock stands still, and the p/e ratio drops; or earnings go up, the price of the stock goes down, and the p/e ratio plummets; or earnings move down, the price of the stock goes up, and the p/e ratio soars. So, in actuality, price/earnings ratios fluctuate widely, and thus in themselves cannot provide any dependable guide to what the price of a stock is going to do. The fallacy of p/e ratios is explained by the *anachronism between price and earnings*. Earnings *lag* the market by about nine months. Price is current but tends to discount the *future*. So, p/e ratios try to relate a current or *futuristic* statistic with a lagging statistic. Result? *Meaningless* fluctuations in the p/e ratio.

Primary Trend. The predominant trend of the market throughout bull and bear markets. When the primary trend turns bullish at the start of a bull market, it stays bullish until the bull market ends. When it turns bearish at the start of a bear market, it stays bearish until the bear market ends.

Pullback. Practically all advances of importance are tested with a subsequent "pullback" to or near the starting point of the advance. The price is easily seen as merely a pullback when the OBV reading is higher on the return trip price than it was the first time it was at that price.

Resistance. Any barrier to progress is resistance. Once a price support level is broken, that support level becomes the *resistance* point on the recovery movement. The theory of resistance holds true in OBV movements.

Rising Bottoms. The ability of a stock to turn up above each preceding important low point traces out a pattern of *rising bottoms,* a bullish formation. This is only half the formation, however. To be complete there should also be an accompanying series of rising tops. Rising bottoms (by definition) precede rising tops and are thus the first technical requirement that must be met if a situation is to be termed a bullish one. The same formation should be looked for in OBV.

Rising Tops. This is the typical pattern best seen in the second- and third-phase stock price movements. It must be seen in the first-phase OBV movements, otherwise the later bullish unfoldment will not be seen. Rising tops beget rising tops until the gravity rule of the third-phase stock price movement takes over.

Secondary Offerings. Planned stock distributions, most numerous during late second phase of a bull market and throughout third phase.

Sell Column. When a stock is down in price at the end of the trading session, all the volume generated for the day is recorded on the downside and the figure is placed in the SELL column.

Selling Climax. This is a situation that occurs when a clear majority of all stocks reach an oversold condition simultaneously. Selling climaxes have the following characteristics: (1) heavy volume, (2) decided plurality of declines over advances, (3) transactions reported long after they occur, the late tape, (4) a strong price reversal occurring before the session has ended, and (5) the move accompanied by a large number of odd lot short sales. If the market had not been closed after the brief period of hectic trading following the Kennedy assassination, it would undoubtedly have ended in such a selling climax. A selling climax implies *ending*

and is one of the finest situations to buy into when seen. However,
they have become increasingly less frequent in recent years. They
are often triggered by *very bad news*, which motivates the badly
timed heavy public selling, thus the great buying opportunity.

Shake-Out. A healthy technical correction of an overbought situation, whether referring to the general market or a specific stock.
The decline is sharp but comparatively short in duration. Shake-
outs often terminate the second-phase stock price movement. If
one counts the shake-out as a full phase of the stock price movement, then it can be said that the bull cycle for individual stocks
consists of four phases. Shake-outs in the general market have
been falsely labeled as major bear markets many times, the surface
appearances often being deceptively similar.

Short Interest. The total number of shares sold short and reported
by the Stock Exchange once a month. A large short interest is
basically bullish but is largely tempered by the volume of trading.
Viewing the short interest, the question that must be answered
is: Are the shorts right or wrong on the market? A mere *quantity*
of short sellers tells us nothing. Short sellers are wrong as a group
in a bull market and right as a group in a bear market. Therefore,
we must ascertain the primary trend *before* we attempt to weigh
the significance of the short interest. If the primary trend is
judged to be bullish, then the short interest is significant, especially if it is rising in relation to the average daily volume. If the
primary trend of the market is judged to be bearish, then a large
short interest is of no help to the bulls because then the shorts
are shorting *with* the trend, and there is no compulsion to cover
their short sales. In a bull market there definitely is an increasing
compulsion to cover, and that is a measurable bullish factor.

Short Interest Ratio. This is the ratio of monthly short interest to
the average daily trading volume for that month. When the ratio
is under 1.00 for a long period of time, it is popularly construed
to be bearish. A ratio above 1.00 is normal. If the ratio climbs
above 1.50, that is bullish, and anything approaching 2.00 is
wildly bullish. This indicator has been a poor one in helping to
detect major market tops but has been among the best in detecting bottoms when the ratio approached the 2.00 level.

Short Selling. This is the process of selling a stock that is not owned
with the expectation of buying it back (covering) at a lower price.

The broker has to borrow the stock in order to make delivery. In a weak market, short selling becomes increasingly popular. When it becomes excessive, then the market either embarks upon a strong technical rally or starts a new bull market according to where the market stands in the four- to four-and-a-half-year market cycle (the shorts taking their profits by buying in or covering).

Shorting Against the Box. This is the process of going short on a stock already owned, a new transaction. To complete the transaction in the case of the stock going down in price, the originally owned stock is merely delivered. If the price goes up after the short sale, then the value of the original holding has also gone up the same amount, and no net loss is incurred. The purpose of shorting against the box is to stretch out the holding period for the originally bought shares so as to qualify for six-month capital gains lower tax rates. Regardless of whether the price of the stock rises or falls on the shorting process, the holder "freezes" his position.

Snapback. A bullish technical property imparted to a stock if the price declines at a faster rate than the OBV. It implies that the stock has reached a true oversold position long before it would have under different circumstances. The price, being out of line with the OBV on the downside, therefore "snaps back."

Smart Money. Is on top of the market game, has read the market message correctly, is operating opposite to the public psychology and not in step with the news. Is accumulating stocks when the market says to accumulate. Is selling stocks when the market says to distribute. Doesn't give a rap for fundamentals if the market dictates otherwise. May at times look like a nut to his friends, but laughs all the way to the bank.

Standard & Poor's 500 Stock Index. Standard index used in computing disparity, the thumb rule being to multiply the index changes by ten and compare those results with the changes in the Dow Jones Industrial Average.

Support. Any barrier to decline is called support. Once a resistance level has been successfully penetrated by a stock advance, the retreat from that level is expected to meet support at the old resistance level. The theory of support also holds true in OBV movements.

Tax Selling. Selling a stock for the purpose of recording a loss for tax purposes, tax selling is often a perfect camouflage for a developing new bull market, the majority mechanically fenced into a time period calling for inappropriate action. The tax selling period should also be related to where it occurs in the typical four- to four-and-a-half-year market cycle.

Technician. One who trys to follow the guidance of the greatest of all market advisors, the market itself. The technician is trained to understand the language of the market and is less prone to interpretive errors by restricting his analysis to this market language. The technician understands the constant struggle between the demand forces and the supply forces and knows that the outcome of that struggle determines prices and not earnings, news, P/E ratios, the economy or anything else.

Topping Out. A term employed to denote loss of upside energy at the top after a long price run-up. Such a loss of energy would also show up in a pattern of declining tops or declining OBV.

Vertical Price Movement. A price run-up is a vertical movement, at high levels always being the chief characteristic of a stock's third phase movement of maturity or, at the very least, the topping out of the second phase price movement just prior to a sharp shake-out.

Volume Advance-Decline Line. Another way of expressing On-Balance Volume, simply substituting the more important volume factor.

Volume Breakout. A new high in a series of On-Balance Volume figures. Such breakouts tend to *precede* price breakouts.

Volume Ratio. A now-antiquated method of detecting significant strength, completely superseded by the new concept of On-Balance Volume.

Index